CASE STUDIES OF U.S. ECONOMIC SANCTIONS

CASE STUDIES OF U.S. ECONOMIC SANCTIONS

The Chinese, Cuban, and Iranian Experience

Hossein G. Askari, John Forrer,
Hildy Teegen, and Jiawen Yang

Westport, Connecticut
London

Library of Congress Cataloging-in-Publication Data

Case studies of U.S. economic sanctions : the Chinese, Cuban, and Iranian experience / Hossein G. Askari . . . [et al.]

p. cm.

Includes bibliographical references and index.

ISBN 1–56720–541–0 (alk. paper)

1. Economic sanctions, American—China—Case studies. 2. Economic sanctions, American—Cuba—Case studies. 3. Economic sanctions, American—Iran—Case studies. I. Title: Case studies of US economic sanctions. II. Title: Economic sanctions. III. Askari, Hossein. IV. Economic sanctions.

HF1604.C27 2003

327.1'17—dc21 2003052888

British Library Cataloguing in Publication Data is available.

Library of Congress Catalog Card Number: 2003052888

ISBN: 1–56720–541–0

First published in 2003

Praeger Publishers, 88 Post Road West, Westport, CT 06881

An imprint of Greenwood Publishing Group, Inc.

www.praeger.com

Printed in the United States of America

The paper used in this book complies with the Permanent Paper Standard issued by the National Information Standards Organization (Z39.48–1984).

10 9 8 7 6 5 4 3 2 1

Contents

Illustrations

Tables

Figures

Appendixes

CHAPTER 1

Introduction

Sanctions are policy tools used by governments to influence other governments and/or firms and citizens in other nations. An *economic sanction* is a restriction on commercial relations between citizens and firms of at least two countries: those in the *sender* (the nation imposing the sanction) and those in the *target* (the nation upon which the sanction is imposed). Economic sanctions may restrict commercial relations of third countries or third parties as well.

Sanctions can include (1) trade embargoes that prohibit all merchandise and/or service trade between the sender and target, (2) more limited trade bans on certain goods or services, (3) restrictions on investment and other financial flows, (4) limitations on travel, and (5) limits on the transfer of nonfinancial assets between nations (as in the case of technology transfer regulations).

HISTORY AS A GUIDE: FINDINGS FROM VOL. I

In the first volume in this series, *Economic Sanctions: Examining Their Philosophy and Efficacy* (Askari, Forrer, Teegen, and Yang, [Praeger, 2003]), we conducted a historical survey of sanctions episodes around the world to gauge extant conditions for their use as foreign policy tools and glean initial insights into the factors associated with sanction effectiveness. The survey identified a marked upward trend in the use of economic sanctions, both unilateral (single sender) and multilateral (two or more senders), as a tool of foreign policy.

Multilateral sanctions provide fewer opportunities for targets to subvert restrictions, and they confer greater moral authority because they are supported by other members of the international community. But enforcement of such sanctions, particularly when imposed by ad hoc coalitions of sender nations (as opposed to senders organized into institutional blocs, as in the case of the League of Nations), is difficult owing to "free rider" problems and other moral hazards that make monitoring costs unwieldy (Mansfield 1995; Drezner 2000). Our survey found that few multilateral sanctions prevented or revoked acts of aggression by targets.

Definitional Refinements

Our historical investigation also prompted us to refine the term "economic sanction" to permit a more precise assessment of sanction effectiveness. Economic sanctions can be classified along several dimensions, and one salient dimension concerns the nature of the rationale(s) for a particular economic sanction. In this volume we extend the work of Bonetti (1998) to propose four distinct, though not necessarily mutually exclusive, rationale-based classifications for economic sanctions. These four classifications—purposeful, palliative, punitive, and partisan—are described in the following paragraphs.

Purposeful economic sanctions are intended by the sender to inflict economic hardship and thus coerce the target into changing objectionable policies. This rationale describes the types of economic sanctions most commonly addressed in the literature (see Hufbauer, Schott, and Elliott 1990).

Palliative economic sanctions are imposed to publicly register displeasure with the actions or policies of the target. The most pertinent audience for such sanctions may be internal to the target or the sender, but as the venue for such protestations is inherently international, the sanctions may be intended for primary consideration by supranational actors, such as global civil society. The value to the sender under this rationale comes from taking a public stand against target policies deemed objectionable; no expectation of policy change by the target is anticipated per se. Additionally, no direct consideration of the harm caused by the sender is germane—any economic sanction that is interpreted by relevant audiences to signal the sender's displeasure with the target is sufficient when referring to a palliative sanction.

Punitive economic sanctions are intended to inflict harm on the target country without explicit consideration of policy change by the target nation. These sanctions offer opportunities for senders to retaliate for specific actions taken (or avoided) by the target nation. This rationale requires an expectation of tangible harm to the target but assumes no explicit anticipation of policy change by the target.

Partisan economic sanctions are intended to promote parochial commercial or other interests. They seek to limit certain activities of the target nation so that particular groups or entities within the sender country (or third countries) might be differentially aided or harmed. For example, sanctions restricting exports of agricultural products from a target nation would serve to promote the interests of domestic producers as well as exporters from trading partners not subject to such sanctions.

Assessing Sanction Efficacy/Success as a Function of Sanction Rationale

Many economic sanctions are imposed for a combination of reasons. Identifying and understanding the underlying rationale(s) for a given economic sanction is a critical first step in assessing the efficacy of the sanction. If a sanction is intended to be purposeful, the relevant gauge of its success or efficacy would be whether the target nation amends or revokes its objectionable policy. If the sender determines that the target's objectionable policies have been changed or withdrawn, it logically should repeal or circumscribe the purposeful economic sanction. Where palliative, punitive, or partisan rationales prompt an economic sanction, no such expectation of policy change by the target is explicitly anticipated.

Drawing a distinction between different types of sanctions based upon their rationales highlights the association of different objectives with different types of sanctions. Using our typology of sanctions helps explain why nations retain sanctions even when they seem ineffective in coercing other countries to change their policies. Longstanding economic sanctions may, in fact, be meeting their objectives—just not the objectives of a *purposeful* economic sanction.

Only in the case of punitive sanctions is the intention of causing significant harm to the target made explicit. Therefore, specific yardsticks are required to gauge the effectiveness of other categories of sanctions in a relevant and defensible way.

Palliative sanctions, for instance, can be judged successful as long as intended audiences perceive the sanctions to convey displeasure by the sender—admittedly a low standard for efficacy. All a sending nation need do in such instances is convince these audiences of its intention to register said displeasure.

Punitive sanctions, on the other hand, cannot be deemed effective unless the sender can demonstrate some significant harm to the target. The form of this harm can vary and can be tailored to affect given sectors or groups within the target.

Partisan sanctions may be assessed according to the benefits that accrue to some groups or associations or the costs that are imposed on others. These benefits and costs may take the form of higher or lower prices, larger or smaller market shares, stronger or weaker business relationships, or better or worse global strategic positions.

Our sanctions survey showed that most sanctions episodes in the past tended toward the purposeful, partisan, and punitive types; we identified few instances of palliative rationales for sanctions. Explicit consideration of the likelihood of achieving stated objectives through purposeful rationales, with specific enforcement measures taken to ensure such achievement, were documented throughout the historical record. Perhaps the nature of commerce, whereby individual nations historically were less integrated economically relative to current times, explains the attention to purpose in motivating, implementing, and enforcing sanctions policy.

Of the four rationales for sanctions, the purposeful and punitive most clearly lend themselves to formal empirical validation of the costs exacted and/or harm inflicted by economic sanctions. This stems from the fact that these two rationales depend upon sufficiency and/or extensiveness of harm for their success.

Using Gravity Models to Assess Efficacy

The extant empirical work on sanctions has tended to focus on merchandise trade costs (with extensions to export sector employment) to both the sender nation and the target nation. The work of Hufbauer, Schott, and Elliott (1990), which uses a basic classification scheme to categorize sanctions events (e.g., comprehensive or selective) and a gravity model to estimate direct trade losses by sanctioning and sanctioned countries, is widely cited.

In our previous volume, we made important refinements to this standard approach for measuring the costs of sanctions by incorporating bilateral trade data (separated into imports and exports) for many more countries and many more years and by utilizing a wider variety of sanctions classification schemes to assess the robustness of our cost estimates. We further advanced the measurement of sanctions costs by incorporating additional explanatory factors into the gravity model (such as common economic bloc membership) and examining the potential benefits of trade diversion from the United States to third countries and regions like Japan and the European Union.

Although our findings did not differ significantly from existing work in this area in terms of the overall costs of sanctions for the United States as a sender country,[1] we did find evidence that sanctions episode classification is a critical determinant of costs (and thus impact) to both senders and targets. We found that Russia and China are the selectively sanctioned nations most affected, in direct trade terms, by U.S. unilateral sanctions, while Iran and Cuba are the comprehensively sanctioned nations most affected by such sanctions.

Although gravity models are useful in gleaning the aggregate merchandise trade costs to a given nation from sanctions, they fall short in terms of fully accounting for all relevant costs to senders and targets. Even in terms of merchandise trade costs, aggregate gravity models are insufficient to distinguish between simple foreign exchange losses from a sanction and deadweight losses in instances where prohibited trade does not result in a redeployment of productive assets to goods tradable elsewhere or consumed domestically. Gravity model assessments of sanctions also ignore spillovers, or indirect trade (through third countries) impacts.

Since purposeful sanctions in particular (and punitive sanctions as well) require a sufficient level of harm to a target nation, improved methods of assessing all relevant costs to the target (as well as to the sender and third parties) are needed to provide a comprehensive and confident appraisal of a particular sanction's success. Even in the case of palliative and partisan sanctions, where specific levels of harm are not required, knowledge of the full costs and benefits associated with sanctions aids in evaluating their utility as foreign and/or commercial policy tools.

The shortcomings of our own (albeit improved) gravity model of aggregate costs of sanctions, coupled with a review of previous work in the area of sanctions, lead us to argue that the following considerations are critical for a more comprehensive assessment of the efficacy of economic sanctions.

SANCTIONS EFFECTIVENESS: PROPOSED CONSIDERATIONS

This section addresses what we believe to be some of the critical factors relevant to assessing the impact and/or effectiveness of economic sanctions beyond the basic delineation of rationales discussed previously. This inventory will serve to guide our efforts in this volume, which is based upon three case studies, to improve and refine our understanding of the specific impacts of economic sanctions. In particular, we will explore economic sanctions imposed unilaterally by the United States on China, Cuba, and Iran.

Scale and Scope of Sanctions

Sanctions may cover all economic interactions between a sender and a target or focus on some relevant subset. Areas of economic activity subject to sanctions include merchandise trade (in aggregate or in certain sectors), services trade (in aggregate or in certain sectors), technology transfers, direct investment, portfolio investment, lending/lending guarantees (commercial, sovereign, and via multilateral institutions), and travel.

The scale and scope of a sanction are often related to the rationale for the sanction. Partisan sanctions, for example, might apply to a certain industrial sector, while palliative sanctions might most readily be imposed in venues involving multiple actors, as in the case of lending by multilateral institutions. So-called "smart" sanctions are often heralded in today's press as inherently more effective and/or just than universal sanctions. A refined view of a sanction's scale and scope must also account for variations in the degree to which a particular sanction is enforced.

Effects of Sanctions: Multilateral versus Unilateral Imposition

Despite the coordination and enforcement concerns inherent in multilateral sanctions, current research favors them, largely because of the moral traction they provide. Although certain sanctions are imposed unilaterally, some degree of "multilateralism creep" exists for most sanctions via sender influence in multilateral fora (e.g., the World Trade Organization and International Monetary Fund) or through quid pro quo commercial relationships (as seen in the case of government procurement among "friendly" nations in support of an otherwise unilateral sanction). Thus, the degree to which a particular sanction truly represents unilateral action on the part of the sender ought to affect the sanction's efficacy.

Sanctions also have the potential to create positive as well as negative impacts for third countries. To the extent a sender can direct a sanction's benefits toward allies and/or impose its negative consequences on third nations with which the sender is at political or economic odds, a sanction may be deemed more successful.

Dependency in Commerce and Investment

Commercial and investment relationships between countries are predicated on a variety of factors, including each nation's economic and political profiles as well as global economic conditions shaping trade and investment patterns. A sanction thus represents merely a *potential* rupture in predicted or "natural" linkages between the sender and the target nation(s).

Where two economies are otherwise linked extensively owing to economic and political factors, the impact of a given sanction should be more acute. Similarly, where one nation's trading or investment success hinges upon participation with another nation—as in the case of selling to a large, wealthy market or laying investment groundwork in markets reflecting high levels of pent-up demand and market growth potential, or where a nation controls access to scarce and valuable commodities—a sanction's impact should be more pervasive.

Most economic linkages involve "sticky" investments in assets, relationships, and knowledge acquisition that are not readily duplicable in short order.[2] Thus, sanctions against targets that depend heavily on economic linkages with the sender will proscribe the targets' ability to evade the sanctions through increased economic engagement with other nations.[3] Multinational firms with carefully calculated strategies that involve economic activity across borders may be able to realign their relationships to thwart the effect of a given sanction. Once a sanction is imposed, however, it may constrain full strategic latitude on the part of firms and other economic actors.

A related issue concerns the degree to which economic linkages affect ubiquitous goods, services, or financial flows. Where ready substitutes exist, the economic impact of a given sanction will easily be dulled through diversion.

Stakeholders: Organization, Location, and Influence

Since economic sanctions are tools of international policy, their efficacy will depend upon the degree to which important and influential stakeholders (1) recognize the sanction and its intended rationale, (2) are sufficiently concerned[4] about issues related to the sanction and/or its rationale to take action for or against the sanction, (3) are organized into effective groups to support or oppose a sanction, (4) can efficiently mobilize their varied resources to influence outcomes in the sender nation, target nation, or other relevant venues, and (5) participate in fora that provide political "space" or "voice" to such groups. One potentially important stakeholder group is a target nation's diaspora community—former citizens of the target who reside overseas and particularly those who reside in the sending nation. If a sanction cannot attract the attention of stakeholders in the sender country, the target country, or elsewhere and motivate them to act, it will not be successful, regardless of its rationale.

Economic Sanctions for Noneconomic Ends: Policy Options and the Credibility Gap

Both economic as well as noneconomic considerations prompt the imposition of sanctions. For intended economic ends, economic sanctions seem a fitting policy prescription, matching the tool to the "problem." Thus, in cases where a sending nation has a particular economic grievance with a target, an economic sanction tends to pass muster on the grounds of appropriateness.

Increasingly, however, economic sanctions are imposed with noneconomic ends in mind. In certain instances, policymakers in the sender country identify economic sanctions as being preferable in terms of potential cost or hardship (principally to the sender itself, but sometimes to "innocent" citizens in the target nation) to other policy options, such as military action. In making these policy tradeoffs, sender nations tend to discount the impact on human life and/or other costs associated with noneconomic policy alternatives. Where such a mismatch between sanction rationale and intended outcome exists, assessments of efficacy will be difficult at best. Like beauty in the eye of the beholder, an economic sanction's effectiveness in producing a primarily political outcome might well depend upon prior notions of legitimate choices among, and the application of, policy instruments.

MOTIVATIONS UNDERLYING AN EXAMINATION OF CHINA, CUBA, AND IRAN

This volume seeks to extend our work in Volume I by overcoming some of the shortfalls of existing research on sanctions. We therefore explicitly consider the relevant factors outlined previously in assessing the efficacy of unilateral U.S. sanctions imposed against three distinct target nations: China, Cuba, and Iran.

These three nations are among the most frequently cited examples of unilateral U.S. economic sanctions in recent years. Our gravity model assessments further point to the important merchandise trade impacts of U.S. sanctions against these three countries.

A Brief History of U.S. Sanctions Against China and Their Rationales

The United States imposed trade sanctions against China in the early 1950s, during the Korean War. The stated purpose of the sanctions was to prevent the spread of communism in the region, so these early restrictions could be considered purposeful or at least palliative in nature.

In 1971 the United States lifted the trade sanctions, signaling a resumption of political relations with China under President Nixon's "Open Door Policy." They were replaced with sanctions on exports of high technology and dual-use (potential commercial as well as military applications) goods and services to China. These sanctions could be considered partisan in nature, imposed in response to pressure from the U.S. military, which feared potential military development in a geopolitically strategic nation.

In the late 1980s, the United States invoked the entire range of rationales for imposing sanctions against China: punitive (in response to human rights abuses in the Tiananmen incident); palliative (to promote democracy and basic human rights, such as freedom of religion and avoidance of objectionable social policies and practices); partisan (to encourage market access and intellectual property rights protection); and purposeful (to effect policy changes across many of these areas).

A Brief History of U.S. Sanctions Against Cuba and Their Rationales

In the case of Cuba, an almost complete economic embargo by the United States has been in place to some degree since the Cuban Revolution of 1959. Until 1990 and the collapse of the Soviet Union—the erstwhile economic and political patron of the Castro regime in Cuba—U.S. sanctions were driven by the global and (to a greater extent) regional threat of communism. This threat was both a purposeful and palliative rationale for sanctions.

Since 1990, U.S. policy toward Cuba has evolved, and sanctions now are intended to bring about a democratically elected government and improve Cuba's human rights practices. Although purposeful and palliative rationales exist for these sanctions, a partisan rationale is also present, considering the important role of the Cuban diaspora in perpetuating U.S. sanctions policy toward the island. Heightened and more extensive enforcement of sanctions also are intended to punish Cuba for certain actions, such as the alleged downing in the early 1980s of a plane being flown by members of the Cuban exile community.

A Brief History of U.S. Sanctions Against Iran and Their Rationales

The United States has imposed sanctions on Iran since 1979. Although these sanctions may be considered comprehensive, they contained for many years an important loophole permitting indirect imports of Iranian oil by the United States. The loophole was closed in 1995, and sanctions against Iran were strengthened in 1996 by the passage of the Iran–Libya Sanctions Act (ILSA).

The taking of U.S. hostages by Iran and alleged Iranian support for terrorism in the region clearly have provoked punitive sanctions, while U.S. desires to deter Iran from developing and disseminating weapons of mass destruction and to encourage Iran's support for Middle East peace have prompted the imposition of purposeful sanctions. The promotion of human rights, particularly for women and certain ethnic groups in Iran, is cited as both a purposeful and palliative rationale for sanctions. Iran's energy resources, coupled with a virtual global oligopoly in such resources, may entail a partisan rationale for sanctions as well.

Summary of Intended Extensions Afforded by Case Analyses

China, Cuba, and Iran have been shown to be important cases for further examination owing to the merchandise trade impact on their economies and to the interest expressed in the popular press concerning U.S. sanctions policy. They also provide interesting cases in terms of rationale classification diversity. As we argued previously, a valid assessment of a sanction's impact first requires a careful analysis of the sanction's motivation(s).

These cases also reflect important economic and political differences that we believe will play a role in sanctions efficacy once the full scale and scope of the relevant sanctions are assessed. China, for example, has a large and growing production platform and internal market for a wide range of goods and services; Cuba depends on traditional Caribbean exports (agriculture, minerals, and tourism); and Iran's economy is dominated by energy exports. Geographic proximity to the United States and an influential diaspora characterize Cuba, but not Iran or China. China represents a case of selective sanctions compared to the more comprehensive sanctions imposed on Iran and Cuba. The particular areas in which sanctions are applied will be assessed to glean insights into the impact of each on the target's economy and the importance of these areas for various stakeholders.

Although all three countries nominally are targets of unilateral U.S. economic sanctions, each has elements of multilateralism that will be explored. In all three cases, explicit economic as well as political ends are incorporated into U.S. sanctions policy. All three also have unique domestic economic structures that highlight the importance (but also complicate the task) of disentangling the effects of the sanctions per se from those of domestic policies on the target's economy and society.

The rich diversity represented by our three cases provides us the opportunity to explore in great detail the impact of unilateral U.S. economic sanctions on target nations, on the United States as the sending nation, and on third countries. With this volume we seek to consider a larger inventory of relevant costs and benefits stemming from these policies so as to provide policymakers with more nuanced evidence and conclusions concerning the efficacy of sanctions. In this way, we will add important insight into questions concerning the use of unilateral economic sanctions and their usefulness in the U.S. foreign policy toolkit.

NOTES

1. We estimate annual losses in exports for the United States at between $14 billion and $23-plus billion, owing largely to the impact of "selectively" sanctioned nations.

2. Portfolio investments are the least "sticky" of sanctionable economic activities. Where they dominate linkages between a target and a sender, prompt and full displacement of sanctioned investment flows by third countries is likely.

3. In our gravity model assessments, we noted some evidence of lingering effects of sanctions subsequent to their lifting.

4. The concern indicated here relates specifically to the degree to which a given sanction is perceived to create "winners" and "losers." Such cleavages serve as rallying cries to stakeholder groups and spur them to organize to support or oppose the sanction.

CHAPTER 2

U.S. Economic Sanctions Against China

INTRODUCTION

U.S. economic sanctions against China have evolved over the past half-century. Viewing China as an adversary and wanting to contain the spread of communism, the United States imposed an embargo on all trade with China from the time of the Korean War until mid-1971. Since the embargo was lifted, U.S. exports to China have been subject to a complex system that restricts exports of goods, services, and technology with military or dual-use military and civilian applications (Lardy 1994). The Tiananmen crisis in June 1989 has made human rights a more prominent basis for U.S. economic sanctions or the threat of sanctions against China. In more recent years, as China's trade with the United States has expanded and U.S. trade deficits with China have grown, U.S. economic sanctions have also been used to address intellectual property rights and market access issues.

The rationale and structure of U.S. economic sanctions against China reflect all of the major goals of U.S. foreign policy (Preeg 1999a). Geopolitical considerations, national security concerns, human rights/democratization issues, domestic politics, and commercial interests all have played a significant role in motivating the various types of sanctions or threats of sanctions against China that exist today. On the grounds of human rights, the United States has threatened to employ broadly based or comprehensive sanctions by terminating China's most-favored-nation (MFN) trading status. On the grounds of arms proliferation and national security, the United States has used export controls restricting China's access to advanced technologies. On the grounds of intellectual property rights protection and market access, the United States has threatened to use punitive tariffs against major imports from China (mainly labor-intensive goods) and to withhold China's application for accession to the World Trade Organization (WTO).

U.S. economic sanctions against China reflect U.S. relations with China, and current U.S.–China relations are characterized by cooperation *and* tension. While interdependence and mutual interest have often brought the two countries together in the international arena, differences in their political systems and cultural backgrounds and a historic lack of mutual trust frequently have generated political tensions. It should be noted at the outset that many of the issues that have motivated U.S. economic sanctions against China are politically sensitive and highly controversial. China has consistently denied the allegations on which U.S. sanctions have been based and has disputed the rationale for the sanctions.

Despite claims in recent years that the two countries are committed to building a constructive and strategic partnership, U.S. economic sanctions against China are likely to persist. This is due to the delicate and fragile nature of their relationship. As Ross (1998a) points out, instability arises from such factors as historical legacies, elite and societal ideological differences, interest groups, and domestic economic and political interests. Thus, U.S. economic sanctions against China pose an issue of long-term relevance for both academic and policy research.

This study focuses on the impact of U.S. economic sanctions against China. The consequences of sanctions are evaluated from both countries' perspectives at both the macroeconomic and microeconomic levels. At the macroeconomic level, we examine how sanctions have affected trade flows (both exports and imports), investments, employment, and overall economic development. At the microeconomic level, we highlight the impact on companies and industry sectors.

This case analysis briefly reviews China's economic development within the context of U.S.–China relations and U.S. economic sanctions against China. It describes the major U.S. economic sanctions against China that are still in effect today, assesses the impact of these sanctions on trade between the two countries, and discusses the overall impact (aside from trade) of sanctions on the Chinese and U.S. economies. It concludes by analyzing the effectiveness of U.S. sanctions against China and offering some perspectives for U.S.–China economic relations in the future.

U.S. ECONOMIC SANCTIONS AND CHINA'S ECONOMIC DEVELOPMENT

Economic and trade relations between the United States and China date back to the early days of the independence of the United States. At the end of World War II, the United States was China's leading trade partner (Xu 1999). But after the Communist Party of China, led by Mao Zedong, gained power in China in 1949, trade between the two countries dried up very quickly. Since then, sanctions against China have been part of U.S.–China economic relations, although the sanctions have assumed different forms and taken on different levels of severity during this period.

This section briefly describes the evolution of U.S. economic sanctions against China and China's economic development since the mid-twentieth century. Based on the nature of U.S. sanctions and China's economic development, this description can be divided into the following time frames: (1) 1950–71, a period marked by a U.S. trade embargo and China's efforts at reconstruction under international isolation; (2) 1972–78, a period of ice-breaking between the two countries while China moved toward the end of the Cultural Revolution; (3) 1979–88, a ten-year period during which U.S.–China economic relations moved toward normalization and China made significant progress toward economic reform; (4) 1989–94, a period of setbacks and attempted improvements in economic relations between the two countries while China pressed forward with its economic reforms; and (5) 1995–2001, a period riddled with trade disputes and political tensions between the United States and China while the latter continued its efforts to join the World Trade Organization (WTO).

1950–71: The U.S. Trade Embargo Against China and China's Reconstruction

The United States imposed selective trade controls on China as soon as the communist forces began to win the civil war early in 1949 (Cohen, Dernberger, and Garson 1971). Export controls were then gradually tightened until a total embargo was imposed on China by the United States following the outbreak of the Korean War. In May 1950 the United Nations, led by the United States, passed a resolution of total embargo on trade with China. The United States also was instrumental in creating the Coordinating Committee on Multilateral Export Controls (COCOM), comprising representatives of the NATO countries and Japan, to supervise the embargo (Lubman 1978). By 1951, there was virtually no trade between China and the United States (Cohen, Dernberger, and Garson 1971).

Given the hostile international environment, China pursued a policy of independence and self-reliance in reconstructing an economy that had been torn through century-long civil conflicts and wars against foreign invaders. With a few dramatic changes—land reform, nationalization of enterprises, and rural communization—China transformed itself in the 1950s from what had been referred to as a semi-colonial economy to a publicly (state-) owned and centrally planned economy modeled after the Soviet Union.

During this period, international isolation, unprecedented natural disasters, and a succession of political movements (including the Cultural Revolution) exerted enduring hardships on the

Table 2.1
China's GDP Growth, 1953–2001

Year	Growth Rate	Year	Growth Rate
1953	15.6	1978	11.7
1954	4.2	1979	7.6
1955	6.8	1980	7.8
1956	15.0	1981	5.2
1957	5.1	1982	9.1
1958	21.3	1983	10.9
1959	8.8	1984	15.2
1960	−0.3	1985	13.5
1961	−27.3	1986	8.8
1962	−5.6	1987	11.6
1963	10.2	1988	11.3
1964	18.3	1989	4.1
1965	17.0	1990	3.8
1966	10.7	1991	9.2
1967	−5.7	1992	14.2
1968	−4.1	1993	13.5
1969	16.9	1994	12.6
1970	19.4	1995	10.5
1971	7.0	1996	9.6
1972	3.8	1997	8.8
1973	7.9	1998	7.8
1974	2.3	1999	7.1
1975	8.7	2000	8.0
1976	−1.6	2001	7.3
1977	7.6		

Note: Calculations based on constant price.
Sources: China National Bureau of Statistics, China Statistics Yearbook (various issues).

Chinese people, yet statistics show China experienced relatively high though volatile economic growth (see Table 2.1). This was due to at least two reasons. First, the Chinese economy was virtually in ruins when the communists took over, so the base for economic growth was very small. Second, despite the internal turmoil in China, these years represented a relatively peaceful period that people in China had long awaited, resulting in great enthusiasm for, and effort toward, reconstruction.

While there was virtually no trade between China and the United States during these years, China traded with other countries, particularly the Soviet Union and Eastern European nations. To the extent the U.S. embargo, coupled with its allied trade controls, limited the movement of goods between China and noncommunist countries, it forced China to rely on the Soviet Union even more than might otherwise have been the case (Cohen, Dernberger, and Garson 1971).

1972–78: Resumption of U.S.–China Trade and the End of China's Cultural Revolution

Several major events took place around the beginning of this time period. In 1971, the People's Republic of China replaced Taiwan in representing China in the United Nations. The following year, President Richard Nixon made his historic visit to China. In the wake of these ice-breaking events, the COCOM agreed to loosen its export controls and allow China to be treated the same as the Soviet Union. Thereafter, U.S. citizens were permitted to make purchases from China and pay for them in dollars. Exports, instead of being under a total embargo, were under the same export control restrictions as sales to the Soviet Union (Lubman 1978). After a more than twenty-year hiatus, trade between the United States and China began to grow.

Mao Zedong, who had led the Communists to power after World War II and served as party chairman since 1949, died in 1976, and with him died the destructive Cultural Revolution. With Deng Xiaoping, a veteran revolutionary, in the country's lead, the Chinese government began in 1978 to shift its focus from political struggle to a modernization campaign that called for a change from self-reliance to opening doors to the outside world. This marked the beginning of China's economic reform.

Together, changes in U.S.–China relations and in China's internal policy brought about a significant increase in U.S.–China trade, from virtually nothing in 1971 to more than $2 billion in 1978.

1979–88: Improved Trade Relations and China's Economic Reform

The beginning of China's economic reform coincided roughly with the normalization of diplomatic relations between China and the United States on 1 January 1979. On 7 July 1979, the two governments signed the Trade Relations Agreement, which accorded each other most-favored-nation treatment (MFN) on a reciprocal basis.[1] In the following years, numerous other agreements were concluded, such as the Textile Trade Agreement (1980) and the Agreement on Civil Aviation and Sea Transportation (1980). In the meantime, three important joint working committees were established (on commerce and trade, science and technology, and economic affairs), and these have been regarded as effective mechanisms to promote dialogue between the two countries.

Starting in 1981, China was given access to higher levels of U.S. technology than the Soviet Union. Then, in December 1985, COCOM adopted what was called a "green line" policy toward China. This policy gave preferential licensing treatment for the export to China of 27 categories of controlled items as compared with other COCOM-proscribed countries (U.S. House 1999).

Internally, China undertook dramatic economic reforms over this time period. Reforms in the agricultural sector were particularly striking: the People's Communes were abolished, farmland was allocated to individual households for production responsibility, and controls on prices of farm products were gradually relaxed. As a result, China reaped bumper-crop harvests several years in a row. The majority of the population, who had suffered from severe food scarcity for centuries, began to enjoy an abundance of food. Many subsistence products that had been rationed for decades, such as wheat flour, rice, meat, and cooking oil, became plentiful. The agricultural reforms released much labor from the land and, in turn, helped spur the growth of the industrial sector. Labor-intensive industries, such as textiles, garments, toys, and other light industrial goods developed rapidly and became the driving force for China's exports. China's economy experienced one of its highest growth periods in history—more than 10 percent annually from 1983 to 1988.

China's economic reforms and open-door policy significantly increased its trade with the rest of the world. China's total trade topped $100 billion in 1990 for the first time in history (see Appendix 2.1). Improvements in U.S.–China relations also fueled China's trade growth, as trade between the two countries increased from $2.3 billion in 1979 to more than $14 billion in 1988 (see Table 2.2). U.S. exports to China more than doubled each year in

Table 2.2
U.S–China Trade, 1978–2001

	Exports to China		Imports from China		Total Trade	
Year	Value	Growth Rate (%)	Value	Growth Rate (%)	Value	Growth Rate (%)
1978	821.0		324.0		1,145.0	
1979	1,724.0	109.99	592.0	82.72	2,316.0	102.27
1980	3,755.0	117.81	1,164.4	96.69	4,919.4	112.41
1981	3,602.7	−4.06	2,062.4	77.12	5,665.1	15.16
1982	2,912.0	−19.17	2,502.4	21.33	5,414.4	−4.43
1983	2,173.1	−25.37	2,476.8	−1.02	4,649.9	−14.12
1984	3,004.3	38.25	3,381.4	36.52	6,385.7	37.33
1985	3,855.7	28.34	4,224.2	24.92	8,079.9	26.53
1986	3,106.3	−19.44	5,240.6	24.06	8,346.9	3.30
1987	3,497.3	12.59	6,910.4	31.86	10,407.7	24.69
1988	5,016.8	43.45	9,261.3	34.02	14,278.1	37.19
1989	5,807.4	15.76	12,901.0	39.30	18,708.4	31.03
1990	4,807.2	−17.22	16,295.8	26.31	21,103.0	12.80
1991	6,287.1	30.79	20,305.1	24.60	26,592.2	26.01
1992	7,469.6	18.81	27,412.5	35.00	34,882.1	31.17
1993	8,767.1	17.37	33,512.7	22.25	42,279.8	21.21
1994	9,286.9	5.93	41,362.4	23.42	50,649.3	19.80
1995	11,748.5	26.51	48,520.7	17.31	60,269.2	18.99
1996	11,977.9	1.95	54,408.9	12.14	66,386.8	10.15
1997	12,805.4	6.91	65,831.7	20.99	78,637.1	18.45
1998	14,258.0	11.34	75,109.2	14.09	89,367.2	13.65
1999	12,943.6	−9.22	86,480.6	15.14	99,424.2	11.25
2000	15,963.7	23.33	106,215.0	22.82	122,178.7	22.89
2001	19,200.0	20.27	109,400.0	3.00	128,600.0	5.26

Note: As reported by the United States; values in $ millions.
Source: U.S. Department of Commerce.

both 1979 and 1980, although U.S. export controls against China remained intact through both unilateral and multilateral sanctions. As Table 2.2 shows, trade between the two countries, though growing, was very volatile during this period due to uncertainty in trade relations.

1989–94: The Tiananmen Sanctions and China's Reaffirmation of Reform

In the early summer of 1989, a student-led movement in Beijing developed into an anti-government confrontation, with demonstrators occupying Tiananmen Square for several weeks.[2] On 4 June, the standoff ended with a government crackdown resulting in the deaths of hundreds of army soldiers, students, and others at the scene. The incident drew immediate and dramatic international reactions. Japan suspended a five-year, $5.5 billion loan to China due to start in April 1990 (Riddell 1989a), and COCOM decided in October 1989 to cancel plans for additional liberalization of export controls toward China. COCOM did not, however, make any changes to the "green line" policy in effect at the time (U.S. House 1999).

The United States reacted by imposing very broad sanctions, including a suspension of official and military exchanges between the two governments, a prohibition on U.S. trade financing and investment insurance for China-related projects, and an embargo on exports to military and police entities in China. The most severe U.S. sanction against China was a linkage of China's MFN status to human rights. Subsequently, China's MFN status with the United States was subject to annual review by the U.S. Congress. The United States began to threaten China to show greater respect for human rights or risk losing its MFN trading status, which would effectively price Chinese goods out of the American market (Ross 1998b).

The Tiananmen crisis also brought changes to China's political leadership. Jiang Zemin, the mayor of Shanghai, replaced Zhao Ziyang as the Communist Party's leader immediately after the Tiananmen incident. Deng Xiaoping, who was instrumental in the Tiananmen event, continued to play a leading role in China's development. The process of economic reform, instead of being halted by the political turmoil, pressed forward. Realizing that political unrest was due at least partly to rising inflation, the Chinese government readjusted its macroeconomic policy and tightened the money supply. Inflation, as measured by the consumer price index, declined from more than 18 percent in 1988 and 1989 to roughly 3 percent in 1990 and 1991 (see Table 2.3). This was accompanied by slower economic growth, at rates of 4.1 percent and 3.8 percent in 1989 and 1990, respectively.

In the spring of 1992, Deng Xiaoping led China to take bolder steps in its economic reform and open-door policies. Dramatic measures were taken to move state-owned enterprises toward a market economy, encourage foreign economic cooperation, and attract foreign investment. Foreign investment in China, including investment from the United States, jumped beginning in 1992: The value of new investment contracts reached $58 billion that year, up from $12 billion in 1991. The Chinese economy resumed its double-digit growth from 1992 to 1995.

Correspondingly, economic sanctions by the industrialized countries started to loosen. A COCOM meeting in June 1990 elimi-

Table 2.3
China's Economic Record, 1970–2000 (Selected Financial Indicators)

Year	Consumer Price Change (% Annual)	End-of-Period Bank Rate (% Annual)	Trade Balance ($ Millions)	Current Account Balance ($ Millions)	International Reserves ($ Millions)	Average Annual Exchange Rate (RMB/$)
1970						2.46
1971						2.46
1972						2.25
1973						1.99
1974						1.96
1975						1.86
1976						1.94
1977					2,345.0	1.86
1978					1,557.0	1.68
1979					2,154.0	1.56
1980					2,545.2	1.50
1981					5,058.1	1.70
1982			4,249.0	5,674.0	11,348.9	1.89
1983			1,990.0	4,240.0	14,986.6	1.98
1984			14.0	2,030.0	17,366.0	2.32
1985			−13,123.0	−11,417.0	12,728.1	2.94
1986			−9,140.0	−7,034.0	11,453.0	3.45
1987	7.22		−1,661.0	300.0	16,304.9	3.72
1988	18.74		−5,315.0	−3,802.0	18,541.3	3.72
1989	18.33		−5,620.0	−4,317.0	17,959.9	3.77
1990	3.06	7.92	9,165.0	11,997.0	29,586.2	4.78
1991	3.54	7.20	8,743.0	13,272.0	43,674.3	5.32
1992	6.34	7.20	5,183.0	6,401.0	20,620.4	5.51
1993	14.58	10.08	−10,654.0	−11,609.0	22,386.9	5.76
1994	24.24	10.08	7,290.0	6,908.0	52,914.1	8.62
1995	16.90	10.44	18,050.1	1,618.4	75,376.7	8.35
1996	8.32	9.00	19,535.0	7,243.0	107,039.0	8.31
1997	2.81	8.55	46,222.0	36,963.0	142,762.0	8.29
1998	−0.84	4.59	46,614.0	31,472.0	149,188.0	8.28
1999	−1.41	3.24	35,982.0	21,115.0	157,728.0	8.28
2000	0.26	3.24	34,473.7	20,518.4	168,278.0	8.28

Source: International Monetary Fund, International Financial Statistics (various issues).

nated or significantly reduced the differences between items that could be exported to China under the "green line" policy and items that could be exported to other proscribed destinations. According to a report by a select committee of the U.S. House of Representatives (1999), China benefited from the decontrols adopted by COCOM for all proscribed destinations subsequent to that meeting. The COCOM member countries reached an agreement in January 1994 to raise the threshold level of computers that would not require an export license to most destinations, including China, from 12.5 million theoretical operations per second (MTOPS) to 260 million.[3]

China's international trade did not suffer much from the Tiananmen crisis. Measured in constant dollars, China's total imports and exports maintained a positive growth rate from 1989 to 1994. U.S.–China trade also increased, from less than $20 billion in 1989 to more than $50 billion in 1994, although U.S. exports to China declined by 17 percent in 1990. U.S. investment in China increased from a mere $284 million in 1989 to about $2.5 billion in 1994.

1995–2001: Escalating Tensions and New Challenges for China

As the twentieth century ended and the twenty-first dawned, U.S.–China political and economic relations began to traverse a bumpier road. A few dramatic events—including a visit by Taiwan's leader to the United States in 1995 and China's ensuing missile test across the Taiwan Strait in 1996, the NATO bombing of the Chinese embassy in Yugoslavia in May 1999, and the collision between a U.S. spy plane and a Chinese fighter jet near China's coast in April 2001—heightened tensions between the two countries. This increasing uneasiness between the United States and China may have had its roots in the broader geopolitical context. According to Ross (1998a), the rapid disappearance of the Soviet threat led to escalated U.S.–China conflict over a wide range of issues and the emergence of a new bilateral bargaining relationship reflecting new dependencies and new sources of negotiating leverage.

The 1990s, particularly the latter half, were riddled with trade conflicts as well as political confrontations between the United States and China. While many of the previous export controls and Tiananmen sanctions were still in effect, the United States began to increase pressure on China on more diversified grounds. Human rights issues continued to haunt China's MFN trading status. Accusations that China stole U.S. military and high-tech secrets (as exemplified by a congressional report on U.S. national security and military/commercial concerns with China[4]) and tensions over Taiwan prompted the United States to further restrict its exports to China.

Moreover, sanctions or the threat of sanctions increasingly were used to target economic issues such as intellectual property rights protection and market access. In the long and strenuous process of China's application to join the WTO, including efforts to join the predecessor organization (the General Agreement on Tariffs and Trade, or GATT), the United States effectively used its leverage as a world trade power to persuade China to agree to open its markets to U.S. exports and allow U.S. investment in agriculture, telecommunications, financial services, and other sectors.

China's economy continued to grow during these years, albeit at a slower rate. China survived the Asian financial crisis that started in the summer of 1997 and maintained its pre-crisis exchange rate. This was due at least in part to its insulation from external financial markets through limited convertibility of its currency. In its ongoing reform of state-owned enterprises, China further loosened its grip on small and medium-sized firms while keeping control of a handful of large ones. Enterprises at local levels and even many large businesses in China are now privately owned. In 1999, non-state-owned enterprises accounted for 72 percent of total industrial production (see Table 2.4). In 2001, the added value of non-state-owned enterprises constituted about two-thirds of total added value in industrial production in China.[5]

Table 2.4
Public and Private Industrial Production in China (Values in 100 Million RMB)

Year	Total Value of Industrial Production	Value of Production of State-owned Enterprises	Share of production of State-owned Enterprises	Share of production of Non-state-owned Enterprises
1952	349	145	41.55%	58.45%
1957	704	378	53.69%	46.31%
1962	920	808	87.83%	12.17%
1965	1,402	1,263	90.09%	9.91%
1970	2,117	1,855	87.62%	12.38%
1975	3,207	2,601	81.10%	18.90%
1978	4,237	3,289	77.63%	22.37%
1980	5,154	3,916	75.98%	24.02%
1985	9,716	6,302	64.86%	35.14%
1990	23,924	13,064	54.61%	45.39%
1991	26,625	14,955	56.17%	43.83%
1992	34,599	17,824	51.52%	18.18%
1993	48,402	22,725	46.95%	53.05%
1994	70,176	26,201	37.34%	62.66%
1995	91,894	31,220	33.97%	66.03%
1996	99,595	36,173	36.32%	63.68%
1997	113,733	35,968	31.62%	68.38%
1998	119,048	33,621	28.24%	71.76%
1999	126,111	35,571	28.21%	71.79%

Note: Values are measured at current prices.
Source: China National Bureau of Statistics.

Two decades of economic reform have made China one of the largest economies in the world. China's gross national product (GNP) reached $1.06 trillion in 2000, ranking it seventh in size globally, compared with $9.60 trillion for the United States, the largest economy in the world (see Table 2.5). According to an estimate based on purchasing power parity by the International Monetary Fund (IMF), China's gross domestic product (GDP) in 2001 was 12.1 percent of the world's total, second only to the United States, whose share was 21.4 percent (IMF 2002b). In terms of trade, as Table 2.6 shows, China's exports and imports totaled $249.3 billion and $225.1 billion, respectively, in 2000, ranking them seventh and eighth among all nations. China was the second-largest recipient (after the United States) of foreign direct investment over the last few years of the twentieth century.

Yet China is still a developing country and among the lowest-income countries in the world. As Table 2.5 shows, China's per-capita income was $840 in 2000, ranking it 141st in the world (compared with $34,100 in the United States, which ranked seventh). Even based on the World Bank's estimate using purchasing power parity, China's per-capita income was only $3,920, ranking it 124th in the world.

China's economic reform faces unprecedented challenges. Nonperforming loans by state-owned banks pose a severe test of the country's financial system. Increased unemployment resulting from reform of the state-owned enterprises has exerted mounting social pressure. The prospect of further liberalization in agricultural trade upon joining the WTO threatens the livelihoods of millions of farmers. Moreover, tensions with the United States may dim the prospect of a peaceful and stable international environment, which China has needed and still needs for its economic development.

TYPES OF U.S. ECONOMIC SANCTIONS AGAINST CHINA

U.S. economic sanctions against China can be divided into three major categories, which this section will describe in turn:

1. U.S. laws and regulations that apply to China but are not exclusive to China;
2. Multilateral sanctions that the United States leads or participates in that apply to China but are not exclusive to China; and
3. U.S. sanctions imposed specifically on China, although such sanctions may not necessarily be unique for China.

Appendix 2.2 lists major U.S. economic sanctions levied against China since 1949. The list contains all three categories of sanctions.

Table 2.5
Development Indicators for China and Selected Countries, 2000

	Area	Population Density		Gross National Income		Gross National Income Per Capita		PPP Estimates Gross National Income			GDP Growth 1999–2000	
Country	Population (millions)	(thousand sq. km.)	(people/ sq. km.)	($ billions)	(rank)	($)	(rank)	($ billions)	($ per capita)	(per-capita rank)	(%)	(% per capita)
United States	282	9,629	31	9,601.5	1	34,100	7	9,601	34,100	3	4.2	3.0
Japan	127	378	348	4,519.1	2	35,620	5	3,436	27,080	12	2.4	2.2
Germany	82	357	230	2,063.7	3	25,120	17	2,047	24,920	20	3.0	2.9
United Kingdom	60	243	248	1,459.5	4	24,430	21	1,407	23,550	27	3.1	2.7
France	59	552	107	1,438.3	5	24,090	23	1,438	24,420	24	3.1	2.6
Italy	58	301	196	1,163.2	6	20,160	30	1,354	23,470	28	2.9	2.8
China	1,262	9,598	135	1,062.9	7	840	141	4,951	3,920	124	7.9	7.2
Canada	31	9,971	3	649.8	8	21,130	26	836	27,170	11	4.5	3.6
Brazil	170	8,547	20	610.1	9	3,580	82	1,243	7,300	83	4.5	3.2
Spain	39	506	79	595.3	10	15,080	38	760	19,260	38	4.1	3.9
Mexico	98	1,958	51	497.0	11	5,070	69	861	8,790	76	6.9	5.3
India	1,016	3,287	342	454.8	12	450	159	2,375	2,340	153	3.9	2.0
South Korea	47	99	479	421.1	13	8,910	54	818	17,300	46	8.8	7.8
Netherlands	16	42	470	397.5	14	24,970	18	412	25,850	15	3.5	2.8
Australia	19	7,741	2	388.3	15	20,240	27	479	24,970	19	1.9	0.8

Note: PPP = Purchasing power parity.
Source: World Bank (2002).

Table 2.6
Leading Exporters and Importers in World Merchandise Trade, 2000

Rank	Exporter	Value ($ billions)	Share (% of world exports)	Annual Percentage Change	Rank	Importer	Value ($ billions)	Share (% of world imports)	Annual Percentage Change
1	United States	781.1	12.3	11	1	United States	1257.6	18.9	19
2	Germany	551.5	8.7	1	2	Germany	502.8	7.5	6
3	Japan	479.2	7.5	14	3	Japan	379.5	5.7	22
4	France	298.1	4.7	−1	4	United Kingdom	337.0	5.1	5
5	United Kingdom	284.1	4.5	6	5	France	305.4	4.6	4
6	Canada	276.6	4.3	16	6	Canada	244.8	3.7	11
7	China	249.3	3.9	28	7	Italy	236.5	3.5	7
8	Italy	237.8	3.7	1	8	China	225.1	3.4	36
9	Netherlands	212.5	3.3	6	9	Hong Kong	214.2	3.2	19
10	Hong Kong	202.4	3.2	16		retained imports	35.4	0.5	24
	domestic exports	23.7	0.4	6	10	Netherlands	198.0	3.0	4
	re-exports	178.8	2.8	18					

Note: Retained imports are defined as imports less re-exports.
Source: World Trade Organization (2001).

U.S. Trade Laws and Regulations that Apply to China

Export Controls

U.S. export controls date to before World War II, when restrictions on exports were imposed to ensure that adequate supplies of commodities would be available to meet wartime needs. After the war, export controls were continued, although changes were made in accordance with developments in the international environment (U.S. House 1999). The two principal statutes that govern U.S. export controls on China today are as follows:

1. The Export Administration Act of 1979, as amended, which controls "dual-use" items. These items comprise what is often called the "Commerce Control List," or CCL.
2. The Arms Export Control Act, which targets munitions items. These items constitute the "U.S. Munitions List," or USML.

These two statutes govern exports of, among other things, commercial communication satellites, high-performance computers, and machine tools.

Export Administration Regulations

The Export Administration Act of 1979 authorizes the U.S. government to regulate exports, improve the efficiency of export regulation, and minimize interference with the ability to engage in commerce.[6] To implement this law and other laws relating to the control of certain exports, re-exports, and activities, the Commerce Department's Bureau of Industry and Security (BIS)[7] issues Export Administration Regulations.

The BIS also maintains the Commerce Control List, which includes items subject to the export licensing authority of the BIS (i.e., commodities, software, and technology). The CCL does not include items exclusively controlled for export or re-export by another department or agency of the U.S. government. In instances where agencies other than the Department of Commerce administer controls over related items, entries in the CCL contain a reference to these controls.

The CCL is divided into ten categories, numbered as follows (EAR 2000):

0–Nuclear materials, facilities, and equipment and miscellaneous

1–Materials, chemicals, "microorganisms," and toxins

2–Materials processing

3–Electronics
4–Computers
5–Telecommunications and information security
6–Lasers and sensors
7–Navigation and avionics
8–Marine
9–Propulsion systems, space vehicles, and related equipment

Within each category, items are arranged by group. Each category contains the same five groups. Each group is identified by the letters A through E, as follows:

A–Equipment, assemblies, and components
B–Test, inspection, and production equipment
C–Materials
D–Software
E–Technology

The BIS also maintains a Commerce Country Chart, which contains licensing requirements based on destination and reasons for control. In combination with the CCL, the Commerce Country Chart allows U.S. enterprises to determine whether a license is required to export items on the CCL to any country in the world.

As Table 2.7 shows, China is among the most export-controlled countries in the world. Of sixteen columns corresponding to sixteen reasons for control, eleven are checked for China. That is, licenses are required for exports to China for almost every major reason, ranging from chemical and biological weapons to national security. Anti-terrorism and firearms conventions are the only reasons that do not apply to exports to China.

For export control purposes, foreign countries are separated into five groups designated by the symbols A, B, C, D, and E (see Appendix 2.3). Although no explicit justification for grouping is given in the EAR, casual observation reveals that Group A contains mostly industrialized countries and Group B mostly developing countries. Group C is reserved for special designations (and is blank as of 26 April 2002). Group E includes only Cuba, Iran, Iraq, North Korea, Libya, Sudan, and Syria, all labeled terrorist-supporting countries. China falls into Group D along with 45 other countries or regions, including countries in South Asia and the Middle East and those that formerly had centrally-planned economies. It should be noted that quite a few countries in this group—Bulgaria, India, Lebanon, and Pakistan, for example—are also listed in one or more

Table 2.7
U.S. Commerce Department Country Chart for Export Control (Selected Countries)

	Chemical/ Biological Weapons			Nuclear Nonpro- liferation		National Security		Missile Tech- nology	Regional Stability		Firearms Conven- tion	Crime Control			Anti- Terror ism	
Country	1	2	3	1	2	1	2	1	1	2	1	1	2	3	1	2
Brazil	X	X				X	X	X	X	X	X	X		X		
Canada											X					
China	X	X	X	X		X	X	X	X	X		X		X		
France	X					X		X	X							
Hong Kong	X	X		X		X		X	X	X		X		X		
India	X	X	X	X	X	X	X	X	X	X		X		X		
Italy	X					X		X	X							
Japan	X					X		X	X							
Korea, North	X	X	X	X	X	X	X	X	X	X		X	X	X	X	X
Korea, South	X					X		X	X	X		X		X		
Russia	X	X	X			X	X	X	X	X		X	X			
United Kingdom	X					X		X	X							

Source: U.S. Department of Commerce.

other groups. Although the grouping system appears to be perplexing and overlapping for some countries, it is clear that exports to China are subject to very restrictive controls.

U.S. Defense Trade Controls

The Arms Export Control Act authorizes the president to control the export and import of defense articles and services. The articles and services so designated constitute the USML (see Appendix 2.4 for its categories). In January 1977, President Ford issued Executive Order 11958, which delegated authority to the secretary of state to promulgate regulations (with the concurrence of the secretary of defense) with respect to exports of defense articles and services.

The general policy of prohibiting exports and sales of articles and services on the USML to certain countries, including China, is stipulated as follows:

> It is the policy of the United States to deny licenses, other approvals, exports and imports of defense articles and defense services, destined for or originating in certain countries. This policy applies to Afghanistan, Armenia, Azerbaijan, Belarus, Cuba, Iran, Iraq, Libya, North Korea, Syria, Tajikistan, and Vietnam. This policy also applies to countries with respect to which the United States maintains an arms embargo (e.g., Burma, China, the Federal Republic of Yugoslavia (Serbia and Montenegro), Haiti, Liberia, Rwanda, Somalia, Sudan and Zaire) or whenever an export would not otherwise be in furtherance of world peace and the security and foreign policy of the United States. (Code of Federal Regulations 2002)

China is among a number of countries that are on the Embargo Reference Chart maintained by the U.S. Defense Department as of June 2002 (see Appendix 2.5). China is being sanctioned under two particular federal regulations. One was issued on 5 June 1989 and suspended munitions exports to China (Public Notice 1109). The other was Amendment 126:1 to the International Traffic in Arms Regulations, prohibiting exports and sales of defense articles to China and other countries.

Multilateral Sanctions

The Export Administration Act of 1979 states that it is U.S. policy to administer such trade controls as necessary to cooperate with other nations and encourage all countries with which the United States has defense treaties or "common strategic objectives" to observe a uniform export control policy (EAA 1979). To this end, the United States has established its own export control regulations and also has led, or participated in, multilateral efforts to control exports. China has often been subject to these multilateral export controls.

Wassenaar Arrangement on Export Controls

As mentioned earlier, until its dissolution in March 1994, the Coordinating Committee on Multilateral Export Controls (COCOM) was the primary multinational export control organization through which the United States and the other member countries controlled the export of items for security purposes. China was a COCOM-proscribed country. In September 1996 COCOM was replaced by a new multinational organization called the Wassenaar Arrangement on Export Controls for Conventional Arms and Dual-Use Goods and Technologies (Wassenaar Arrangement). The Wassenaar Arrangement maintains a control list of export items similar to the previous COCOM list as it existed in 1993. Some items in the Wassenaar control list are included in the Commerce Control List and the remainder are included in the U.S. Munitions List (U.S. House 1999).

The Wassenaar Arrangement has a "no undercut agreement" on denials. Under this agreement, when a member country reports a denial of a sensitive item to the Wassenaar Secretariat, no other member will approve the sale of the same item to the same end user without first consulting the country that initially denied the export (U.S. House 1999). This agreement, in theory, obligates other member countries to impose the same export controls on China as the United States imposes.

The Australia Group

The Australia Group was established in 1984 as an informal forum for countries that seek to discourage and impede the proliferation of chemical and biological weapons. The Australia Group pursues these goals by sharing information on proliferation and harmonizing national export controls on chemical-weapons precursor chemicals, biological-weapons pathogens, and dual-use equipment that may be used for chemical or biological weapons. There is a "no undercut agreement" on denials by Australia Group members (U.S. House 1999).

Missile Technology Control Regime

The Missile Technology Control Regime (MTCR) was created in April 1987 by Canada, France, Germany, Italy, Japan, the United

Kingdom, and the United States. The purpose of the MTCR is to limit the proliferation of missiles capable of delivering weapons of mass destruction. The missile-related items subject to MTCR controls are included in either the Commerce Control List or the U.S. Munitions List (U.S. House 1999). Although not a member of the MTCR and subject to periodic sanctions itself, China agreed in 1992 to adhere to the original MTCR guidelines.

The Nuclear Suppliers Group

The Nuclear Suppliers Group was established in 1992 to control exports of nuclear and nuclear-related dual-use commodities. Member countries adhere to safeguards established by the International Atomic Energy Agency. There is a "no undercut rule" on denials by member countries.

U.S. Sanctions Imposed Specifically on China

Much of the authority to impose, waive, or lift sanctions rests with the U.S. president. In the case of China, however, Congress has played an active part in constructing the U.S. sanctions regime (Rennack 1997).

In addition to more general export controls administered by the Department of Commerce and the Department of State, the United States imposes specific sanctions against China, including the following:

- Suspension of nuclear trade and cooperation;
- Suspension of U.S. support for multilateral development bank financing;
- Suspension of operations of the Overseas Private Investment Corporation (OPIC);
- Prohibition of exports for crime-control and detection equipment and exports of U.S. satellites;
- Ban on importation of Chinese munitions and ammunition and certain imports produced by prison labor;
- Blocking of United Nations Population Fund financing for China programs; and
- Denial of Generalized System of Preferences (GSP) treatment for China.

Prohibition of Nuclear Trade and Cooperation

On 23 July 1985, China and the United States signed the "Agreement for Cooperation Between the Government of the United States of America and the Government of the People's Republic of China Concerning Peaceful Use of Nuclear Energy."

When Congress took up the matter, it enacted a resolution that conditions nuclear cooperation under the agreement on presidential certification of certain conditions. The resolution stipulates that no export licenses (including for end use, transfer, or retransfer) shall be issued for nuclear material, facilities, or components covered by the agreement until the president certifies that: (1) reciprocal arrangements ensure all goods in question are for peaceful purposes; (2) China has provided additional information regarding its nuclear nonproliferation policies and from such information it can be concluded that China is not in violation of section 129 of the Atomic Energy Act of 1954; and (3) certain terms of the agreement will not prejudice U.S. licensing procedures (Rennack 1997). This prohibition is still in effect.

Suspension of Arms Trade and Military Exchanges

Following the Tiananmen crisis, President Bush suspended all government-to-government exchanges, commercial arms sales, and military exchanges to express U.S. condemnation of China's actions. The suspension was later modified to allow for government-to-government and military exchanges and commercial arms sales at times.

Suspension of Financing Support

The Foreign Assistance Appropriation Act (1964) prohibited the U.S. Export-Import Bank (Ex-Im Bank) from financing transactions with communist countries, including China, unless the president determined it was in the national interest and reported so to Congress. The prohibition was reenacted annually in subsequent foreign aid appropriations measures. The 1986 Export-Import Bank Act prohibits Ex-Im Bank guarantees, insurance, or credits for any purchases by Marxist-Leninist countries. China is on the list of countries identified as Marxist-Leninist.

Before 1989, several presidential waivers were granted for the Ex-Im Bank to extend credits for exports to China. Following the Tiananmen crisis in 1989, the United States again prohibited Ex-Im Bank financing for China. But many times since then, the president has determined it is in the national interest of the United States for the Ex-Im Bank to extend credits to China.

After the Tiananmen crisis, the United States also postponed its support for new multilateral development bank (MDB) loans for China and stopped China-related activities of the U.S. Overseas Private Investment Corporation (OPIC) and the Trade and Development Agency (TDA).

Prohibition of Other Exports and Programs

Section 902 of the Foreign Relations Authorization Act for fiscal years 1990 and 1991 codified some steps the United States had already taken against China and required the imposition of additional sanctions to express U.S. condemnation of the Tiananmen incident. The act required the following (Rennack 1997):

1. The continued suspension of OPIC insurance, reinsurance, financing, or guarantees;
2. The suspension of funds obligated by the Trade and Development Agency for new projects in China;
3. The continued suspension of exports of any defense article on the USML, except systems and components for civil products not destined for the Chinese military or security forces;
4. The prohibition of export licenses for crime control and detection equipment;
5. The continued suspension of U.S. satellite exports;
6. The suspension of nuclear trade and cooperation with China; and
7. The suspension of, and opposition to, the liberalization of export controls by COCOM.

These sanctions could be terminated in part or wholly if the president reported to Congress that China had made progress in implementing political reforms, including those related to Tibet. The president also was given authority to terminate the sanctions if it was determined to be in the national interest of the United States (Rennack 1997).

Some requirements of the 1990–91 Foreign Relations Authorization Act have become irrelevant due to changing circumstances, such as the dissolution of COCOM, and some have been lifted, such as TDA operations. Most of the export controls remain binding, however, though some one-time terminations or waivers have been granted.

Prohibition of Certain Imports Produced by Prison Labor

On several occasions since 1992, the U.S. Customs Service has determined that certain products imported from China were manufactured with the use of convict, forced, and/or indentured labor and therefore could be prohibited from importation into the United States or seized by customs officials on importation. Some of these restrictions have since been lifted, while others remain active.

Prohibition of Imports of Munitions and Ammunition

On 26 May 1994, President Clinton announced that he would renew MFN status for China and de-link the extension to human rights conditions. At the same time he announced that, effective May 28, the importation of munitions and ammunition from China would be prohibited. This sanction remains active today (see Appendix 2.2).

Prohibition of U.S. Funding for Certain U.N. Programs

The Foreign Operations Appropriations Act for fiscal year 1995 prohibited U.S. contributions to the United Nations Population Fund (UNFPA) from being made available for programs in China. If the UNFPA spent in excess of $7 million in China in 1995, U.S. payments to the UNFPA would be reduced by the amount over $7 million. This restriction was enacted again in the fiscal 1996 Foreign Operations Appropriations Act. For fiscal year 1997, the Foreign Operations Appropriations Act required that no U.S. funds allocated for the UNFPA be made available for activities in China, U.S. contributions to the UNFPA be limited to $25 million, and U.S. payments to the UNFPA be reduced by the amount the organization expends in China (Rennack 1997).

These sanctions remain in effect as of 2002. President Bush blocked $34 million earmarked for the United Nations Population Fund in 2002 in response to the concerns of a group of 55 members of Congress led by Christopher Smith, a Republican representative from New Jersey. They had complained in a letter to the White House that the fund's program in China "supports coercive abortion and sterilization and therefore is in violation of our conscience and our law" (Kristof 2002).

Prohibition of Procurement Contracts With, and Importation From, Certain Individuals and Companies

The U.S. State Department from time to time issues public notices determining that certain Chinese entities and persons have engaged in chemical weapons proliferation activities that require the imposition of sanctions. The U.S. government is prohibited from entering into procurement contracts with, or importing from, the sanctioned Chinese individuals and entities.

On 16 January 2002, the United States imposed penalties on two Chinese companies and one Chinese national pursuant to the Iran

Nonproliferation Act of 2000. The penalties were imposed for the transfer to Iran of sensitive equipment and technology controlled by the Australia Group. As described earlier, the Australia Group is a 33-nation organization that seeks to prevent the proliferation of chemical and biological weapons. The penalties imposed on the three Chinese entities are as follows:

- No department or agency of the U.S. government may procure, or enter into any contract for the procurement of, any goods, services, or technology from the three Chinese entities;
- No department or agency of the U.S. government may provide any assistance to the three Chinese entities;
- The three entities shall not be eligible to participate in any assistance program of the U.S. government;
- U.S. government sales of any item on the U.S. Munitions List to any of these Chinese entities are prohibited, and sales of any defense articles, defense services, or design and construction services controlled under the Arms Export Control Act are to be terminated; and
- New licenses are to be denied, and existing licenses suspended, for transfer to these three entities of items controlled under the Export Administration Act of 1979 or the Export Administration Regulations.

The determination was published in the *Federal Register* on 24 January 2002. The penalties are to remain in effect until 15 January 2004 (Department of State 2002).

Similarly, since February 1997, the *Federal Register* has published several Commerce Department rules that have added people and organizations to the Entity List, a compilation of foreign end-users involved in proliferation activities. The Commerce Department's Bureau of Industry and Security (BIS) maintains the Entity List to inform the public of certain entities subject to such licensing requirements. China is among the few countries with firms, agencies, and citizens on this list.

Denial of Generalized System of Preferences Status

The preceding sanctions are mostly related to U.S. export controls. On the import side, the most significant discrepancy in the treatment of China is reflected in the U.S. designation of beneficiary countries for the Generalized System of Preferences (GSP).

Intergovernmental negotiations held in the 1960s under the auspices of the United Nations Conference on Trade and Development (UNCTAD) resulted in the adoption of the Generalized System of Preferences (GSP), whereby preferential tariff treatment is granted on a non-reciprocal and non-discriminatory basis by most developed countries to exports from developing countries. Under the GSP, specific products are allowed to enter the markets of preference-giving countries with most-favored-nation (MFN) duties reduced or eliminated. The underlying idea is to help the developing world industrialize. Countries of the European Union were the first to implement the GSP, in 1971, and most industrialized countries, including the United States, Australia, Japan, and fifteen member states of the European Union, now have GSP operations.

The United States differs with other industrialized nations on whether China should be a "beneficiary" of GSP treatment. In the 1960s, nations that considered themselves to be developing countries created the Group of 77, with a view to cooperating and strengthening their position in the UNCTAD and other U.N. fora. Up to now, the main (if not only) criterion for being considered a developing country is membership of the Group of 77, which amounts today to roughly twice that figure. China does not belong to the Group of 77 but forms a separate one-country group within the framework of UNCTAD. China nevertheless is considered to be a developing country and is accorded that status for purposes of the European Union's GSP.[8]

The U.S. GSP provides preferential duty-free entry for more than 4,650 products from approximately 140 designated beneficiary countries and territories. The GSP program was instituted on 1 January 1976 and authorized under Title V of the Trade Act of 1974 for a 10-year period. Congress has renewed the program's authorization several times. GSP-eligible beneficiaries designated by the United States are divided into three groups: independent countries, nonindependent countries and territories, and least-developed beneficiary developing countries. The three groups contain the majority of countries in the nonindustrialized world, including Argentina, Brazil, Chile, and Russia, whose per-capita income has been much higher than that of China. Yet China is noticeably absent from the three groups.

In addition to being considered a developing country, nations seeking GSP status from the United States must satisfy other criteria as well. These criteria are as follows:

1. A GSP beneficiary may not be a communist country unless such a country receives normal trade relations treatment, is a member of the General Agreement on Tariffs and Trade (GATT, now the WTO) and the International Monetary Fund, and is not dominated by international communism.
2. A GSP beneficiary may not be a party to an arrangement of countries and participate in actions the effect of which is to withhold supplies of vital commodities or raise the price of such commodities to an unreasonable level and cause serious disruption of the world economy.

3. A GSP beneficiary may not afford preferential treatment to products of a developed country that has, or is likely to have, a significant adverse effect on United States commerce.
4. A beneficiary may not have nationalized, expropriated, or otherwise seized property of U.S. citizens or corporations without providing, or taking steps to provide, prompt, adequate, and effective compensation, or submitting such issues to a mutually agreed forum for arbitration.
5. A GSP beneficiary may not have failed to recognize or enforce arbitral awards in favor of U.S. citizens or corporations.
6. GSP beneficiary may not aid or abet, by granting sanctuary from prosecution, any individual or group that has committed an act of international terrorism.
7. A beneficiary must have taken, or be taking, steps to afford internationally recognized worker rights, including the right of association, the right to organize and bargain collectively, freedom from compulsory labor, a minimum age for the employment of children, and acceptable conditions of work with respect to minimum wages, hours of work, and occupational safety and health.

Failure to meet criteria (4) through (7) may not prevent the granting of GSP eligibility if the president determines that such a designation would be in the national economic interest of the United States. The fact that China has been withheld from the beneficiary list reveals that the United States has serious reservations about China, and its exclusion from the U.S. Generalized System of Preferences represents the imposition of virtual economic sanctions on China.[9]

Conditions on China's WTO Membership

In November 1999, the United States and China reached a bilateral agreement on China's WTO membership that has built-in conditions to allow future U.S. restrictions on imports from China. Under the product-specific safeguard included in the agreement, the United States has the option of imposing unilateral restrictions on imports from China under conditions that no other member of the WTO has ever been required to accept. According to Lardy (2001), these conditions are relatively easy to meet, and restrictions based on them can be directed solely against imports from China. Under normal WTO safeguard arrangements, import restrictions must be imposed proportionately on all supplying countries. Since the product-specific safeguard conflicts with the fundamental WTO principle of equal treatment for all countries, Lardy recommends that the United States invoke this instrument against China only under extraordinary circumstances.

Similarly, China has agreed to a special textile safeguard that allows the United States to impose unilateral restrictions on the import of Chinese textiles and apparel for a period of four years after the current quota system is phased out. During the period 2005–08, China will be the only member of the WTO potentially subject to quota restrictions on its textile and apparel products (Lardy 2001).

U.S. legislation to allow permanent normal trade relations (PNTR) with China, signed into law by President Clinton on 10 October 2000, set stringent measures and conditions that may become the source of future trade tensions and the basis for future sanctions against China. The law—

- Established a special congressional–executive commission to monitor and report on various aspects of China's policies on human rights, including labor practices and religious freedom;
- Codified the anti-surge mechanism established under the November 1999 U.S.–China trade agreement and created procedures for obtaining relief from import surges;
- Authorized additional funding for various U.S. government agencies to monitor and seek enforcement of China's compliance with its WTO trade commitments;
- Created a special government task force to halt U.S. imports from China of products suspected of using prison labor;
- Authorized funding for programs to promote the development of the rule of law in China (Morrison 2002); and
- Mandated that the United States trade representative (USTR) issue a report annually assessing China's compliance with its WTO trade obligations.

IMPACT OF U.S. ECONOMIC SANCTIONS ON U.S.–CHINA TRADE

Trade statistics seem to suggest that U.S. economic sanctions against China have had no apparent adverse impact on trade between the two countries. Both nations are considered large traders in the world, although China is far behind the United States. According to the WTO, the United States accounted for 12.3 percent of total world exports and 18.9 percent of total world imports in 2000, while China accounted for 3.9 percent and 3.4 percent of world exports and imports, respectively (see Table 2.6).

China became a major trading partner of the United States in the last decade of the twentieth century by all broad measures. According to U.S. statistics for 2000, China was the fourth-leading supplier of U.S. imports, the eleventh-largest purchaser of U.S. exports, and the fourth-largest trading partner for the United States after Canada, Mexico, and Japan (see Table 2.8). As Table 2.9 shows, China surpassed Japan in 2000 as the country with which the United States has the largest trade deficit on an annual basis, although (as will be discussed shortly) trade data reported by China have differed significantly from statistics reported by the United States.

The United States figures more prominently in China's international trade. As Table 2.10 shows, the United States was China's top export market and third-largest import source in 2000, accounting for 20.93 percent and 8.98 percent of China's total exports and imports, respectively.

The gravity model of international trade predicts that trade between two countries should be proportional to the size of their economies and retarded by the geographical distance between them. On the positive side, China's economy has grown faster than that of most countries in the last two decades and is now one of the largest in the world. Correspondingly, China has become one of the top ten countries in world trade and in trade with the United States.

On the negative side, few countries in the world are farther away from the United States (China is literally on the other side of the globe). This distance, a factor often regarded as a proxy for trans-

Table 2.8
Leading U.S. Trade Partners, 2000

U.S. Exports				U.S. Imports			
Rank	Destination	Amount ($ millions)	Share (%)	Rank	Source	Amount ($ millions)	Share (%)
1	Canada	174,616.0	22.62	1	Canada	229,191.0	18.51
2	Mexico	108,751.0	14.09	2	Japan	149,520.0	12.08
3	Japan	64,537.6	8.36	3	Mexico	135,080.0	10.91
4	United Kingdom	41,360.6	5.36	4	China	106,215.0	8.58
5	Germany	29,216.7	3.78	5	Germany	59,480.5	4.80
6	South Korea	27,337.6	3.54	6	United Kingdom	43,676.8	3.53
7	Taiwan	24,406.0	3.16	7	South Korea	40,911.0	3.30
8	Netherlands	21,693.6	2.81	8	Taiwan	40,503.0	3.27
9	France	20,398.0	2.64	9	France	30,084.4	2.43
10	Singapore	17,497.2	2.27	10	Italy	26,000.8	2.10
11	China	15,963.7	2.07	11	Malaysia	25,990.0	2.10
12	Brazil	15,182.8	1.97	12	Singapore	19,630.4	1.59
13	Hong Kong	14,567.3	1.89	13	Venezuela	18,612.1	1.50
14	Belgium	13,873.8	1.80	14	Thailand	17,161.4	1.39
15	Australia	12,331.8	1.60	15	Ireland	15,825.0	1.28

Source: International Monetary Fund (2001a). Data for Taiwan from Department of Commerce (2002b).

Table 2.9
Top Contributors to U.S. Trade Deficit as Reported by the United States, 1993–2000 ($ Millions)

Country	1993	1994	1995	1996	1997	1998	1999	2000
China	−22,777	−29,505	−33,790	−39,520	−49,695	−56,927	−68,677	−83,833
Japan	−59,355	−65,668	−59,137	−47,580	−56,115	−64,014	−73,398	−81,555
Canada	−10,772	−13,967	−17,144	−21,682	−15,467	−16,653	−32,111	−51,897
Germany	−9,630	−12,515	−14,450	−15,450	−18,663	−23,185	−28,428	−29,064
Mexico	1,664	1,350	−15,809	−17,506	−14,549	−15,857	−22,812	−24,577
Taiwan	−8,934	−9,597	−9,682	−11,447	−12,263	−14,960	−16,073	−16,097
Malaysia	−4,499	−7,013	−8,639	−9,283	−7,247	−10,043	−12,364	−14,631
Italy	−6,752	−7,620	−7,487	−9,528	−10,413	−11,968	−12,266	−13,982
Venezuela	−3,550	−4,332	−5,124	−8,424	−6,876	−2,666	−5,981	−13,073
South Korea	−2,336	−1,604	1,196	3,966	1,873	−7,456	−8,220	−12,478

Source: Department of Commerce (2002b).

Table 2.10
China's Leading Trade Partners, 2000

Exports				Imports			
Rank	Destination	Amount ($ millions)	Share (%)	Rank	Source	Amount ($ millions)	Share (%)
1	United States	52,161.7	20.93	1	Japan	41,511.8	16.66
2	Hong Kong	44,519.8	17.87	2	South Korea	23,207.3	9.31
3	Japan	41,654.0	16.72	3	United States	22,374.6	8.98
4	South Korea	11,292.5	4.53	4	Germany	10,408.8	4.18
5	Germany	9,278.1	3.72	5	Hong Kong	9,429.2	3.78
6	Netherlands	6,687.2	2.68	6	Russia	5,769.9	2.32
7	United Kingdom	6,310.2	2.53	7	Malaysia	5,480.0	2.20
8	Singapore	5,761.3	2.31	8	Singapore	5,059.7	2.03
9	Italy	3,802.3	1.53	9	Australia	5,024.1	2.02
10	France	3,714.6	1.49	10	Indonesia	4,402.0	1.77
11	Australia	3,428.9	1.38	11	Thailand	4,380.8	1.76
12	Canada	3,158.0	1.27	12	France	3,951.5	1.59
13	Indonesia	3,061.9	1.23	13	Canada	3,751.1	1.51
14	Malaysia	2,565.0	1.03	14	United Kingdom	3,592.5	1.44
15	Belgium	2,300.8	0.92	15	Oman	3,261.8	1.31
	European Union	38,230.3	15.34		European Union	30,846.7	12.38
	World	249,195.0	100.00		World	225,096.0	90.33

Source: International Monetary Fund (2001a).

portation costs in international trade, should hinder trade between the two countries. The fact that China has become a major trading partner with the United States confirms that the economic size factor in the gravity model wields significant explanatory power. On the other hand, the greater trade volumes between the United States and Canada and Mexico, whose economies (as measured by GDP) are not as large as China's, seem to suggest that distance matters.

With GDP and geographical distance as explanatory variables in the gravity model, estimated U.S. imports from China and exports to China for the years 1987 to 1998 are actually lower than the corresponding actual imports and exports (see Table 2.11). This seems to suggest that U.S. economic sanctions against China have had no adverse impact on U.S. trade with China. In fact, as Table 2.11 shows, gravity model residuals assume an increasing trend, particularly for U.S. imports from China. One plausible interpretation of the positive residuals and the increasing trend is that China is relatively more open to trade than the world norm, which would explain why U.S.–China trade has grown faster than the world average.

Table 2.11
Differences in Actual U.S. Trade with China vs. Gravity Model Estimates ($ Millions)

	Exports			Imports		
Year	Actual	Estimated	Residual	Actual	Estimated	Residual
1987	3,497.30	2,593.20	904.1	6,293.50	4,904.07	1,389.43
1988	5,021.40	3,345.04	1,676.36	8,510.90	3,617.85	4,893.05
1989	5,755.40	3,404.99	2,350.41	11,989.90	6,642.47	5,347:43
1990	4,806.40	3,694.82	1,111.58	15,237.30	5,158.99	10,078.31
1991	6,278.30	3,875.00	2,403.30	18,969.00	4,506.67	14,462.33
1992	7,418.40	4,069.10	3,349.30	25,727.60	3,125.26	22,602.34
1993	8,762.80	4,392.86	4,369.94	31,539.90	3,192.60	28,347.30
1994	9,281.80	6,698.79	2,583.01	38,786.70	7,338.72	31,447.98
1995	11,753.60	8,505.76	3,247.84	45,543.20	8,160.02	37,383.18
1996	11,992.60	7,736.95	4,255.65	51,512.60	12,800.59	38,712.01
1997	12,862.30	10,069.77	2,792.53	62,557.60	14,169.00	48,388.60
1998	14,241.30	10,345.74	3,895.56	71,168.70	21,728.75	49,439.95

Note: Export figures are obtained by subtracting estimated exports from actual exports; import figures are obtained in the same manner. The estimation model is specified as:

$$\log(T_{ij}) = \alpha + \beta_1 \log(GDP_i^{*}GDP_{US}) + \beta_3 \log(DIST_{ij}) + \nu_i$$

where T denotes imports or exports between the United States and its trade partner, GDP_{US} is U.S. gross domestic product, GDP_i is the corresponding gross domestic product for the trade partner, and DIST is the geographical distance between the United States and the trade partner. See Askari et al. (2003) for details of data and variable descriptions.

It is important to note that the results presented in Table 2.11 appear to be different from those presented in Askari et al. (2002), where export losses are estimated on the model parameters rather than the model residuals. Estimates based on parameters are more relevant for total U.S. export losses with all its trade partners than for losses with individual countries.

Given the gravity model assessment, can one conclude that U.S. sanctions against China have had no impact on trade between the two countries? Such a conclusion may be premature. The gravity model does not capture certain aspects of the Chinese economy that underlie China's trade with the rest of the world and, in particular, with the United States. Therefore, the model may fail to reveal the full impact of sanctions.

One fundamental factor that may have been overlooked in discussions of China's economic growth is per-capita income. Despite a high economic growth rate and significant improvements in living standards, China's per-capita income is still among the lowest in the world. It can be argued that a lower per-capita income represents a lower purchasing power for foreign goods and, thus, a negative impact on the country's total trade and on imports in particular. Gravity models for trade studies often include per-capita income to capture the effects of intra-industry trade, which is assumed to occur among high per-capita income countries.

But lower per-capita income can also translate into lower production costs, particularly for labor-intensive industries, thus representing a comparative advantage in international trade. It is true that such a translation is not automatic; in many instances, low per-capita income may be associated with low productivity and, hence, high production costs. In the case of China, which has a huge labor force that is willing to work hard and improve its fortunes, low per-capita income does represent, and has translated into, low production costs.

Its comparative advantage in labor costs has made China a leading source of low-priced manufactured products for the world and for the United States in particular. Table 2.12 presents the industry distribution of U.S.–China trade in 2001, with industries categorized by the United Nations' Standard International Trade Classification (SITC). It can be seen that the United States has an overall surplus in the five sectors that constitute basically agricultural products and raw materials, but a relatively large deficit in the five sectors that are considered manufacturing industries.

The one-digit SITC classification codes may be too broad to reveal trade patterns between the United States and China in manufactured products. For example, SITC 7 (machinery and transport

Table 2.12
Composition of U.S.–China Trade, 2001 ($ Millions)

SITC	Description	U.S. Exports to China	U.S. Imports from China	U.S. Balance
0	Food and Live Animals	510.78	1,143.72	−632.94
1	Beverages and Tobacco	6.07	40.37	−34.30
2	Crude Materials, Inedible, Except Fuels	3,145.86	594.76	2,551.10
3	Mineral Fuels, Lubricants and Related Materials	93.45	387.22	−293.77
4	Animal and Vegetable Oils, Fats and Waxes	14.16	5.68	8.48
5	Chemicals and Related Products, N.E.S.	2,211.23	2,064.68	146.55
6	Manufactured Goods Classified Chiefly by Material	1,106.52	10,803.65	−9,697.13
7	Machinery and Transport Equipment	10,284.63	34,943.68	−24,659.05
8	Miscellaneous Manufactured Articles	1,653.25	51,068.26	−49,415.01
9	Commodities and Transactions, N.E.S.	208.89	1,228.47	−1,019.58
	Total	19,234.83	102,280.48	−83,045.65

Note: The Standard International Trade Classification (United Nations Statistical Papers, Series M, No. 34/Rev.3) is a statistical classification of the commodities entering external trade. It is designed to provide the commodity aggregates needed for purposes of economic analysis and to facilitate the international comparison of trade-by-commodity data.
Source: Census Bureau (2002).

equipment) includes highly diversified products ranging from non-motorized cycles, which represent products with moderate-level technology, to high-tech aircraft. According to Hecker (1996), the top five U.S. imports from China in 1995—which accounted for about 65 percent of total U.S. imports from China—were (1) miscellaneous manufactured articles, such as toys and games, (2) clothing and apparel, (3) footwear, (4) telecommunications, sound recording, and reproduction equipment, and (5) electrical machinery. Hecker also quotes a U.S. Department of Commerce official as saying that China acted as a provider of low-cost goods to the United States that largely compete with similar products from India and Indonesia (Hecker 1996).

In the same year, the top five U.S. exports to China—which accounted for about 45 percent of total U.S. exports to China—were (1) fertilizers, (2) transport equipment (mainly aircraft and aircraft parts), (3) cereals and cereal preparations, (4) textile fibers, and (5) telecommunications and sound equipment. According to the U.S. Department of Agriculture, China has become an increasingly important market for U.S. agricultural exports. In 1995, China purchased nearly 40 percent of all U.S. fertilizer exports and nearly 10 percent of all wheat and corn exports sold by U.S. farmers (Hecker 1996).

Low labor costs and price competitiveness have allowed China's labor-intensive products to survive and at times thrive in the U.S. market, even though China has not been afforded GSP treatment by the United States. The increased presence of Chinese products in U.S. markets has caused ongoing concern in the United States, particularly among labor unions and their representatives in political circles. China's textile products have been subject to U.S. quota restrictions, and the two countries often have disputes over U.S. reductions in quota allocations to China. As mentioned earlier, fear of increased Chinese textile exports to the United States prompted the inclusion of a textile safeguard in the U.S.–China agreement on China's accession to the WTO. The safeguard, which permits U.S. companies and workers to respond to increased imports of textile and apparel products from China, will remain in effect until 31 December 2008, four years after the WTO agreement on textile and clothing expires.[10]

China's export performance also has been helped by foreign investment in China. According to Lardy (1996), the U.S. trade deficit with China primarily reflects China's openness to foreign investment, not unfair trading practices. Investors from Hong Kong, Taiwan, and South Korea have moved facilities that produce footwear, garments, toys, sporting goods, and other labor-intensive products to China to take advantage of low labor costs. These products account for a large share of U.S. imports from China. The growing U.S. trade deficit with China has been accompanied by declining U.S. deficits with Hong Kong, Taiwan, and South Korea.

In addition to low labor costs, an improving investment environment—including preferential treatment for foreign investment—also has attracted investors from industrial countries, including the United States. As part of their international business strategy, a number of multinational firms have shifted production to China and distributed their products made in China to the rest of the world, including their home markets. Such business strategies are reflected in the trade balances between China and its partners.

For example, many U.S. firms produce goods in China and sell their products back to the United States. Such sales are recorded as Chinese exports and U.S. imports. These multinational firms have been a major contributing factor in China's increasing exports and economic growth. According to Lardy (2001), almost half of China's exports were produced by firms either fully or partly owned by foreign companies operating in China in 2000.

In sum, given China's huge population and its comparative advantage in labor-intensive products, trade between the United

States and China might have increased even more if U.S. economic sanctions had not been in place.

The Position of Hong Kong

While it seems that the price competitiveness of Chinese products has helped China weather some price-based U.S. economic sanctions (e.g., the denial of GSP treatment), more severe sanctions such as the trade embargo and export controls have had long-lasting effects on China's development and on trade between the two countries. These effects are reflected in the role Hong Kong has played for decades in economic relations between China and the rest of the world and, more recently, in the burgeoning U.S. trade deficit with China.

The position of Hong Kong—and, to a lesser extent, that of Taiwan—in trade between the United States and China is prominently reminiscent of U.S. economic sanctions against China in recent history. During the years of the U.S. trade embargo against China, Hong Kong served as a window for China to reach out to the world and a gateway for the world to reach out to China. After years of isolation caused by the embargo, China and the industrialized world needed time to understand each other and build the trust necessary for commercial exchange. This has been a long and complex process, as evidenced by the periodic tensions that continue to flare some three decades after the lifting of the U.S. trade embargo against China.

Hong Kong's unique position has allowed it to serve as an intermediary in trade between China and the world. This role has helped Hong Kong emerge as a major trader—the tenth largest exporter and ninth largest importer in the world in 2000 (see Table 2.6).

Hong Kong's exports to and imports from its major trading partners are presented in Tables 2.13 through 2.16. From 1980 to 2000, Hong Kong's exports and imports experienced annual growth rates of 12.87 percent and 12.56 percent, respectively. China, the United States, the European Union, and Japan (in that order) have been Hong Kong's main export markets, while China, Japan, the European Union, and the United States have been the main suppliers of its imports.

The extraordinarily large volumes of trade that Hong Kong has reported include significant amounts of re-exports and reflect Hong Kong's position as an intermediary between China and its other trade partners. As Table 2.17 shows, re-exports represented 77.2 percent, 83.9 percent, and 84.7 percent of Hong Kong's imports and

Table 2.13
Hong Kong's Exports to Major Destinations ($ Millions)

Year	China	United States	European Union	Japan	United Kingdom	All Exports
1980	1,249.1	5,157.3	4,869.0	909.2	1,526.7	19,720.0
1981	1,964.5	6,056.3	4,444.9	1,021.7	1,540.1	21,815.5
1982	1,939.0	6,040.1	4,029.8	940.9	1,283.8	20,893.2
1983	2,494.8	7,069.2	3,845.3	966.0	1,269.1	21,949.2
1984	5,030.6	9,404.8	4,403.6	1,251.3	1,467.1	28,313.9
1985	7,857.4	9,300.6	4,053.0	1,279.1	1,255.4	30,181.8
1986	7,550.6	11,107.9	5,605.5	1,651.3	1,590.1	35,437.8
1987	11,290.5	13,511.0	8,335.7	2,469.7	2,202.4	48,473.3
1988	17,028.7	15,689.4	10,696.8	3,696.0	2,810.8	63,182.3
1989	18,816.8	18,504.6	12,134.6	4,524.6	3,019.9	73,113.8
1990	20,331.5	19,817.1	15,231.4	4,679.9	3,286.6	82,144.1
1991	26,736.0	22,391.3	18,540.3	5,307.5	3,651.3	98,579.4
1992	35,411.7	27,582.6	20,400.4	6,261.6	4,281.1	119,512.0
1993	43,684.4	31,158.9	21,762.6	6,959.0	4,563.9	134,996.0
1994	49,668.7	35,179.4	22,916.9	8,436.3	4,866.4	151,379.0
1995	57,861.2	37,850.6	25,959.1	10,596.4	5,584.0	173,556.0
1996	61,979.6	38,368.9	26,866.4	11,829.1	6,023.4	180,530.0
1997	65,583.8	40,949.1	27,676.1	11,414.0	6,431.7	187,870.0
1998	59,840.7	40,700.2	27,398.6	9,122.1	6,755.1	173,693.0
1999	57,994.2	41,502.3	28,003.4	9,413.3	7,211.6	173,793.0
2000	69,743.9	47,084.1	30,725.2	11,194.9	8,095.8	201,871.0

Note: Hong Kong's export numbers include re-exports.
Source: International Monetary Fund (2001a).

84.8 percent, 88.5 percent, and 89.6 percent of Hong Kong's exports in 1996, 2000, and 2001, respectively. China and the United States are the main destinations for Hong Kong's re-exports, accounting for more than 55 percent of its total re-exports in 1996, 2000, and 2001. China, Japan, Taiwan, and the United States are the main sources of Hong Kong's imports and hence re-exports, accounting for more than two-thirds of its total imports for the same years.

The success of Hong Kong's economy is due to many factors. The government of the Hong Kong Special Administrative Region (HKSAR) of China claims the following:

[Hong Kong's success] owes much to a simple tax structure and low tax rates, a versatile and industrious workforce, an excellent infrastructure, free flow of capital and information and the government's firm commitment to free trade and free enterprise. The government believes its task is to facilitate commerce and industry within the framework of a free market. The HKSAR maintains no tariffs and no regulatory trade and investment measures other than those required to discharge its international

Table 2.14
Hong Kong's Exports to Major Destinations (By Percentage Share)

Year	China	United States	European Union	Japan	United Kingdom	Subtotal
1980	6.33	26.15	24.69	4.61	7.74	61.79
1981	9.01	27.76	20.37	4.68	7.06	61.82
1982	9.28	28.91	19.29	4.50	6.14	61.98
1983	11.37	32.21	17.52	4.40	5.78	65.49
1984	17.77	33.22	15.55	4.42	5.18	70.96
1985	26.03	30.82	13.43	4.24	4.16	74.52
1986	21.31	31.34	15.82	4.66	4.49	73.13
1987	23.29	27.87	17.20	5.09	4.54	73.46
1988	26.95	24.83	16.93	5.85	4.45	74.56
1989	25.74	25.31	16.60	6.19	4.13	73.83
1990	24.75	24.12	18.54	5.70	4.00	73.12
1991	27.12	22.71	18.81	5.38	3.70	74.03
1992	29.63	23.08	17.07	5.24	3.58	75.02
1993	32.36	23.08	16.12	5.15	3.38	76.72
1994	32.81	23.24	15.14	5.57	3.21	76.76
1995	33.34	21.81	14.96	6.11	3.22	76.21
1996	34.33	21.25	14.88	6.55	3.34	77.02
1997	34.91	21.80	14.73	6.08	3.42	77.51
1998	34.45	23.43	15.77	5.25	3.89	78.91
1999	33.37	23.88	16.11	5.42	4.15	78.78
2000	34.55	23.32	15.22	5.55	4.01	78.64

Source: International Monetary Fund (2001a).

obligations or to protect health, the environment and access to high technology. (Howlett 1998)

The open-door policy and economic reforms in China have not only provided a huge production base and market outlet for Hong Kong's manufacturers but also have created an abundance of business opportunities for a wide range of service activities in Hong Kong (Howlett 1998). Since mid-1980, Hong Kong's economy has become increasingly oriented toward services. The share of services in Hong Kong's GDP has risen steadily, from around 67 percent in 1980 to 74 percent in 1990, 84.4 percent in 1996, and 85.6 percent in 2000. The service sector that includes wholesale, retail, and import/export trades and restaurants and hotels accounted for 26.1 percent of Hong Kong's GDP in 2000 (HKSAR 2002).

It is undeniable that a unique set of events in the international arena contributed to Hong Kong's position and its success today. The isolation of China following the U.S. trade embargo set Hong

Table 2.15
Hong Kong's Imports from Major Sources ($ Millions)

Year	China	United States	European Union	Japan	United Kingdom	World
1980	4,400.6	2,652.9	2,862.6	5,141.9	1,094.2	22,399.4
1981	5,271.5	2,588.5	3,012.6	5,755.7	1,125.3	24,767.6
1982	5,396.5	2,538.0	2,987.9	5,176.3	1,127.5	23,443.8
1983	5,846.6	2,637.5	2,926.8	5,516.3	1,026.9	24,005.1
1984	7,130.6	3,121.0	3,371.6	6,729.6	1,113.2	28,557.6
1985	7,567.9	2,814.6	3,621.6	6,847.9	1,084.4	29,700.8
1986	10,462.2	2,979.5	4,297.7	7,228.4	1,197.8	35,359.7
1987	15,048.7	4,141.4	5,698.4	9,220.5	1,501.9	48,462.7
1988	19,937.7	5,302.4	7,046.7	11,914.9	1,655.4	63,900.2
1989	25,212.9	5,933.4	7,647.1	11,950.2	1,662.2	72,148.8
1990	30,313.4	6,653.3	8,557.3	13,269.0	1,812.3	82,481.8
1991	37,757.9	7,575.7	9,754.2	16,396.8	2,128.8	100,274.0
1992	45,784.6	9,128.3	12,410.5	21,472.8	2,483.3	123,430.0
1993	51,987.3	10,271.2	14,216.6	23,014.8	2,770.9	138,595.0
1994	60,863.9	11,565.0	16,676.9	25,238.1	3,287.1	161,771.0
1995	69,737.5	14,881.6	20,732.4	28,601.9	3,935.9	192,765.0
1996	73,756.8	15,657.9	22,050.8	26,924.0	4,300.8	198,551.0
1997	78,587.3	16,200.0	22,968.3	28,630.7	4,686.7	208,623.0
1998	74,973.6	13,767.1	19,630.0	23,250.5	3,832.7	184,602.0
1999	78,338.0	12,719.5	16,414.1	21,001.8	3,480.9	179,650.0
2000	91,803.8	14,498.6	18,554.0	25,597.5	4,085.2	213,183.0

Note: Hong Kong's import numbers include re-exports to other destinations.
Source: International Monetary Fund (2001a).

Kong apart from the mainland while keeping it abreast of the West. This created an enormous opportunity for Hong Kong to bridge the gap between China and the industrialized world when relations were normalized between China and the United States and other countries. Hong Kong also has been the intermediary between the mainland and Taiwan, as there are no direct commercial dealings between the two sides despite the willingness of businesses on both sides to trade with each other.

Such a position has its challenges, however. The importance of this intermediary position depends on relations between China and the industrialized world, particularly the United States. At one extreme, with a total trade embargo against China, Hong Kong would have no role to play; at the other, with China fully integrated into the world economy, Hong Kong's role also would diminish. Hong Kong thus faces challenges in both directions. Its economy is at risk when trade tensions between China and the United States

Table 2.16
Hong Kong's Imports from Major Sources (By Percentage Share)

Year	China	United States	European Union	Japan	United Kingdom	Subtotal
1980	19.65	11.84	12.78	22.96	4.88	67.23
1981	21.28	10.45	12.16	23.24	4.54	67.14
1982	23.02	10.83	12.74	22.08	4.81	68.67
1983	24.36	10.99	12.19	22.98	4.28	70.52
1984	24.97	10.93	11.81	23.57	3.90	71.27
1985	25.48	9.48	12.19	23.06	3.65	70.21
1986	29.59	8.43	12.15	20.44	3.39	70.61
1987	31.05	8.55	11.76	19.03	3.10	70.38
1988	31.20	8.30	11.03	18.65	2.59	69.17
1989	34.95	8.22	10.60	16.56	2.30	70.33
1990	36.75	8.07	10.37	16.09	2.20	71.28
1991	37.65	7.56	9.73	16.35	2.12	71.29
1992	37.09	7.40	10.05	17.40	2.01	71.94
1993	37.51	7.41	10.26	16.61	2.00	71.78
1994	37.62	7.15	10.31	15.60	2.03	70.68
1995	36.18	7.72	10.76	14.84	2.04	69.49
1996	37.15	7.89	11.11	13.56	2.17	69.70
1997	37.67	7.77	11.01	13.72	2.25	70.17
1998	40.61	7.46	10.63	12.59	2.08	71.30
1999	43.61	7.08	9.14	11.69	1.94	71.51
2000	43.06	6.80	8.70	12.01	1.92	70.57

Source: International Monetary Fund (2001a).

rise, but with China joining the WTO and direct trade between the mainland and Taiwan expected to materialize in the future, Hong Kong's intermediary role will likewise be marginalized. The continued success of Hong Kong's economy will depend on a structural change that will make Hong Kong less dependent on being an entrepôt in international trade.

The U.S. Trade Deficit

The U.S. trade deficit with China increasingly has become a political as well as an economic issue between the two countries. Current analyses of the issue address not only the causes of the trade deficit, but also its actual size (see Yang 1998 and Lardy 1997 for discussions of the issue). The statistical treatment of Hong Kong's re-exports between the United States and China and U.S. export restrictions on China are believed to be among the relevant factors for understanding this deficit.

The unusually large discrepancies in the U.S. trade deficit with China as reported by the United States and China (see Table 2.18)

Table 2.17
Hong Kong's Imports, Exports, and Re-exports (Leading Sources and Destinations)

	Value ($H.K. billions)			Share		
	1996	2000	2001	1996	2000	2001
Imports (total)	1,535.6	1,658.0	1,568.2	100.0%	100.0%	100.0%
China	570.4	715.0	682.0	37.1%	43.1%	43.5%
Japan	208.2	199.0	176.6	13.6%	12.0%	11.3%
Taiwan	123.2	124.2	107.9	8.0%	7.5%	6.9%
United States	121.1	112.8	104.9	7.9%	6.8%	6.7%
Singapore	81.5	75.0	72.9	5.3%	4.5%	4.6%
Asia-Pacific Economic Co-operation	1,294.0	1,436.9	1,340.9	84.3%	86.7%	85.5%
European Union	170.6	144.3	151.2	11.1%	8.7%	9.6%
Exports (total)	212.2	181.0	153.5	100.0%	100.0%	100.0%
China	61.6	54.2	49.5	29.0%	29.9%	32.2%
United States	53.9	54.4	47.6	25.4%	30.1%	31.0%
United Kingdom	10.6	10.7	8.6	5.0%	5.9%	5.6%
Germany	11.4	9.3	5.8	5.4%	5.1%	3.8%
Taiwan	6.7	6.1	5.3	3.2%	3.4%	3.5%
Asia-Pacific Economic Co-operation	163.0	139.6	121.6	76.8%	77.1%	79.2%
European Union	37.0	32.9	25.5	17.4%	18.2%	16.6%
Re-exports (total)	1,185.8	1,391.7	1,327.5	100.0%	100.0%	100.0%
China	417.8	488.8	496.6	35.2%	35.1%	37.4%
United States	242.3	311.0	282.2	20.4%	22.3%	21.3%
Japan	80.2	82.1	83.6	6.8%	5.9%	6.3%
United Kingdom	36.0	52.4	46.8	3.0%	3.8%	3.5%
Germany	47.2	50.6	45.8	4.0%	3.6%	3.5%
Asia-Pacific Economic Co-operation	907.4	1,078.9	1,042.8	76.5%	77.5%	78.6%
European Union	170.8	206.9	188.2	14.4%	14.9%	14.2%
Re-exports as percentage of:						
Total imports				77.2%	83.9%	84.7%
Total exports				84.8%	88.5%	89.6%

Source: Census and Statistics Bureau, Hong Kong.

began to attract attention in the early 1990s. The U.S. Department of Commerce and its Chinese counterpart, the Ministry of Foreign Trade and Economic Relations (MOFTEC), together with China Customs, conducted a study of the issue for 1992 and 1993 (DOC 1995). The study found that the primary cause of the discrepancies was the large amount of U.S.–China trade shipped through Hong Kong and other intermediaries. Both nations followed international guidelines in their published trade statistics, but these guidelines created some inconsistencies between corresponding import and export statistics. Most importantly, exports were attributed to the

Table 2.18
U.S. Trade Balance with China, 1985–2001 ($ Millions)

	As Reported by China			As Reported by the United States		
Year	Exports to United States	Imports from United States	U.S. Trade with China	Exports to China	Imports from China	U.S. Trade Balance with China
1985	2,336.2	5,198.7	2,862.5	3,855.7	3,861.7	−6.0
1986	2,632.7	4,718.2	2,085.5	3,106.2	4,770.9	−1,664.7
1987	3,030.4	4,835.6	1,805.2	3,497.3	6,293.5	−2,796.2
1988	3,398.7	6,633.0	3,234.3	5,021.4	8,510.9	−3,489.5
1989	4,413.6	7,863.6	3,450.0	5,755.4	11,989.9	−6,234.5
1990	5,313.9	6,591.0	1,277.1	4,806.4	15,237.3	−10,430.9
1991	6,198.0	8,010.3	1,812.3	6,278.3	18,969.0	−12,690.7
1992	8,598.8	8,902.7	303.9	7,418.4	25,727.6	−18,309.2
1993	16,976.5	10,632.8	−6,343.7	8,762.8	31,539.9	−22,777.1
1994	21,421.4	13,976.7	−7,444.7	9,281.8	38,786.7	−29,504.9
1995	24,743.9	16,123.2	−8,620.7	11,753.6	45,543.2	−33,789.6
1996	26,730.6	16,178.9	−10,551.7	11,992.6	51,512.6	−39,520.0
1997	32,743.9	16,289.8	−16,454.1	12,862.3	62,557.6	−49,695.3
1998	38,000.6	16,997.3	−21,003.3	14,241.3	71,168.7	−56,927.4
1999	42,003.1	19,488.7	−22,514.4	13,111.0	81,788.2	−68,677.2
2000	52,161.7	22,374.6	−29,787.1	16,185.3	100,018.4	−83,833.1
2001				19,234.8	102,280.5	−83,045.7

Source: IMF (2002a).

country of final destination known at the time of export, which might not, in fact, be the final destination. For example, for east-bound trade (Chinese exports/U.S. imports), many of the goods identified by the United States as imports from China were shown by China as exports to Hong Kong. Since many of China's exports were shipped through Hong Kong, China's export statistics were much lower than U.S. import statistics.

According to the report, about 80 percent of U.S. imports from China traveled via intermediaries, with Hong Kong accounting for all but 3 to 4 percent of the intermediary trade. Nearly 30 percent of the value of Chinese goods re-exported by Hong Kong to the United States consisted of Hong Kong's markup, equivalent to a 41 percent increase in the cost of the Chinese goods when imported by Hong Kong. The initial values and the markup of the re-exports by Hong Kong were both counted as imports from China in U.S. statistics. About 25 percent of China's imports from the United States traveled via Hong Kong or other intermediaries, and many of these exports were reported by the United States as exports to Hong Kong or elsewhere.

A plausible inference from this study is that the United States may have overestimated U.S. trade deficits, while China may have underestimated them. As Table 2.18 shows, the study correctly predicted that the two countries' trade statistics would continue to differ. "Not only is the final destination frequently unknown at the time of exportation from China, but the U.S. import value includes the value added in the intermediary," the report noted. "There were also differences in the methods used to determine country of origin."

By definition, a U.S. trade deficit with China means U.S. exports to China have lagged behind imports from China. Export controls have played a significant role in the export performance of the United States. Trade between the two countries should be a classic example of gains for both nations: China is abundant in labor resources and has a comparative advantage in labor-intensive products, while the United States is abundant in capital and technology and has a comparative advantage in high-tech goods. In addition, given the high labor cost in the United States and China's enthusiasm for modernizing its economy, trade between the two countries should complement each other's needs.

However, export controls imposed by the United States on China have held back exports of products that represent new and high technologies, as they can easily be classified as "dual-use" items. The fear of being caught exporting high-tech goods to China may make U.S. exporters wary as well. One *Financial Times* report stated, "If the U.S. had removed the sanctions on high technology exports, which are worth several billion [U.S. dollars] each year, it is thus questionable who would be enjoying the surplus" (Harding 1997).

IMPACT OF U.S. ECONOMIC SANCTIONS ON CHINA

It is extremely difficult, if not impossible, to evaluate the full impact of U.S. economic sanctions against China given the complex nature of both the sanctions and the Chinese economy. We would, however, like to highlight a few major areas where U.S. economic sanctions against China are obviously seen or felt. These areas include the lingering impact of U.S. sanctions long after they are lifted, specific effects on some sectors of the Chinese economy that are subject to U.S. export controls, effects on trade-related programs such as U.S. and international financing for China, and the effects on Hong Kong, Taiwan, and other economies that have a significant stake in China.

The Lingering Effects of U.S. Economic Sanctions

The complex impact of U.S. economic sanctions against China has its origins in a number of factors. First, unlike a total trade embargo, U.S. economic sanctions against China since the normalization of diplomatic relations between the two countries in 1979 have been imposed within the context of mutual normal trade status. Despite periodic tensions between the two countries, normal trading status—or most-favored-nation (MFN) treatment, as it was called previously—has not been denied China by the United States since 1979. The most noticeable sanctions on China have been the U.S. denial of Generalized System of Preferences (GSP) treatment and restrictions on some specific imports from China, such as textiles. Second, China's trade with the United States has grown rapidly since 1979 and to such an extent that the economic interests of the two countries have increasingly become intertwined and interdependent. Third, China's economy has experienced the fastest growth in its history and in comparison with the rest of the world since the beginning of economic reform in 1978, which coincided with the normalization of relations with the United States.

In addition, U.S. investment in China has achieved a prominent presence and made significant contributions to the growth of the Chinese economy and trade between the two countries. Given the fast growth of the Chinese economy, the increase in trade between the United States and China, and the rise in U.S. investment in China, it is reasonable to argue that U.S. sanctions have had minimal impact on the Chinese economy.

Yet the Cold War, during which many U.S. economic sanctions against China originated, created lingering suspicions toward business relations between the two countries. The recursive tensions between the two countries and the frequent imposition or threat of U.S. sanctions against China have taken a toll on the Chinese economy, albeit often of a transitory nature. Immediately after the Tiananmen crisis, for example, many U.S. businesses closed their offices in China or withdrew their prospective investment projects. China's imports and economic growth suffered a temporary setback in 1990 following the Tiananmen-related sanctions imposed by the United States and other industrialized countries.

Increased political tensions between the two countries, coupled with a few dramatic events such as the NATO bombing of the Chinese embassy in Yugoslavia in May 1999 and the collision between U.S. and Chinese aircraft along the Chinese coast in April 2001, have had chilling effects on the overall atmosphere between the two countries. From time to time, events like these and the accompanying rhetoric and reactions on both sides remind people of the Cold War and cause anxiety over the future course of relations between the two countries. This uncertainty has a direct economic impact on both the United States and China.

Effects on U.S. Investment in China

As Tables 2.19 and 2.20 show, the United States has become a major investor in China, accounting for more than 10 percent of external direct investment in China at the end of the twentieth century and ranking second after Hong Kong in 1999. U.S. investment in China in 2000 was concentrated in manufacturing (59.13 percent), petroleum (19.28 percent), and financial services (7.73 percent), as Table 2.21 indicates. Many U.S. multinational companies have gained brand recognition and dominance in some consumer markets in China: General Motors automobiles, Dell computers, Motorola cell phones, Kodak film, Coca-Cola and Pepsi-Cola soft drinks, McDonalds hamburgers, and Marlboro cigarettes (to name just a few) have become household names and are popular in major cities such as Beijing and Shanghai. In fact, one can find almost all brand-name consumer products in major cities in China that one can find in other major cities around the world.

Table 2.22 shows market shares and rankings for some American products, based on a market survey for consumer products conducted in 32 major cities in China in October 1997. For example, the market shares of Motorola, Coca-Cola, and Kodak were more than 40 percent of their respective markets in China.

U.S. investment in China has, however, been confined largely to major U.S. multinational companies. The majority of U.S. businesses, particularly small and medium-sized companies, still shy away from China in their long-term investment strategies. This is evidenced by the relatively low overall U.S. investment in China compared with total U.S. investment abroad and with U.S. investment in other specific countries. As is apparent from Appendix 2.6, U.S. direct investment in China accounted for only 1.05 percent of its total direct investment abroad in 2001, compared with 16.66 percent in the United Kingdom, 14.18 percent in Canada, and 12.40 percent in Mexico. On a cumulative basis, U.S. direct investment in China accounted for 0.77 percent of its total overseas direct investment as of 2000, compared with 18.75 percent in the United Kingdom, 10.16 percent in Canada, and 2.85 percent in Mexico (see Appendix 2.7).

The relatively low level of U.S. investment in China may reflect the effects of U.S. economic sanctions, as investment in China has been subject to the same restrictions that the U.S. government has

Table 2.19

U.S. Direct Investment in China, 1979–2001 (Values in $ Millions)

	Total FDI in China			U.S. Direct Investment in China					
Year	Number of New Contracts	Value of New Contracts	Actual FDI Utilized	Number of New Contracts	Share of New Contracts	Value of New Contracts	Share of Value of New Contracts	Value of Actual Investment Utilized	Share of Value of Actual Investment Utilized
1979–82	922	4,608	1,771	21	2.28%	281	6.10%	13	0.73%
1983	470	1,731	916	25	5.32%	470	27.15%	5	0.55%
1984	1,856	2,650	1,419	62	3.34%	165	6.23%	256	18.04%
1985	3,073	5,931	1,956	100	3.25%	1,152	19.42%	357	18.25%
1986	1,498	2,834	1,875	102	6.81%	527	18.60%	315	16.80%
1987	2,233	3,709	2,647	104	4.66%	342	9.22%	263	9.94%
1988	5,945	5,297	3,194	269	4.52%	370	6.99%	236	7.39%
1989	5,779	5,600	3,774	276	4.78%	641	11.45%	284	7.53%
1990	7,273	6,596	3,487	357	4.91%	358	5.43%	456	13.08%
1991	12,978	11,977	4,366	694	5.35%	548	4.58%	323	7.40%
1992	48,764	58,124	11,008	3,265	6.70%	3,121	5.37%	511	4.64%
1993	83,437	111,437	27,515	6,750	8.09%	6,813	6.11%	2,063	7.50%
1994	47,549	82,680	33,767	4,223	8.88%	6,010	7.27%	2,491	7.38%
1995	37,011	91,282	37,521	3,474	9.39%	7,471	8.18%	3,083	8.22%
1996	24,556	73,276	41,726	2,517	10.25%	6,915	9.44%	3,444	8.25%
1997	21,001	51,004	45,257	2,188	10.42%	4,940	9.69%	3,240	7.16%
1998	19,799	52,102	45,463	2,238	11.30%	3,898	7.48%	6,484	14.26%
1999	16,918	41,223	40,319	2,028	11.99%	4,200	10.19%	6,000	14.88%
2000	22,347	62,380	40,715	2,609	11.67%	8,001	12.83%	4,384	10.77%
2001	26,150	69,120	46,842	2,594	9.92%	7,505	10.86%	4,858	10.37%

Source: China National Bureau of Statistics, China Statistics Yearbook (various issues).

Table 2.20
Major External Sources of Direct Investment in China, 1999 (Values in $ Millions)

Source	Number of New Contracts	Value of New Contracts	Average Contract Size	Actual FDI Utilized
Hong Kong	5,902	13,330	2.26	16,360
United States	2,028	6,020	2.97	4,220
Japan	1,167	2,590	2.22	2,970
Virgin Islands	495	3,490	7.05	2,660
Singapore	503	2,260	4.49	2,640
Taiwan	2,499	3,370	1.35	2,600
Germany	196	940	4.80	1,370
South Korea	1,547	1,480	0.96	1,270
United Kingdom	230	1,090	4.74	1,040
France	110	470	4.27	880

imposed on exports. It may also reflect the influence of daily political rhetoric and media coverage regarding China as well as legitimate concerns about China's business environment. The majority of U.S. business executives and managers, even those in non-controlled sectors of the economy, have been reluctant even to explore the possibility of doing business with or in China.

Impact on Technology Transfer

The key impact of U.S. export controls is their hindrance of U.S. technology transfer to China. While pressing China to further liberalize markets for U.S. investment in telecommunications, retail trade, and financial services (such as banking and insurance), the United States maintains control over technology transfer by U.S. companies to China. Technological improvements in China's production facilities have caused constant concern in the United States.

Semiconductors

A report by the U.S. General Accounting Office (2002) argued that rapid advances in China's semiconductor industry underscore a need for fundamental U.S. export control policy review. The report states that since 1986, China's efforts to improve its semiconductor manufacturing capability have narrowed the gap between U.S. and Chinese semiconductor manufacturing technology from between seven to ten years to two years or less. China's most advanced commercial manufacturing facilities, in fact, can

Table 2.21

U.S. Direct Investment Abroad on a Historical-Cost Basis: Industry Distribution, 2000 (Amounts in $ Millions)

	All Countries		China			Latin America and Other Western	Asia and	European
Industries	Value	Share	Value	Share	Canada	Hemisphere	Pacific	Union
All destinations	1,244,654	100.00%	9,577	100.00%	126,421	239,388	199,599	573,416
Petroleum	105,486	8.48%	1,846	19.28%	18,018	9,084	29,736	26,051
Manufacturing	343,992	27.64%	5,663	59.13%	50,425	50,696	60,710	168,648
Food and kindred products	36,840	2.96%	181	1.89%	4,445	10,595	4,117	15,594
Chemicals and allied products	86,081	6.92%	245	2.56%	8,929	10,616	10,314	52,605
Primary and fabricated metals	18,713	1.50%	183	1.91%	3,630	3,304	1,623	9,385
Industrial machinery and equipment	42,523	3.42%	931	9.72%	3,447	3,361	11,111	23,141
Electronic and other electric equipment	43,441	3.49%	3,208	33.50%	3,271	1,987	18,189	17,490
Transportation equipment	41,099	3.30%	147	1.53%	12,707	7,683	4,496	15,497
Other manufacturing	75,294	6.05%	768	8.02%	13,996	13,150	10,861	34,936
Wholesale trade	88,090	7.08%	362	3.78%	9,834	9,076	17,744	34,365
Depository institutions	37,155	2.99%	78	0.81%	1,999	−1,639	11,578	18,083
Finance (except depository institutions), insurance, and real estate	497,267	39.95%	740	7.73%	29,125	140,655	51,439	239,523
Services	79,857	6.42%	295	3.08%	8,297	7,301	13,638	47,243
Other industries	92,809	7.46%	594	6.20%	8,724	24,215	14,755	39,504

Source: Department of Commerce (2002a).

Table 2.22
Market Share of Selected U.S. Firms in China, 1997

Firm	Market Share	Rank
Motorola	48.32%	1
Coca-Cola	43.68%	1
Kodak	40.44%	2
Sprite	26.26%	2
Pepsi-Cola	12.20%	3
Maxwell	11.46%	2
Compaq (computers)	6.77%	2
Apple (computers)	6.02%	3

Source: People's Daily (1997).

produce chips that are only one generation behind current, commercial state-of-the-art technology. The growing sophistication of these facilities, which has improved China's ability to develop more capable weapons systems and advanced consumer electronics, has been fueled by China's success in acquiring manufacturing technology from abroad.

According to the GAO report, U.S. practice has aimed at keeping China at least two generations (about three to four years) behind state-of the-art semiconductor manufacturing capabilities. The current U.S. export control system has not, however, effectively slowed China's ability to obtain billions of dollars in advanced semiconductor equipment as part of its national strategy to modernize its semiconductor industry. To improve the system, the GAO report recommends that the secretary of commerce, in consultation with the secretaries of defense and state, reassess and document U.S. export policy on semiconductor manufacturing equipment and materials to China. Specifically, it recommends that these agencies complete the analyses needed to serve as a sound basis for an updated policy; develop new export controls, if appropriate, or alternative means for protecting U.S. security interests; and communicate the results of these efforts to the U.S. Congress and industry.

High-Performance Computers

Exports of high-performance computers (HPC) to China also are subject to restrictive U.S. controls. U.S. policy with respect to the export of computers and other sensitive technology is to seek a balance between the economic interest in promoting exports and the

Table 2.23
U.S. Exports of High-Performance Computers, Fiscal Years 1996 and 1997 (Ranked by Total MTOPS Exported)

Country	Tier	FY1996 Machines	FY1997 Machines	Total Machines	Total MTOPS	Share
Germany	1	111	488	599	2,600,949	18.48%
United Kingdom	1	87	489	576	2,359,761	16.76%
Japan	1	74	233	307	1,667,745	11.85%
South Korea	2	62	269	331	1,128,945	8.02%
France	1	29	229	258	1,070,385	7.60%
Italy	1	16	142	158	601,979	4.28%
Switzerland	1	23	147	170	500,327	3.55%
Spain	1	10	123	133	484,862	3.44%
Sweden	1	20	77	97	441,541	3.14%
Australia	1	32	88	120	398,198	2.83%
Netherlands	1	10	95	105	321,352	2.28%
Belgium	1	12	88	100	288,194	2.05%
Hong Kong	2	9	73	82	259,072	1.84%
China	3	23	54	77	239,037	1.70%
Brazil	2	2	68	70	214,350	1.52%
Israel	3	7	41	48	200,177	1.42%
Mexico	1	12	45	57	199,133	1.41%
Malaysia	2	23	53	76	194,805	1.38%
Singapore	2	5	60	65	189,729	1.35%
South Africa	2	8	28	36	132,675	0.94%
Thailand	2	2	35	37	110,536	0.79%
Austria	1	6	25	31	108,449	0.77%
Norway	1	1	15	16	107,388	0.76%
Indonesia	2	0	27	27	91,561	0.65%
Russia	3	7	21	28	84,961	0.60%
Finland	1	1	23	24	81,571	0.58%
Total		592	3036	3628	14,077,682	100.00%

Source: GAO (1998).

national security interest in maintaining a military advantage over potential adversaries and denying the spread of technologies used to develop weapons of mass destruction. The United States has long controlled the export of high-performance computers to "sensitive" destinations, such as Russia and China (Johnson 2000), as part of a policy that organizes countries into four "tiers," with each higher-numbered tier representing a successively higher level of concern related to U.S. national security interests. China is designated a Tier 3 country. This control system has significantly limited China's imports of U.S. computers. According to a 1998 GAO report, Tier 1 countries, mainly U.S. friends and allies, accounted for 72.1 percent of high-performance computer exports for the period January 1996 to September 1997 (see Table 2.23), while China accounted for only 1.7 percent of total U.S. exports.

Table 2.24
World Operable Nuclear Capacities by Region, 1997–98 (Net Gigawatts)

	1997		1998	
Country	Capacity	Share	Capacity	Share
Industrialized	283.6	80.59%	278.6	79.85%
United States	99.0	28.13%	97.1	27.83%
Other North America	13.3	3.78%	11.6	3.32%
Japan	43.9	12.48%	43.7	12.53%
France	62.9	17.87%	61.7	17.68%
United Kingdom	13.0	3.69%	13.0	3.73%
Other Western Europe	51.5	14.63%	51.6	14.79%
Eastern Europe/Former Soviet Union	46.3	13.16%	46.6	13.36%
Eastern Europe	9.8	2.78%	10.2	2.92%
Russia	19.8	5.63%	19.8	5.67%
Ukraine	13.8	3.92%	13.8	3.96%
Other Former Soviet Union	2.8	0.80%	2.8	0.80%
Developing Countries	22.0	6.25%	23.7	6.79%
China	2.2	0.63%	2.2	0.63%
South Korea	9.8	2.78%	11.4	3.27%
Other	10.1	2.87%	10.1	2.89%
Total World	351.9	100.00%	348.9	100.00%

Notes: Totals may not equal sum of components due to independent rounding.
Source: Department of Energy (2000).

Nuclear Technology

Besides semiconductors and high-performance computers, the United States also has restricted exports and technology transfer to China in many other industries on the basis of national security concerns. The nuclear power industry is a clear example. China has been building nuclear power plants to meet rapid growth in electricity demand. Two nuclear power plants are operating in China: one was designed and built independently by China and began operating in 1991, while the other was imported from France and began operating in 1994. Four more nuclear power plants are under construction, one designed by China and the other three imported from France, Canada, and Russia, respectively. These plants are expected to begin operating in the early 2000s. Even with these additional plants, however, China's nuclear power generating capacity will still be very limited. In the late 1990s, China's operable nuclear capacity, as Table 2.24 shows, was only 0.63 percent of the world's total, and accounted for only 1.2 percent of China's total energy supply (CAEA 2002).

The United States has long prohibited American companies from selling nuclear power-generating equipment to China.

Although there has been no specific evaluation of how this export ban has affected China's nuclear power development, the lack of U.S. participation in China's nuclear power industry may reflect missed opportunities for both sides.

Exports of Satellites

In part to promote better ties with China, the Reagan administration, in September 1988, first notified Congress of its decision to approve licenses for exports of satellites for launch from China (Kan 1998). It is believed that such exports are mutually beneficial. For the United States, as the Clinton administration argued, "Satellite exports to China have benefits for commercial competitiveness, nonproliferation goals, spread of democracy, and the policy of engagement" (Kan 1998). China, on the other hand, gains several benefits from launching satellites for foreign customers, including foreign capital, technical expertise, and international prestige. However, considerations of post-Tiananmen sanctions and missile proliferation activities have been added to the export control process since 1990. Presidential waivers are now needed before licenses can be approved for export of satellites or parts to China.

The debate over whether to allow satellite exports to China has been very tense in the United States since 1990, but one common theme prevails—forbidding the transfer of technology to China. Kan (1998) provides a list of views from both sides of the debate. On one side is the White House, which believes there are several advantages to the United States in allowing satellite exports to China. First, such a policy would help U.S. firms compete in the world satellite export market yet still protect U.S. security interests through export licensing procedures and strict security measures (including escorts of satellites by Pentagon officials) that would preclude any assistance to Chinese missile programs. Allowing Pentagon officials access to China's secretive aerospace and missile complex might provide a second benefit, while the satellites themselves could prove advantageous by promoting the spread of democratic values.

Opponents of U.S. satellite exports to China say, first, that the practice indirectly subsidizes and assists China's missile research and development efforts. They also argue that exporting small amounts of technology or technical assistance with each satellite may, over time, have the cumulative effect of conveying valuable expertise to China. Third, satellite exports may enable Chinese engineers to learn important quality control processes and other lessons in missile technology development from their American and European counterparts. Finally, opponents say, allowing the Chinese to launch U.S. satellites may jeopardize U.S. efforts to prevent missile proliferation.

From December 1989 to February 1998, Presidents Bush and Clinton issued 13 waivers out of 20 proposed satellite projects, a denial rate of 35 percent (Kan 1998). Responding to continued criticism of satellite exports to China, the Clinton Administration announced on 22 February 1999 that it would refuse to license the export of a $450 million American-made satellite to China. Those arguing for denial of the export license maintained that the Hughes satellite was a new design that had not been launched by the Chinese before and would give China the opportunity to learn the new technology.

U.S. Investment Insurance and Export Financing

U.S. sanctions prohibiting several U.S. government agencies from operating in China have contributed to losses of investment and trade opportunities for both countries. One such agency is the U.S. Overseas Private Investment Corporation (OPIC), which sells investment services to American companies. Its stated mission is "to mobilize and facilitate the participation of United States private capital and skills in the economic and social development of less developed countries and areas, and countries in transition from non-market to market economies, thereby complementing the development assistance objectives of the United States." OPIC claims that its political risk insurance and loans help U.S. businesses of all sizes invest and compete in more than 140 developing nations and emerging markets (OPIC 2002). Yet, more than a decade after it suspended its activities in China in 1989, OPIC is still prohibited from resuming its operations in China. This may partly explain the lack of investment in China by small and medium-sized U.S. companies.

The U.S. Trade and Development Agency (TDA) is a U.S. agency that helps create jobs for Americans by assisting U.S. companies in pursuing overseas business opportunities. The TDA funds feasibility studies, orientation visits, specialized training grants, business workshops, and various forms of technical assistance to "enable American businesses to compete for infrastructure and industrial projects in middle-income and developing countries" (TDA 2002). In January 2002, the TDA reopened its program in China following a national interest waiver lifting a 1989 sanction that had suspended the agency's operations in China. Prior to 1989, the TDA had a very successful program in China, with $24 million in grants facilitating $1.4 billion in U.S. exports (TDA 2001).

The Export-Import Bank of the United States (Ex-Im Bank) is a federal agency that provides financing for American exports. Its primary products and services are guarantees, insurance, loans that protect against nonpayment by a foreign buyer, guarantee loans to produce goods or provide a service for export, and assistance to importers to obtain financing at advantageous terms (Ex-Im Bank 2002b). After the Tiananmen crisis in 1989, the U.S. government ordered the selective withholding of Ex-Im Bank loans and credit guarantees for exports to China for non-economic or non-security reasons.

Environmental protection also has become a rationale for denying financing programs. In 1992, China launched the Three Gorges Dam project, a hydroelectric power project being built over the Yangtze River, the world's third largest river after the Amazon and the Nile. The Three Gorges Dam, according to some claims, will be the largest water control project in the world when completed. In September 1994, the International Rivers Network (IRN) and a coalition of U.S. environmental, development, and human rights groups encouraged the Clinton administration to withhold financial support for U.S. companies interested in bidding on the project. After more than a year, the U.S. National Security Council concluded that the U.S. government should stay clear of the Three Gorges Dam. In May 1996, the Export-Import Bank announced it would not guarantee loans to U.S. companies seeking contracts for the dam (IRN 2001).

Multilateral Development Bank Financing

Since 1989, the U.S. government has required the U.S. director on the Executive Board of the World Bank to vote against or abstain from voting on all China loans not devoted strictly to meeting basic human needs. This sanction had an initial impact on World Bank financing for China: Immediately after the Tiananmen crisis, the World Bank announced it would defer consideration of about $780 million in new loans to China but would continue to disburse funds under existing commitments (Riddell 1989b).

U.S. opposition to China loans from the World Bank and other multilateral development banks has seldom been effective, however. Based on data in a Congressional Research Service report (Rennack 1997), from November 1990 to March 1997, 200 loans for China were considered by multilateral development banks such as the Asian Development Bank (ADB), Global Environmental Facility

(GEF), International Bank for Reconstruction and Development (commonly called the World Bank), International Development Association (IDA), International Finance Corporation (IFC), Asian Development Foundation (ADF), and the Japanese Special Fund (JSF) of the ADB. The United States voted "no" in 27 cases and abstained in 173 cases. All the loans were approved.

There was one case, however, in which a World Bank loan for a China poverty reduction project failed to materialize.[11] The project, called the Qinghai project, was a component of China's Western Poverty Reduction Project (WPRP) aimed at alleviating poverty in Gansu, Inner Mongolia, and Qinghai, three poor provinces in western and northwestern China. A campaign against the project began shortly after negotiations between the World Bank and China had been completed in April 1999. The protest was led by the International Campaign for Tibet (ICT) in the United States and Tibetan support groups around the world and focused mainly on the proposed resettlement of large numbers of non-Tibetans in the project area and on environmental damage the project allegedly would cause.

According to Bottelier (2001), opposition to the project was essentially political in nature, but the conflict took the form of a proxy battle over compliance with World Bank operational guidelines and safeguard policies. The president of the bank, James Wolfensohn, and bank directors, were inundated with thousands of letters and e-mails from all over the world protesting the Qinghai project and World Bank support for it. Wolfensohn also was urged to drop support for the project by 60 members of the U.S. Congress as well as the U.S. secretary of the treasury in his capacity as the U.S. representative on the bank's Board of Governors. In the end, the United States and Japan were the only two member countries of the World Bank to oppose the project. All other shareholders supported it in principle, but some (including European shareholders as well as Canada and Australia) required that it be resubmitted for Board approval after completion of additional studies and assessments. China refused to accept this condition and decided to use its own resources to implement the project.

Impact on Hong Kong and Taiwan

As discussed earlier, trade between the United States and China is crucial to Hong Kong's economy. As Taiwan increasingly orients its economy toward China and exports from the mainland to the United States, U.S.–China trade has become instrumental to Taiwan's business success. Rising land and labor costs in Taiwan

Table 2.25
U.S. Footwear Imports from Taiwan and China, 1986–96 (Values in $ Thousands)

	Taiwan		China	
Year	Value	Share	Value	Share
1986	2,167,442	96.59%	76,585	3.41%
1987	2,477,707	94.55%	142,887	5.45%
1988	2,408,681	87.58%	341,668	12.42%
1989	2,004,545	73.55%	720,956	26.45%
1990	1,528,163	50.84%	1,477,406	49.16%
1991	1,168,771	31.58%	2,532,053	68.42%
1992	843,421	19.86%	3,402,557	80.14%
1993	582,917	11.42%	4,519,553	88.58%
1994	455,571	7.97%	5,259,130	92.03%
1995	351,322	5.69%	5,823,739	94.31%
1996	256,633	3.86%	6,391,558	96.14%

Source: United States–China Business Council.

have prompted many Taiwanese firms to relocate their export-oriented, labor-intensive operations to the mainland. As a result, many labor-intensive products that previously were exported from Taiwan to the United States are now being exported from China to the United States.

U.S. footwear imports from China and Taiwan, shown in Table 2.25, exemplify the switch of U.S. imports from Taiwan to China. In terms of percentages, Taiwan and China have literally reversed their positions in U.S. footwear imports. According to one researcher, more than half of Taiwan's footwear manufacturers have moved to the mainland (Klintworth 1995), where they operate 300-plus factories and employ 100,000 workers to produce brand-name shoes such as Nike and Reebok for export to the United States and elsewhere. While Taiwan's shoe exports to the entire world dropped from 800 million pairs in 1987 to 370 million pairs in 1991, exports of shoe parts to China ballooned by almost 60 percent in 1991 alone. That same year, 40 percent of the 500 million Chinese-made shoes sold in the United States were manufactured in Taiwanese factories on the mainland. China has now replaced Taiwan as the biggest shoe supplier to the United States.

Many Taiwanese manufacturers in other industries also have moved to the mainland. By 1995, more than 80 percent of Taiwan's ceramic manufacturers, one-third of its plastics industry, and a quarter of its toy and leather goods factories had shifted operations to China. The majority of their mainland production (up to 70 percent) was exported to the United States and elsewhere, with 20 per-

Table 2.26
Changing Patterns in Taiwan's Exports, 1986–94 (Selected Products; Values in $ Millions)

Year	All Exports Value	Footwear		Garments		Ceramic Products		Subtotal
		Value	Share	Value	Share	Value	Share	
1986	39,861.5	3,107.6	7.80%	3,790.6	9.51%	416.3	1.04%	18.35%
1987	53,678.7	3,691.6	6.88%	4,439.1	8.27%	674.9	1.26%	16.40%
1988	60,667.4	3,856.1	6.36%	4,068.2	6.71%	671.4	1.11%	14.17%
1989	66,304.0	3,799.5	5.73%	3,946.9	5.95%	665.2	1.00%	12.69%
1990	67,214.4	3,528.3	5.25%	3,109.3	4.63%	616.9	0.92%	10.79%
1991	76,178.3	3,810.8	5.00%	3,518.6	4.62%	626.1	0.82%	10.44%
1992	81,470.3	3,703.6	4.55%	3,128.5	3.84%	618.4	0.76%	9.15%
1993	85,091.5	2,772.6	3.26%	2,768.0	3.25%	463.8	0.55%	7.06%
1994	93,048.8	1,726.4	1.86%	2,538.1	2.73%	377.2	0.41%	4.99%

Source: CEPD (1995).

cent sold in China and 10 percent sold back to Taiwan (Klintworth 1995). Based on Taiwan's trade statistics (see Table 2.26), Taiwan's shares of world exports of footwear and parts, garments, and ceramic products fell from 7.80 percent, 9.51 percent, and 1.04 percent, respectively, in 1986 to 1.86 percent, 2.73 percent, and 0.41 percent in 1994. These three groups of products comprised 18.35 percent of Taiwan's total exports in 1986, but accounted for less than 5 percent in 1994.

The threat of U.S. economic sanctions on imports from China is seen as a threat to the well-being of both Hong Kong and Taiwan. Indeed, all countries that have investment stakes in China or ties to the Chinese economy can be hurt by U.S. sanctions on China. When China's trade status was being debated in the 1990s, the United States was constantly being urged by its trading partners in Asia not to deny MFN status for China.

In an interview with the *Financial Times* in London in 1994, Goh Chok Tong, Singapore's prime minister, cautioned that a break in Sino–U.S. relations over China's human rights policies would have severe long-term consequences for the world (Nicoll 1994). Jeffrey Koo, chairman of Taiwan's Chinese National Association of Industry and Commerce and a prominent advisor to the Taiwanese government, stated in a *Wall Street Journal* article that MFN status for China was also good for Taiwan (Koo 1996). According to Koo, at least 25,000 Taiwanese enterprises had invested in China by 1996, but the actual number could have been higher than 50,000 as there were no official statistics. By taking advantage of China's low-cost labor and land, these firms turned out products at competitive prices for export to developed countries, including the United States.

Christopher Patten, the former governor of Hong Kong, also favored MFN status for China. In a speech on 8 May 1996, Patten stated, "If China loses MFN, Hong Kong will lose a colossal amount of business at a stroke" (BCUSCT 1997).

Impact on China's Policies

U.S.–China economic relations in general, and U.S. economic sanctions in particular, have had important consequences for China's overall economic policies. During the years of total embargo, China had no choice but to adopt a policy of self-reliance and hard struggle. China's alliance with the former Soviet Union was to some extent both a cause and a result of the U.S. embargo. The lifting of the embargo in the early 1970s and the subsequent normalization of diplomatic relations between the two countries provided a prelude to, and a necessary external environment for, China's open-door policy and economic reform that began in 1978.

As China's trade with the United States has increased, so has its dependence on the U.S. market for its exports. Although China has objected to almost all the rationales that have motivated U.S. sanctions against it, China has cooperated with the United States in solving issues and averting escalations of tensions that might have led to trade wars. Since the beginning of China's economic reform, China has established many trade-related laws and regulations (including those on intellectual property rights protection and nuclear exports), improved trade transparency, liberalized its domestic market, and generally established harmonization with international commercial practices.

IMPACT OF U.S. ECONOMIC SANCTIONS ON THE UNITED STATES

Economic sanctions interfere with normal trade and exchange between countries. If free trade is good for all trading nations, as most economists agree in theory, then economic sanctions hurt both the target country and the sanctioning country. Thus, basic economic theory suggests that U.S. sanctions against China should inflict economic costs not only upon China but upon the United States as well. U.S. import restrictions, for example, will raise prices of its imports and reduce consumer welfare, while U.S. export restrictions will deprive U.S. exporters of international markets and hurt U.S. employment, thus reducing the welfare of U.S. workers.

The assumption underlying this argument is that both the United States and China are large economies that can influence supply and demand, and hence prices, in each other's markets. Economic theories also suggest that a small economy (in terms of market power) is more dependent on a large economy in terms of export market and international price determination. Accordingly, a large country's economic sanctions against a small economy will cause more economic pain to the small country than vice versa. Indeed, it is believed that U.S. economic sanctions against China hurt China more than the United States, since China presumably is more dependent on the trade relationship. This belief is substantiated by the fact that the United States accounts today for more than 20 percent of China's export market and about 9 percent of its imports (see Table 2.10), while China accounts for only about 2 percent of the U.S. export market and less than 10 percent of its imports (see Table 2.8). In addition, the United States is better able to find substitutes for its imports from China as they are basically low-priced manufactures, while its exports to China can be high in technology content and command high prices.

But the assumption that China depends more on trade with the United States than vice versa should not trivialize the fact that U.S. economic sanctions against China do exert costs—at times, very large costs—on the United States itself. This can be particularly true in a global economy in which China is perceived as a relatively large market.

As a study of U.S. sanctions policy by the European-American Business Council pointed out, measuring the impact of sanctions on the U.S. economy and on multinational companies is a complex and challenging task (EABC 1997). Few, if any, companies have analyzed thoroughly the dollar and employment losses they have suffered from U.S. sanctions. From the aggregate U.S.–China trade statistics, one may draw only very rough estimates of the losses that U.S. economic sanctions may have caused the United States.

On the import side, U.S. losses due to economic sanctions on China may be seen in how U.S. consumers have been affected. U.S. imports from China in 2000 were somewhere between $52 billion (Chinese data; see Table 2.18) and $100 billion (U.S. data). Since China has been denied GSP treatment (which eliminates tariffs for most goods from developing countries) by the United States, U.S. consumers have had to pay higher prices for imports from China. Assuming that the average duty on imports from China is 4 percent—the average U.S. tariff charged in normal trade—U.S. consumers paid between $2.04 and $4.24 billion in duties on imports from China.

One should be cautioned that this estimate is very primitive and based on plausible but rudimentary assumptions. The added cost is not a net national loss but a simple income transfer from U.S. consumers to the U.S. government. Still, the reduction in consumption of imports from China due to higher prices and quantity limitations can result in large deadweight losses that are not recovered by anyone else within the United States. These deadweight losses include increased domestic production costs for import substitutes as well as consumers' welfare losses due to reduced consumption.

On the export side, U.S. export controls have contributed at least partly to the U.S. trade deficit with China ($83.83 billion based on U.S. data and $29.79 billion based on Chinese data for 2000; see Table 2.18). According to a U.S. Department of Commerce study, $1 billion of goods exported in 1992 supported 15,500 jobs, both directly in the exporting firms and indirectly in their suppliers (Davis 1996). If the same estimates still applied in 2000, U.S. job losses due to its trade deficit with China would have ranged from 461,745 (based on China's data) to as many as 1,299,365 (based on U.S. data). These estimates are grounded in the assumption that the U.S. trade deficit with China can be eliminated through U.S. exports, which is plausible in the absence of U.S. export controls. A loss of more than a million jobs sounds unbelievable, but it indicates how large an impact U.S. export controls on China may have.

Even more difficult to calculate are losses from the "chilling effect" of U.S. economic sanctions on certain trade and investment opportunities. A chilling effect occurs when companies forego certain business opportunities rather than risk being subject to sanctions (EABC 1997). With China labeled a "sensitive" country by the United States, one can easily imagine that U.S. firms are very wary of doing business with China. It is true that many U.S. companies are operating in China, but it is hard to estimate the damage these barriers to entry impose on U.S. firms.

Political tensions are often coupled with economic sanctions and can produce the same chilling effect. As Mastel (1997) explained, this chilling effect is one of two factors underlying the poor performance of U.S. exports to China. First, as discussed before, the United States has at several points held up export financing to China and barred China from many of its aid programs. The second factor has been the ongoing political tension between the United States and China.

According to Mastel, the United States, in its role as a world leader, has been prominent in criticizing China for violations of human rights, arms sales, piracy of intellectual property, and a raft of other issues. This had led to significant ongoing tensions between the United States and China and claims by China that the United States is seeking to "contain" Chinese influence. The U.S. Congress, in an effort to apply leverage on these issues, has also threatened to impose high tariffs on Chinese exports to the United States. The combined effect of all these tensions has been to insert acrimony and uncertainty into the U.S.–China relationship, which can only damage U.S. export prospects (Mastel 1997).

Given the difficulties in compiling more systematic and comprehensive estimates of the impact of U.S. economic sanctions, most analyses have been anecdotal. Even anecdotal figures, however, illustrate the high cost that U.S. sanctions impose on U.S. companies (EABC 1997). As mentioned before, from 1988 to 1998 the U.S. government refused seven of twenty satellite export projects to China. One such refusal cost Hughes $450 million in exports to China. To protest U.S. trade policies toward China, Beijing passed up Boeing in favor of Airbus in placing a $1.89 billion order for 34 planes in 1996 (Burstein and De Keijzer 1998). Caterpillar reported in 1998 that the prohibition of U.S. Ex-Im Bank financing for sales of construction equipment for the Three Gorges Dam project gave foreign companies a competitive edge (ITC 1998). According to a *Financial Times* report, a Chinese official once specifically mentioned Westinghouse as a "very strong competitor in bidding for China's nuclear power construction" (Harding 1997). But U.S. sanctions on nuclear power plant exports to China pushed the opportunities to competitors from other nations—through 1996, China had purchased or contracted for approximately $8 billion of nuclear power equipment from France, $3 billion from Canada, and $4 billion from Russia.

Anecdotal evidence also highlights the cost or potential cost of U.S. unilateral sanctions on broad U.S. economic sectors. According to an editorial in the *Washington Post,* restrictions on U.S. credit guarantees for China as proposed in legislation (S. 2645) in the 106th Congress sponsored by Senators Thompson and Torricelli would have dealt a devastating blow to American farmers, who were suffering a serious economic downturn because of the steep drop in U.S. farm exports to Asia. The editorial stated as follows:

> Losing China—which the U.S. Department of Agriculture projects could account for one-third of growth in U.S. farm exports—would be a major setback. In short, Thompson-Torricelli sanctions won't strengthen U.S. leverage. Instead, the bill would ensure that China buys European aircraft, Japanese cars, Canadian wheat and Australian beef—all of which benefit from subsidized export financing. (Donohue 2000)

In 1999, following the release of the House report on illegal technology transfers to China, the U.S. Congress decided to transfer authority over satellite export licensing from the Commerce Department to the State Department. A year later, U.S. Rep. Sam Gejdenson, D-Connecticut, ranking member of the House International Relations Committee, claimed that "[T]he new process has led to a loss of almost 40 percent of the market share to our competitors, while sales internationally have increased. This jeopardizes our commercial advantage as well as our national defense capabilities" (Gejdenson 2000).

The uncertain supply of U.S. products caused by U.S. economic sanctions has long-term effects on U.S. companies and their exports. According to a report published by the Center for Strategic & International Studies, the reputation of the United States as an unreliable supplier has led foreign firms to avoid U.S. laws by designing products that have few, if any, U.S.-made components or developing foreign replacements for U.S.-made components. Airbus Industries, for example, was once dependent on a significant number of U.S. parts for its aircraft, but it changed designs so that it could, when necessary, manufacture an Airbus composed of less than 10 percent U.S. parts, thereby escaping U.S. trade controls. Similar tactics have been adopted by the foreign subsidiaries of U.S. firms (Collins and Bowdoin 1999).

This supply uncertainty can help explain the weak performance of U.S. exports to China. China has for many years tried to diversify its sources of imports for its development. Such diversification is seen in many key industries, such as telecommunications, power generation, and machine tools, to name just a few. Multinational companies from the EU and Japan as well as the United States are major players in these industries in China.

Some indication of the overall third-country effect of U.S. economic sanctions against China may be found in the changing trade shares of China's major trade partners. As Table 2.27 shows, China's imports from the United States, Japan, the EU, and Hong Kong have followed different paths. The U.S. share of China's total imports has been declining, from more than 20 percent in the early 1980s to less than 10 percent in 2000. Similarly, Japan's share of China's total imports has declined from almost 36 percent in 1985 to less than 20 percent in 2000. On the other hand, China's imports from the EU have remained relatively stable at about 15 percent over the same time period. The fact that the U.S. share declined more than Japan's and the European Union's may reflect the diversion of China's imports from the United States to other industrialized countries. The sharp decline in the share of China's imports

Table 2.27

Major Suppliers of China's Imports, 1980–2000 (Values in $ Millions)

Year	Hong Kong		European Union		Japan		United States		Subtotal	All Countries
	Value	Share	Value	Share	Value	Share	Value	Share	(Share)	(Value)
1980	569.8	2.92%	3,072.6	15.75%	5,168.9	26.50%	3,830.2	19.64%	64.81%	19,505.0
1981	1,236.3	5.72%	3,129.9	14.47%	6,183.0	28.58%	4,682.4	21.65%	70.42%	21,630.5
1982	1,314.2	6.95%	2,340.6	12.37%	3,901.7	20.62%	4,304.6	22.75%	62.69%	18,920.4
1983	1,709.8	8.02%	3,654.5	17.15%	5,495.2	25.78%	2,753.0	12.92%	63.87%	21,312.6
1984	2,830.2	10.90%	3,716.0	14.32%	8,056.9	31.04%	3,837.1	14.78%	71.05%	25,953.3
1985	4,762.1	11.21%	6,699.3	15.77%	15,178.4	35.73%	5,198.7	12.24%	74.95%	42,479.9
1986	5,572.0	12.88%	8,472.9	19.59%	12,463.2	28.82%	4,718.2	10.91%	72.20%	43,247.4
1987	8,437.0	19.52%	8,026.0	18.57%	10,087.2	23.34%	4,835.6	11.19%	72.61%	43,222.2
1988	12,004.7	21.69%	8,860.9	16.01%	11,062.1	19.99%	6,633.0	11.98%	69.66%	55,351.7
1989	12,540.4	21.20%	9,784.8	16.55%	10,533.9	17.81%	7,863.6	13.30%	68.86%	59,140.1
1990	14,565.0	27.07%	9,146.5	17.00%	7,655.9	14.23%	6,591.0	12.25%	70.54%	53,809.4
1991	17,543.3	27.47%	9,296.8	14.55%	10,031.7	15.71%	8,010.3	12.54%	70.27%	63,874.9
1992	20,538.7	25.09%	10,862.9	13.27%	13,685.6	16.72%	8,902.7	10.87%	65.95%	81,870.8
1993	10,501.1	10.13%	15,738.5	15.19%	23,302.5	22.49%	10,632.8	10.26%	58.07%	103,622.0
1994	9,487.8	8.20%	18,604.2	16.08%	26,318.9	22.75%	13,976.7	12.08%	59.11%	115,705.0
1995	8,599.0	6.51%	21,313.3	16.13%	29,007.3	21.95%	16,123.2	12.20%	56.78%	132,163.0
1996	7,839.0	5.64%	19,882.5	14.31%	29,190.2	21.01%	16,178.9	11.64%	52.60%	138,949.0
1997	6,997.3	4.92%	19,204.5	13.51%	28,989.6	20.39%	16,289.8	11.46%	50.28%	142,163.0
1998	6,666.7	4.75%	20,730.7	14.77%	28,306.8	20.16%	16,997.3	12.11%	51.79%	140,385.0
1999	6,892.4	4.16%	25,466.1	15.37%	33,768.2	20.38%	19,488.7	11.76%	51.66%	165,718.0
2000	9,429.2	4.19%	30,846.7	13.70%	41,511.8	18.44%	22,374.6	9.94%	46.27%	225,096.0

Note: Imports are based on c.i.f.
Source: International Monetary Fund (2001a).

from Hong Kong, from more than 25 percent in the early 1990s to less than 5 percent in 2000, is an indication that U.S. sanctions may have reduced the role of Hong Kong as a re-exporter of U.S. products to China.

The share of China's imports from the four major sources—namely Japan, the European Union, the United States, and Hong Kong—has experienced a steady overall decline, from about 70 percent in the 1980s to less than 50 percent today. There may be two interpretations for this overall decline. First, the multilateral sanctions that the industrialized countries imposed on China after the 1989 Tiananmen crisis have had a long-lasting impact on China's imports from these sources. Indeed, the early 1990s seemed to be a turning point—that is, China's imports from these four sources were increasing until 1990, at which point they reversed direction. Second (and correspondingly), China has effectively diversified its import sources. As Table 2.10 shows, South Korea became the second largest source of China's imports in 2000. Other countries in the Asia-Pacific area, such as Malaysia, Singapore, and Australia, also have become major sources of China's imports.

The third-country effect of U.S. sanctions against China is not apparent on China's exports. The share of China's exports to the United States has increased from around 8 percent in the 1980s to more than 20 percent in 2000 (see Table 2.28). The share of China's exports to the EU has remained relatively stable, with a slight upward trend. But the share of China's exports to Japan has declined steadily, from better than 20 percent in the early 1980s to around 17 percent in the late 1990s. The overall share of China's exports to the four major destinations—the United States, Hong Kong, Japan, and the EU—increased from around 65 percent in the early 1980s to more than 75 percent in the early 1990s, then declined to a little over 70 percent in 2000.

EFFECTIVENESS AND RATIONALE OF U.S. SANCTIONS AGAINST CHINA

Measuring the effectiveness of economic sanctions is not only difficult, but controversial. There are at least two points at issue: objective and causality. If the objective is to cause pain and suffering in the target economy, economic sanctions should be considered effective, albeit to different degrees for different countries under different circumstances. After all, economic sanctions interfere with normal trade. But if the objective is too ambitious, economic sanctions may be considered ineffective. According to Thomas J. Donohue (2000), president and chief executive officer of the U.S.

Table 2.28

Major Destinations of China's Exports, 1980–2000 (Values in $ Millions)

	Hong Kong		European Union		Japan		United States		Subtotal	All Countries
Year	Value	Share	Value	Share	Value	Share	Value	Share	Share	Value
1980	4,353.2	24.00%	2,490.5	13.73%	4,032.2	22.23%	982.6	5.42%	65.37%	18,139.2
1981	5,262.7	24.51%	2,682.4	12.49%	4,746.6	22.10%	1,505.1	7.01%	66.11%	21,475.9
1982	5,180.6	23.69%	2,268.9	10.38%	4,806.4	21.98%	1,764.7	8.07%	64.12%	21,864.9
1983	5,796.7	26.23%	2,601.8	11.78%	4,517.0	20.44%	1,713.0	7.75%	66.20%	22,095.8
1984	6,586.1	26.53%	2,330.2	9.39%	5,155.0	20.77%	2,312.5	9.32%	66.00%	24,824.2
1985	7,148.1	26.16%	2,383.8	8.72%	6,091.4	22.29%	2,336.2	8.55%	65.72%	27,329.3
1986	9,776.3	31.17%	4,141.1	13.20%	5,078.6	16.19%	2,632.7	8.39%	68.95%	31,366.7
1987	13,764.2	34.88%	4,101.7	10.39%	6,391.8	16.20%	3,030.4	7.68%	69.15%	39,464.2
1988	18,239.2	38.27%	4,977.5	10.44%	8,046.4	16.88%	3,398.7	7.13%	72.72%	47,662.8
1989	21,915.9	41.42%	5,113.7	9.66%	8,394.7	15.86%	4,413.6	8.34%	75.29%	52,913.8
1990	27,162.6	43.28%	6,275.1	10.00%	9,210.4	14.68%	5,313.9	8.47%	76.42%	62,759.8
1991	32,137.6	44.66%	7,127.4	9.90%	10,251.8	14.25%	6,198.0	8.61%	77.42%	71,965.9
1992	37,511.3	43.81%	8,004.1	9.35%	11,699.3	13.66%	8,598.8	10.04%	76.87%	85,620.1
1993	22,067.5	24.07%	12,257.7	13.37%	15,782.3	17.21%	16,976.5	18.51%	73.16%	91,692.8
1994	32,365.4	26.78%	15,418.0	12.76%	21,489.8	17.78%	21,421.4	17.72%	75.04%	120,865.0
1995	36,003.5	24.17%	19,258.2	12.93%	28,466.4	19.11%	24,743.9	16.61%	72.82%	148,955.0
1996	32,904.0	21.77%	19,868.1	13.14%	30,888.3	20.43%	26,730.6	17.68%	73.03%	151,165.0
1997	43,798.4	23.94%	23,870.8	13.05%	31,819.8	17.40%	32,743.9	17.90%	72.29%	182,917.0
1998	38,782.2	21.11%	28,161.9	15.33%	29,718.1	16.17%	38,000.6	20.68%	73.29%	183,744.0
1999	36,890.6	18.92%	30,244.8	15.52%	32,399.1	16.62%	42,003.1	21.55%	72.61%	194,931.0
2000	44,519.8	17.87%	38,230.3	15.34%	41,654.0	16.72%	52,161.7	20.93%	70.85%	249,195.0

Note: Exports are based on f.o.b.

Source: International Monetary Fund (2001a).

Chamber of Commerce, "In the past century, we've imposed unilateral sanctions 120 times against country after country, hoping that one day they would achieve their stated purpose of destroying economies or destabilizing governments. They never do."

U.S. economic sanctions did cause China a lot of pain and suffering during the embargo years, as evidenced by the absence of trade between the two countries even when China was in severe need of food during a three-year famine in the early 1960s. The sanctions also have hindered the transfer of U.S. technology to China since the embargo was lifted, although the impact of this hindrance is almost impossible to quantify. But despite the difficulties that these sanctions may have imposed, China has made remarkable progress in both economic growth and technological improvement in the last two decades. China has become a major trading nation in the world and has accumulated a high level of international reserves. Judging from the overall performance of the Chinese economy, U.S. economic sanctions have not had a significant adverse impact.

While economic losses may be appropriate measures of the cost of economic sanctions, they are not, in many cases, the objective or purpose of sanctions. Indeed, the effectiveness of an economic sanction should be measured not by the volume of business activity deterred, but rather by the desired behavioral changes on the part of the target regime(s) (EABC 1997). To some, U.S. economic sanctions against China have been very effective. According to a recently declassified analysis by the U.S. Arms Control and Disarmament Agency, "The history of U.S.–China relations shows that China has made specific nonproliferation commitments only under the threat or imposition of sanctions" (Helms 1999).

U.S. Senator Jesse Helms, R-North Carolina, former chairman and now ranking member of the Senate Foreign Relations Committee, views unilateral sanctions as the linchpin of U.S. nonproliferation policy, saying, "Short of war, sanctions are the main leverage the United States has over China" (Helms 1999). He also believes U.S. sanctions against China have played a crucial role in trade disputes between the two countries:

> The threat of unilateral sanctions on China over intellectual property rights and unfair trade barriers has forced China several times to yield. In November 1991, the U.S. trade representative threatened $1.5 billion in trade sanctions if an intellectual property rights agreement was not reached by January 1992. Not surprisingly, such an agreement was struck on January 16, 1992. No wonder business lobbyists are so keen to retain unilateral sanctions in the trade arsenal—even as they campaign to remove them from our nation's foreign policy. (Helms 1999)

It is true that China has made nonproliferation commitments and signed various trade agreements with the United States over the past decades. It is believed that China made huge concessions to the United States in its negotiations to join the WTO. But if these Chinese actions are seen as a result of U.S. economic sanctions or the threat of U.S. economic sanctions, one might wonder about the value of the commitments and agreements. The causality of these same commitments and agreements may, in fact, be seen in an entirely different light: cooperative efforts by the two countries to avert confrontation that would be good for neither.

There have been different evaluations of the effectiveness of U.S. economic sanctions against China. James Dorn, vice president for academic affairs at the Cato Institute, a public policy research foundation that advocates limited government, individual liberty, free markets, and peace, believes economic sanctions have little chance of success against China (Dorn 1996). He cites three factors behind his thinking.

First, U.S. sanctions against China are politically and operationally infeasible. American consumers would see higher prices and immediately protest. China, meanwhile, could transship products through Hong Kong or other channels, and U.S. customs officials would find it hard to identify the point of origin. Likewise, restricting American exports to China or curtailing the billions of dollars U.S. investors have poured into China would cause a political backlash from stakeholders and be difficult to enforce.

Second, third-country effects exist. Dorn argues that even if the U.S. government could block flows of goods and capital to China, there is no guarantee other countries would not step in to fill the gap. For example, instead of buying from Boeing or looking to American investors, the Chinese would shift to Airbus Industries and look to European and Asian trading partners for additional capital. U.S. investors, for their part, would try to reroute their funds into China rather than abandon their invested capital.

Third, China could retaliate if America were to ban trade with China. The ensuing trade war would harm both countries as well as the so-called Asian tigers and do irreparable damage to the evolution of economic and civil society in China.

CONCLUSION

China has been subject to different types of U.S. economic sanctions for more than half a century: a trade embargo from 1949 to 1971 and targeted sanctions afterwards. At present, the United States still maintains a broad spectrum of economic sanctions against China ranging from export controls to a prohibition on certain imports.

The impact of these sanctions on China can be summarized as follows. First, from a macroeconomic perspective, U.S. sanctions have caused pain to China but had no obvious adverse effect on China's economic growth. The U.S. trade embargo effectively blocked all trade between China and the Western world, isolating China and contributing to the hardships it suffered in those years. After the embargo was lifted, trade between the United States and China increased, making both countries major trade partners with each other. In the past two decades, China has achieved significant economic growth.

Second, based on estimates from a simple gravity model, U.S. economic sanctions against China apparently have not held back trade between the two countries since the mid-1980s. However, the U.S. denial of GSP treatment for China may have caused U.S. consumers more than $2 billion each year in higher costs for Chinese imports. U.S. restrictions on imports from China also may have caused deadweight losses due to higher domestic production costs for import substitutes and a reduction in consumption.

Third, U.S. export controls have hindered U.S. exports to China and contributed to large U.S trade deficits with China. The export controls may have caused losses of about 500,000 to more than a million jobs in the United States in 2000.

Fourth, U.S. export controls on China have benefited U.S. competitors (e.g., France and Japan) in some high-tech industries, such as nuclear power generation and telecommunications. In the nuclear power industry alone, U.S. competitors have generated revenues of several billion U.S. dollars in exports to China over the past few years. This third-country effect is also evident in China's overall trade with countries other than the United States. While China's share of imports from the United States has been declining, its share of imports from other sources, particularly the European Union, has remained steady or increased.

Fifth, U.S. economic sanctions against China also have affected economies that are involved in trade between China and the United States. Hong Kong, Taiwan, and (to some extent) Korea have moved a significant part of their manufacturing operations to China and export their products to the United States. U.S. economic sanctions on China have a direct impact on the viability of these economies.

Sixth, China's diversification of imports to sources other than the United States may have a long-term effect on U.S. exports to China even after U.S. economic sanctions against China are lifted.

Seventh, U.S. economic sanctions against China may have contributed to the relatively small share of U.S. investment in China as compared with total U.S. overseas investment. The sanctions also have held back U.S. financing of exports to China and financing for China from international institutions.

Despite the U.S. sanctions against China, economic relations between the two countries have become increasingly interdependent. The United States has become a major investor in China, and U.S. multinational companies have achieved market dominance in a number of sectors of the Chinese economy. With China joining the WTO at the end of 2001, it is believed that U.S. companies will have even more business opportunities in China in the future.

But as long as China is viewed as a potential adversary to the United States and sanctions are considered an effective source of leverage against China to solve differences between the two countries, U.S. economic sanctions against China likely will continue. Periodic tensions between the two countries can only serve to intensify the application of sanctions. The economic impact of such sanctions will be more severe than ever before for both countries, given the extent of their interdependence. Third-country effects may help alleviate some pains, but cannot totally negate the adverse effects on two such large economies.

Future studies of U.S. economic sanctions against China should focus on the issues that have motivated these sanctions. While there may be many alternative ways to approach the conflict areas (economic sanctions being one), enhancing mutual understanding may work in the best interests of both countries.

NOTES

1. The term "most favored nation" was changed to "normal trade relations" (NTR) by the Internal Revenue Service Restructuring and Reform Act of 1998 (Public Law 105–206), signed into law 22 July 1998 by President Bill Clinton.

2. Descriptions and analyses of the event differ. One opinion is that the use of force was a necessary measure against a rebellious movement aimed at overthrowing the Chinese government, while others, particularly media in the West, consider the incident a crackdown on a democratic movement. Tiananmen Square, a large square at the center of Beijing surrounded by historic monuments and buildings, is the symbolic political center of China.

3. The composite theoretical performance of a computer is measured in millions of theoretical operations per second (MTOPS). In principle, more theoretical operations indicate greater raw power to solve computations

quickly but do not describe the actual performance of a given machine for a given application (GAO 1998).

4. On 3 January 1999, the Select Committee on U.S. National Security and Military/Commercial Concerns with the People's Republic of China, chaired by Rep. Christopher Cox, issued a three-volume report describing a pattern of systematic and successful Chinese espionage to learn American nuclear secrets (Gerth and Risen, 1999).

5. The ratio is calculated from the 2001 statistical report on China's economic and social development, published by the China National Bureau of Statistics (2002).

6. The Export Administration Act of 1979 (Public Law 96–72) expired 20 August 1994 and was reauthorized by Public Law 106–508, signed 13 November 2000. During the interim, a national emergency declared under Executive Order 12924 (issued 19 August 1994 and extended by annual presidential notices) ensured that the provisions of the Export Administration Act remained in effect. Public Law 106–508 lapsed on 20 August 2001, but President Bush, asserting that "unrestricted access of foreign parties to U.S. goods and technology . . . constitute[s] an unusual and extraordinary threat to the national security, foreign policy, and economy of the United States," declared a national emergency and ordered that the export control system continue in full force until revoked or amended by the Commerce Department (Executive Order 13222 2001).

7. The Bureau of Industry and Security (BIS) originally was named the Bureau of Export Administration. It was renamed in April 2002.

8. General information about the Generalized System of Preferences is available from the United Nations Council for Trade and Development (UNCTAD) and its Web site, http://www.unctad.org. Information about the European Union's GSP operations is posted on two Web sites, http://www.eurunion.org and http://www.europa.eu.int.

9. The GSP operations of the United States are managed by the Office of the United States Trade Representative. For specific information, see the office's Web site at http://www.ustr.gov.

10. The WTO agreement on textile and clothing permits industrial countries to phase out their quota restrictions on textile and clothing imports by the end of 2004 (China Trade Relations Working Group 2000).

11. For a detailed description of the project and the World Bank loan process for the project, see Bottelier (2001).

Appendixes

Appendix 2.1
China's Economic Record, 1961–2000

	1961	1962	1963	1964	1965	1966	1967	1968	1969	1970
Population (millions)	660.00	666.00	682.00	698.00	715.00	735.00	755.00	775.00	796.00	818.00
GDP (billions of current $)	50.10	46.50	50.30	58.60	69.70	75.90	72.10	70.00	78.70	91.50
GDP per capita (current $)	75.91	69.82	73.75	83.95	97.48	103.27	95.50	90.32	98.87	111.86
GDP (billions of constant 1995 $)	54.30	51.00	56.30	65.20	75.90	82.20	80.30	78.10	86.00	98.10
GDP per capita (constant 1995 $)	82.28	76.63	82.50	93.37	106.09	111.76	106.36	100.79	108.01	119.88
Exports (billions of current $)										1.65
Exports (billions of constant 1995 $)										
Imports (billions of current $)										1.71
Imports (billions of constant 1995 $)										
External debt ($ billions)										
INDICES (1995 = 100)										
Population index	55.00	55.50	56.83	58.17	59.58	61.25	62.92	64.58	66.33	68.17
GDP index (current $)	7.16	6.64	7.19	8.37	9.96	10.84	10.30	10.00	11.24	13.07
GDP per capita index (current $)	13.01	11.97	12.64	14.39	16.71	17.70	16.37	15.48	16.95	19.18
GDP index (constant $)	7.76	7.29	8.04	9.31	10.84	11.74	11.47	11.16	12.29	14.01
GNP per capita index (constant $)	14.16	13.19	14.20	16.07	18.25	19.23	18.30	17.34	18.59	20.63
Export index (current $)										0.98
Export index (constant $)										
Import index (current $)										1.13
Import index (constant $)										

Appendix 2.1 (continued)
China's Economic Record, 1961–2000

	1961	1962	1963	1964	1965	1966	1967	1968	1969	1970
Population (millions)	841.00	862.00	882.00	900.00	916.00	931.00	943.00	956.00	969.00	981.00
GDP (billions of current $)	98.60	112.00	137.00	142.00	161.00	152.00	172.00	147.00	176.00	202.00
GDP per capita (current $)	117.24	129.93	155.33	157.78	175.76	163.27	182.40	153.77	181.63	205.91
GDP (billions of constant 1995 $)	104.00	107.00	115.00	118.00	126.00	124.00	131.00	145.00	155.00	164.00
GDP per capita (constant 1995 $)	123.32	123.60	130.45	131.22	137.86	133.63	139.16	151.33	160.20	167.63
Exports (billions of current $)	1.88	2.71	5.08	6.15	6.78	6.41	7.43	6.78	11.20	15.40
Exports (billions of constant 1995 $)								9.63	16.70	27.80
Imports (billions of current $)	2.06	2.92	4.43	6.51	6.75	5.96	6.83	7.26	12.40	15.90
Imports (billions of constant 1995 $)								12.90	22.70	35.70
External debt ($ billions)										
INDICES (1995 = 100)										
Population index	70.08	71.83	73.50	75.00	76.33	77.58	78.58	79.67	80.75	81.75
GDP index (current $)	14.09	16.00	19.57	20.29	23.00	21.71	24.57	21.00	25.14	28.86
GDP per capita index (current $)	20.10	22.27	26.63	27.05	30.13	27.99	31.27	26.36	31.14	35.30
GDP index (constant $)	14.86	15.29	16.43	16.86	18.00	17.71	18.71	20.71	22.14	23.43
GNP per capita index (constant $)	21.22	21.27	22.45	22.58	23.72	22.99	23.95	26.04	27.57	28.84
Export index (current $)	1.12	1.61	3.02	3.66	4.04	3.82	4.42	4.04	6.67	9.17
Export index (constant $)								5.73	9.94	16.55
Import index (current $)	1.36	1.92	2.91	4.28	4.44	3.92	4.49	4.78	8.16	10.46
Import index (constant $)								8.49	14.93	23.49

Appendix 2.1 (continued)
China's Economic Record, 1961–2000

	1981	1982	1983	1984	1985	1986	1987	1988	1989	1990
Population (millions)	994.00	1,010.00	1,020.00	1,040.00	1,050.00	1,070.00	1,080.00	1,100.00	1,120.00	1,140.00
GDP (billions of current $)	193.00	202.00	227.00	256.00	305.00	296.00	268.00	307.00	342.00	355.00
GDP per capita (current $)	194.16	200.00	222.55	246.15	290.48	276.64	248.15	279.09	305.36	311.40
GDP (billions of constant 1995 $)	174.00	191.00	211.00	243.00	274.00	298.00	331.00	366.00	381.00	396.00
GDP per capita (constant 1995 $)	175.00	188.95	206.46	234.79	260.78	278.90	305.14	332.31	340.73	349.15
Exports (billions of current $)	16.50	18.00	18.80	24.10	30.50	35.00	36.60	40.10	43.60	62.20
Exports (billions of constant 1995 $)	31.90	32.90	33.60	41.40	41.00	46.30	53.30	61.00	68.20	84.90
Imports (billions of current $)	15.90	14.80	17.10	24.30	43.00	43.50	36.70	43.40	46.20	50.80
Imports (billions of constant 1995 $)	36.10	31.90	35.60	49.10	69.00	59.50	55.10	66.50	72.40	72.30
External debt ($ billions)	5.80	8.36	9.61	12.10	16.70	23.70	35.30	42.40	44.90	55.30
INDICES (1995 = 100)										
Population index	82.83	84.17	85.00	86.67	87.50	89.17	90.00	91.67	93.33	95.00
GDP index (current $)	27.57	28.86	32.43	36.57	43.57	42.29	38.29	43.86	48.86	50.71
GDP per capita index (current $)	33.29	34.29	38.15	42.20	49.80	47.42	42.54	47.84	52.35	53.38
GDP index (constant $)	24.86	27.29	30.14	34.71	39.14	42.57	47.29	52.29	54.43	56.57
GNP per capita index (constant $)	30.11	32.51	35.53	40.40	44.87	47.99	52.51	57.18	58.63	60.08
Export index (current $)	9.82	10.71	11.19	14.35	18.15	20.83	21.79	23.87	25.95	37.02
Export index (constant $)	18.99	19.58	20.00	24.64	24.40	27.56	31.73	36.31	40.60	50.54
Import index (current $)	10.46	9.74	11.25	15.99	28.29	28.62	24.14	28.55	30.39	33.42
Import index (constant $)	23.75	20.99	23.42	32.30	45.39	39.14	36.25	43.75	47.63	47.57

Appendix 2.1 (continued)
China's Economic Record, 1961–2000

	1991	1992	1993	1994	1995	1996	1997	1998	1999	2000
Population (millions)	1,150.00	1,160.00	1,180.00	1,190.00	1,200.00	1,220.00	1,230.00	1,240.00	1,250.00	1,260.00
GDP (billions of current $)	377.00	418.00	432.00	543.00	700.00	816.00	898.00	946.00	991.00	1,080.00
GDP per capita (current $)	327.83	360.34	366.10	456.30	583.33	668.85	730.08	762.90	792.80	857.14
GDP (billions of constant 1995 $)	433.00	495.00	561.00	634.00	700.00	767.00	835.00	900.00	964.00	1,040.00
GDP per capita (constant 1995 $)	376.08	424.49	476.47	531.54	581.16	630.19	678.91	724.73	768.79	824.04
Exports (billions of current $)	73.20	81.60	73.70	137.00	168.00	172.00	207.00	207.00	218.00	280.00
Exports (billions of constant 1995 $)	99.00	114.00	124.00	154.00	168.00	121.00	148.00	159.00	181.00	239.00
Imports (billions of current $)	60.60	75.10	80.30	127.00	152.00	154.00	164.00	164.00	190.00	251.00
Imports (billions of constant 1995 $)	84.80	106.00	134.00	147.00	152.00	110.00	122.00	126.00	154.00	192.00
External debt ($ billions)	60.30	72.40	85.90	100.00	118.00	129.00	147.00	155.00	154.00	150.00
INDICES (1995 = 100)										
Population index	95.83	96.67	98.33	99.17	100.00	101.67	102.50	103.33	104.17	105.00
GDP index (current $)	53.86	59.71	61.71	77.57	100.00	116.57	128.29	135.14	141.57	154.29
GDP per capita index (current $)	56.20	61.77	62.76	78.22	100.00	114.66	125.16	130.78	135.91	146.94
GDP index (constant $)	61.86	70.71	80.14	90.57	100.00	109.57	119.29	128.57	137.71	148.57
GNP per capita index (constant $)	64.71	73.04	81.99	91.46	100.00	108.44	116.82	124.70	132.29	141.79
Export index (current $)	43.57	48.57	43.87	81.55	100.00	102.38	123.21	123.21	129.76	166.67
Export index (constant $)	58.93	67.86	73.81	91.67	100.00	72.02	88.10	94.64	107.74	142.26
Import index (current $)	39.87	49.41	52.83	83.55	100.00	101.32	107.89	107.89	125.00	165.13
Import index (constant $)	55.79	69.74	88.16	96.71	100.00	72.37	80.26	82.89	101.32	126.32

Source: World Bank, World Development Indicators (various issues).

Appendix 2.2
Selected U.S. Sanctions Against China Since 1949

Date	Authority for Action	Description	Status
Early 1949	Export Control Act of 1949	Trade restrictions. Imposed selective controls on trade with China.	Replaced by new export administration regulations on 1 Jan. 1965.
December 1950	Trading with the Enemy Act	Trade embargo. Effectively embargoed all trade with China, forbade any financial transactions involving or on behalf of China (including transactions related to travel), and blocked the assets of residents of the People's Republic of China that were subject to U.S. jurisdiction.	Travel prohibition lifted 7 May 1971; financial transaction controls revised 10 June 1971 and lifted 31 Jan. 1980; trade embargo lifted 11 June 1971 and 31 Jan. 1980.
1 Sept. 1951	Trade Agreements Extension Act of 1951; Presidential Proclamation 2935; Trade Agreement Letter of 1 Aug. 1951	Suspension of MFN treatment. Suspended most-favored-nation (MFN) trade status for all communist countries except Yugoslavia.	Modified on 3 Jan. 1975 and lifted 1 Feb. 1980.
26 Aug. 1955	Mutual Security Act of 1954	Prohibition of arms trade. Banned exports of defense articles and services to, and imports from, certain countries and areas, including the People's Republic of China.	Modified in March 1980 and lifted 16 June 1981.
1 Aug. 1962	Foreign Assistance Act of 1961 (as amended)	Prohibition of aid. Prohibited aid to communist countries unless the president certified that it was vital to the national security of the United States. The People's Republic of China was identified as a communist state, along with Tibet.	Waived 11 Dec. 1985.

Appendix 2.2 (continued)
Selected U.S. Sanctions Against China Since 1949

Date	Authority for Action	Description	Status
6 Jan. 1964	Title III of 1964 Foreign Assistance Appropriation Act; Export-Import Bank Act of 1945 (as amended in 1986)	Prohibition of Export-Import Bank programs. Prohibited the Export Import Bank from engaging in financing transactions with communist countries listed in section 620(f) of the Foreign Assistance Act of 1961, as amended (including China and Tibet), unless the president determined it was in the national interest and reported so to Congress. The prohibition was re-enacted annually in subsequent foreign aid appropriations legislation.	Selectively waived and periodically re-imposed since 1980.
1 Jan. 1965	Originally at 15 CFR Part 370; country groups currently at 15 CFR Part 785	Export controls. A completely revised system of export control regulations categorized country groups by various levels of restrictions. China was placed in the most severely restricted country group (Z).	China placed in Group Y just before President Nixon's visit to China in 1972, moved to Group P on 25 April 1980, and moved to Group V on 23 Nov. 1983.
22 Oct. 1968	Sec. 3 of Arms Export Control Act	Restrictions on government-to-government arms sales and transfers. Prohibited countries from receiving U.S. defense articles or services unless the president certified (1) that providing such articles or services would strengthen U.S. security and promote world peace, (2) that a recipient country would be transparent about the end use and would guarantee that certain security conditions would be maintained, and (3) that a recipient country was otherwise eligible.	Lifted 12 June 1984.

Appendix 2.2 (continued)
Selected U.S. Sanctions Against China Since 1949

Date	Authority for Action	Description	Status
3 Jan. 1975	Trade Act of 1974	Restriction of trade relations. Continued the denial of MFN status to China but provided a means of conditionally restoring the trade status. Tied nondiscriminatory treatment of trade to freedom of emigration and required the president to make annual determinations to waive the freedom of emigration conditions or make semiannual determinations that a country was fully compliant with the emigration requirements.	Suspended 1 Feb. 1980 by Executive Order 12167.
1 Jan. 1976	Title V of Trade Act of 1974	Withholding of Generalized System of Preferences (GSP) status. The Trade Act of 1974 requires a communist country to meet certain conditions for the president to designate it a "beneficiary developing country" and thereby receive preferential treatment under the Generalized System of Preferences (GSP).	Active.
8 Aug. 1980	Sec. 239(g) (redesignated subsection (f) in 1981) of the Foreign Assistance Act of 1961 (as amended 8 Aug. by Public Law 96-327); Presidential Determination No. 80-25 (issued 8 Aug. 1980)	Prohibition of OPIC transactions. Prohibits the Overseas Private Investment Corporation from operating in China unless the president determines that such activity is important to the U.S. national interest. President Carter made such a determination.	Prohibition suspended on 8 Aug. 1980; Re-imposed in 1989. Active.
16 Dec. 1985	Public Law 99-183	Prohibition of exports of nuclear materials, facilities, or components. China and the United States had signed a bilateral agreement concerning the peaceful use of nuclear energy. When Congress took up the matter, it enacted a resolution that conditions nuclear cooperation under the agreement on presidential certification of certain conditions.	Active.

Appendix 2.2 (continued)
Selected U.S. Sanctions Against China Since 1949

Date	Authority for Action	Description	Status
22 Oct. 1987		Suspension of high-tech exports. Suspended the process of gradually allowing more sophisticated high-technology items to be sold to China.	Lifted on 9 March 1988 when the Reagan administration became satisfied that China was not selling Silkworm missiles to Iran.
5 June 1989	Secs. 38 and 42 of Arms Export Control Act	Suspension of arms trade and military exchanges. Suspended all government-to-government and commercial arms sales and military exchanges.	Modified 7 July 1989 to allow sale of four Boeing 757-200 commercial jets with navigation system capable of being converted for military uses; modified in Oct. 1989 to allow Chinese military officers to return to work upgrading China's F-8 fighter with U.S. avionics; and modified 22 Dec. 1992 to allow transfer of military articles paid for by China prior to the Tiananmen incident.
20 June 1989		Suspension of high-level government exchanges. Suspended all high-level exchanges between the U.S. government and China.	Modified in Jan. 1990 and lifted on 30 Nov. 1990, when China's foreign minister, Qian Qishen, visited the United States.

Appendix 2.2 (continued)
Selected U.S. Sanctions Against China Since 1949

Date	Authority for Action	Description	Status
20 June 1989		Postponement of loans from multilateral development banks. President Bush indicated the United States would seek a postponement on new loans to China from MDBs.	Modified in Jan. 1990 to support a limited number of World Bank loans.
1 Oct. 1989	National Defense Authorization Act (FY 1989)	Restriction of sale of defense articles to third countries. Prohibited defense articles subject to Sec. 36(b) of the Arms Export Control Act from being sold to any country that had acquired intermediate-range ballistic missiles from China. Was applicable only for FY 1989.	Expired.
21 Nov. 1989	Title I of the Foreign Operations, Export Financing, and Related Programs Appropriations Act (FY 1990)	Withholding of funds for IDA. Stipulated that $115 million of the total obligations for the International Development Association (IDA) be withheld until 1 Jan. 1990 and released after that date only if the president certified to Congress that China had not received any new loans from IDA since 27 June 1989 or that the loans would support political reforms. A similar provision was included in the FY1991 appropriations bill.	Lifted 3 Jan. 1990 by Presidential Determination 90-6.
21 Nov. 1989	The Departments of Commerce, Justice, and State, the judiciary, and Related Agencies Appropriations Act (FY 1990)	Prohibition of export licenses. Prohibited funds appropriated for the Departments of Commerce, Justice, State, and the Judiciary from being used to reinstate or approve export licenses for the launch of U.S.-built satellites on Soviet- or Chinese-built vehicles. The prohibition could be terminated if the president certified to Congress that China had made progress on political reforms or if the president determined the issuance of licenses was in the national interest.	Waived 19 Dec. 1989. President Bush approved the granting of three export licenses to enable the launch of U.S.-built AUSSAT and AsiaSat satellites on China's launch vehicles, amounting to about $300 million in business for U.S. firms.

Appendix 2.2 (continued)
Selected U.S. Sanctions Against China Since 1949

Date	Authority for Action	Description	Status
19 Dec. 1989	International Development and Finance Act of 1989	Prohibition of Export-Import Bank financing. Notwithstanding other prohibitions on Ex-Im Bank programs with China, Congress stipulated that unless certain conditions were met, the Export-Import Bank could not provide financing, credit, guarantees, insurance, or reinsurance for any trade with China. The sanctions could be waived if the president reported to Congress that China had implemented political reforms (including reforms in Tibet) or if the president determined it was in the national interest to do so.	Selectively waived.
16 Feb. 1990	Foreign Relations Authorization Act, (as amended) FY1990 and FY1991	Suspension of certain programs and activities. Codified some steps the president had already taken against China and required the imposition of additional sanctions to express U.S. condemnation of the Chinese government's actions in the Tiananmen crisis.	Modified.
30 April 1991	Foreign Relations Authorization Act, FY1990 and FY1991 (as amended)	Prohibition on U.S. satellite exports. President Bush informed Congress of his intent to waive the prohibition against export licenses for AUSSAT and FREJA, allowing the satellites to be launched from China. However, he also upheld the prohibition, in the same communication to Congress, against the export of U.S. satellite components because of proliferation concerns surrounding a Chinese domestic communications satellite, the Dong Fang Hong 3.	Selectively waived.

Appendix 2.2 (continued)
Selected U.S. Sanctions Against China Since 1949

Date	Authority for Action	Description	Status
27 May 1991	Arms Export Control Act, as amended; Export Administration Act of 1979, as amended; Department of State Public Notice 1423	Prohibition of export of missile-related computer technology and satellites. The Bush administration announced new sanctions against China to restrict the export of missile technology, missile-related computers, and satellites.	Waived 23 March 1992 after the White House received written assurances of compliance with MTCR guidelines; modified 4 Dec. 1992 for export of a super computer to China.
1 Sept. 1991	15 CFR Part 799; amended at 56 F.R. 66559, 57 F.R. 4572, 58 F.R. 33510, and 59 F.R. 30686	Modification of certain export license requirements. In an effort to deregulate export procedures for civilian-use and dual-use goods and technologies, COCOM eliminated licensing requirements for low-level items exported to China. The Department of Commerce revised Export Administration Regulations to relax some national security controls imposed against China, the Soviet Union, and Warsaw Pact countries since the Cold War.	Expired.
6 Oct. 1992	Sec. 543 of the Foreign Operations, Export Financing, and Related Programs Appropriations Act (FY 1993)	Prohibition of indirect aid. Added China to the list of countries banned from receiving indirect aid. Prohibited the use of any funds appropriated under the act for indirect assistance to China and other countries unless the president certified that the withholding of funds was contrary to the national interest.	Waived by Presidential Determinations for each of the fiscal years that China has been listed.

Appendix 2.2 (continued)
Selected U.S. Sanctions Against China Since 1949

Date	Authority for Action	Description	Status
5 Jan. 1993	Title I as continued by Sec. 119 of the Further Continuing Appropriations for FY1992 (as amended); Presidential Determination 93-7	Modification for withholding of funds for IDA. President Bush determined it was in the national interest of the United States to obligate funds appropriated for the U.S. contribution to the International Development Association during FY1992. These funds had been withheld because of restrictive provisions concerning China.	Expired.
28 May 1993	Executive Order 12850	Conditions on China's MFN treatment. President Clinton renewed MFN status for China. At the same time, he issued an Executive Order requesting the secretary of state to assess whether renewal in 1994 would substantially promote freedom of emigration in China and whether China was complying with a 1992 agreement concerning the use of prison labor. Clinton further linked the 1994 renewal of MFN for China to Beijing's adherence to the Universal Declaration of Human Rights, release of those detained in connection with the Democracy Wall and Tiananmen Square actions of 1989, general prisoner treatment, protection of Tibet's religious and cultural heritage, and admission into China of international radio and television broadcasts.	Expired.

Appendix 2.2 (continued)
Selected U.S. Sanctions Against China Since 1949

Date	Authority for Action	Description	Status
24 Aug. 1993	Sec. 73(a)(2)(A) of the Arms Export Control Act (as amended); Sec. 11B(b)(1)(B)(i) of the Export Administration Act of 1979 (as amended); Department of State Public Notice 1857	Prohibition of export of MTCR items and U.S. government contracts. The State Department determined that China and Pakistan had engaged in missile technology proliferation activities. This finding required the imposition of sanctions against the two government entities involved and all their subsidiaries, divisions, subunits, or successors, a denial of export licenses for items covered by the Missile Technology Control Regime (MTCR) Annex for two years, and the denial of U.S. government contracts relating to these same items. The finding further imposed sanctions against Chinese government organizations involved in the development or production of electronics, space systems or equipment, and military aircraft.	Waived Nov. 1994.
9 Dec. 1993	15 CFR Parts 771 and 799	Modification of license requirements for computers. The Department of Commerce issued revised Export Administration Regulations to allow for the export to China (and other controlled destinations), without a validated license, of computers with a data processing speed of up to 67 million theoretical operations per second (MTOPS)	Modified in 1996.
Jan. 1994		Modification of license requirements for fiber optics and telecommunications. COCOM participants agreed to ease licensing requirements for export of advanced telecommunications equipment and fiber optics to China and the former Soviet Union.	Expired.

Appendix 2.2 (continued)
Selected U.S. Sanctions Against China Since 1949

Date	Authority for Action	Description	Status
31 March 1994	15 CFR Parts 771 and 774	Establishment of new export license. COCOM agreed to cease operations on 31 March 1994. Member nations agreed to retain current control lists until a successor organization was established. The Commerce Department established a new general license, GLX, for exporters to Country Groups QWY and the People's Republic of China.	Modified.
28 May 1994	Secs. 2, 38, 40, 42, and 71 of the Arms Export Control Act; 22 CFR Part 126.1; 27 CFR Part 47.52	Prohibition of importation of munitions and ammunition. On 26 May 1994, President Clinton announced he would renew MFN status for China,but de-linked the extension from human rights conditions imposed a year earlier. He also announced that, effective 28 May, the importation of munitions and ammunition from China would be prohibited.	Active.
23 Aug. 1994	Foreign Operations Appropriations Act for FY1995 and subsequent acts	Prohibition of U.S. payments to UNFPA for programs in China. Prohibits U.S. contributions to the United Nations Population Fund (UNFPA) from being made available for programs in China.	Active.

Appendix 2.2 (continued)
Selected U.S. Sanctions Against China Since 1949

Date	Authority for Action	Description	Status
22 June 1995	Sec. 902(b)(2) of Foreign Relations Authorization Act, FY1990 and FY1991	Modification of license requirement for cryptographic items. President Clinton informed Congress on 22 June 1995 that it was in the national interest of the United States to terminate the suspension of license issuance for export to China of certain cryptographic items covered by category XIII of the USML. Licenses are required and applications are reviewed on a case-by-case basis by the Departments of State and Defense.	Active.
22 Jan. 1996	15 CFR Parts 770-776, 785, 787, and 799	Modification of license requirements for computers. The Department of Commerce issued interim Export Administration Regulations (EAR) establishing a new four-tier system of licensing. China, Vietnam, Pakistan, the former Soviet Union, countries of the Middle East, Maghreb, and several Eastern European countries are in Tier 3. Exports to Tier 3 countries are authorized under General License G-DEST for computers less than or equal to 2,000 MTOPS. Exports of computers greater than 2,000 but less than 7,000 MTOPS are authorized under General License G-CTP. Where concerns arise if end-use is military, nuclear, chemical, biological, or missile-related, licenses will be reviewed on a case-by-case basis.	Active.

Appendix 2.2 (continued)
Selected U.S. Sanctions Against China Since 1949

Date	Authority for Action	Description	Status
20 May 1998	National Defense Authorization Act for FY 1999	Prohibition of space and missile technology transfer. Prevents the United States from entering into new agreements with China involving space or missile-related technology; prohibits U.S. participation in investigations of Chinese launch failures; prohibits transfers of missile equipment or technology to China; and prohibits the export or re-export of U.S. satellites to China. Also, Section 1212 would return control over licensing exports of satellites to the State Department.	Active.

Source: Adapted from Rennack (1997).

Appendix 2.3(a)
U.S. Commerce Control List: Country Groups (Country Group A)

	[A:1]	[A:2] Missile Technology Control Regime	[A:3] Australia Group	[A:4] Nuclear Suppliers Country Group
Argentina		x	x	x
Australia	x	x	x	x
Austria[1]		x	x	x
Belgium	x	x	x	x
Brazil		x		x
Bulgaria				x
Canada	x	x	x	x
Cyprus				x
Czech Republic			x	x
Denmark	x	x	x	x
Finland[1]		x	x	x
France	x	x	x	x
Germany	x	x	x	x
Greece	x	x	x	x
Hong Kong[1]				
Hungary		x	x	x
Iceland		x	x	
Ireland[1]		x	x	x
Italy	x	x	x	x
Japan	x	x	x	x
Korea, South[1]			x	x
Latvia			x	x
Luxembourg	x	x	x	x
Netherlands	x	x	x	x
New Zealand[1]		x	x	x
Norway	x	x	x	x
Poland			x	x
Portugal	x	x	x	x
Romania			x	x
Russia		x		x
Slovakia			x	x
South Africa		x		x
Spain	x	x	x	x
Sweden[1]		x	x	x
Switzerland[1]		x	x	x
Turkey	x		x	
Ukraine				x
United Kingdom	x	x	x	x
United States	x	x	x	x

[1]Cooperating countries

Appendix 2.3(b)
U.S. Commerce Control List: Country Groups (Country Group B)

Countries

Afghanistan
Algeria
Andorra
Angola
Antigua
Argentina
Australia
Austria
Bahamas
Bahrain
Bangladesh
Barbados
Barbuda
Belgium
Belize
Benin
Bhutan
Bolivia
Bosnia & Herzegovina
Botswana
Brazil
Brunei
Burkina Faso
Burma
Burundi
Cameroon
Canada
Cape Verde
Central African Republic
Chad
Chile
Colombia
Comoros
Congo
Costa Rica
Cote d'Ivoire
Croatia
Cyprus
Czech Republic
Denmark
Djibouti
Dominica
Dominican Republic
Ecuador
Egypt
El Salvador
Equatorial Guinea
Eritrea
Ethiopia
Fiji
Finland
France
Gabon
Gambia, The
Germany
Ghana
Greece
Grenada
Guatemala
Guinea
Guinea-Bissau
Guyana
Haiti
Honduras
Hong Kong
Hungary
Iceland
India
Indonesia
Ireland
Israel
Italy
Jamaica
Japan
Jordan
Kenya
Kiribati
Korea, South
Kuwait
Lebanon
Lesotho
Liberia
Liechtenstein
Luxembourg
Macedonia, the Former Yugoslav Republic of
Madagascar
Malawi
Malaysia
Maldives
Mali
Malta
Marshall Islands
Mauritania
Mauritius
Mexico
Micronesia, Federated States of
Monaco
Morocco
Mozambique
Namibia
Nauru
Nepal
Netherlands
New Zealand
Nicaragua
Niger
Nigeria
Norway
Oman
Pakistan
Palau
Panama
Papua New Guinea
Paraguay
Peru
Philippines
Poland
Portugal
Qatar
Rwanda
Saint Kitts & Nevis
Saint Lucia
Saint Vincent
San Marino
Sao Tome & Principe
Saudi Arabia
Senegal
Seychelles
Sierra Leone
Singapore
Slovakia
Slovenia
Solomon Islands
Somalia
South Africa
Spain
Sri Lanka
Surinam
Swaziland
Sweden
Switzerland
Taiwan
Tanzania
Thailand
Togo
Tonga
Trinidad & Tobago
Tunisia
Turkey
Tuvalu
Uganda
United Arab Emirates
United Kingdom
United States
Uruguay
Vanuatu
Vatican City
Venezuela
Western Sahara
Western Samoa
Yemen
Yugoslavia (Serbia and Montenegro, Federal Republic of)
Zaire
Zambia
Zimbabwe

Appendix 2.3(c)
U.S. Commerce Control List: Country Groups (Country Group C)

[Reserved]

Appendix 2.3(d)
U.S. Commerce Control List: Country Groups (Country Group D)

Country	[D:1] National Security	[D:2] Nuclear	[D:3] Chemical and Biological	[D:4] Missile Technology
Afghanistan			x	
Albania	x			
Armenia	x		x	
Azerbaijan	x		x	
Bahrain			x	x
Belarus	x		x	
Bulgaria	x		x	
Burma			x	
Cambodia	x			
China	x		x	x[1]
Cuba		x	x	
Egypt			x	x
Estonia	x			
Georgia	x		x	
India		x	x	x[1]
Iran		x	x	x[1]
Iraq		x	x	x
Israel		x	x	x
Jordan			x	x
Kazakhstan	x		x	
Korea, North	x	x	x	x[1]
Kuwait			x	x
Kyrgyzstan	x		x	
Laos	x			
Latvia	x			
Lebanon			x	x
Libya		x	x	x
Lithuania	x			
Macau	x		x	x
Moldova	x		x	
Mongolia	x		x	
Oman			x	x
Pakistan		x	x	x[1]
Qatar			x	x
Romania	x			
Russia	x		x	x
Saudi Arabia			x	x
Syria			x	x
Taiwan			x	
Tajikistan	x		x	
Turkmenistan	x		x	
Ukraine	x		x	
United Arab Emirates			x	x
Uzbekistan	x		x	
Vietnam	x		x	
Yemen			x	x

[1]Certain missile technology projects have been identified in the following countries:

China	M Series Missiles CSS-2
India	Agni, Prithvi, SLV-3 Satellite Launch Vehicle, Augmented Satellite Launch Vehicle (ASLV), Polar Satellite Launch Vehicle (PSLV), Geostationary Satellite Launch Vehicle (GSLV)
Iran	Surface-to-Surface Missile project, Scud Development Project
North Korea	No Dong I, Scud Development Project
Pakistan	Haft Series Missiles

Appendix 2.3(e)
U.S. Commerce Control List: Country Groups (Country Group E)

Country	[E:1] Terrorist-Supporting Countries	[E:2] Unilateral Embargo[1]
Cuba	x	x
Iran	x	
Iraq	x	
Korea, North	x	
Libya	x	x
Sudan	x	
Syria	x	

[1]In addition to the controls of the EAR that the Bureau of Export Administration administers, note that the Treasury Department's Office of Foreign Assets Control administers:
(a) A comprehensive embargo against Cuba, Iran, Iraq, Libya, Sudan, and the Taliban and areas of Afghanistan controlled by the Taliban;
(b) A ban on arms and specified items destined to the National Union for the Total Independence of Angola (UNITA) located in Angola; and
(c) An embargo against certain individuals and entities, e.g., Specially Designated Terrorists (SDT). (Note: The Department of State also imposes sanctions on certain individuals and entities; please consult with the Department of State for further information regarding these controls.)
Source: Department of Commerce

Appendix 2.4
Defense Trade Controls: United States Munitions List Categories

Code	Description
I	Firearms
II	Artillery Projectors
III	Ammunition
IV	Launch Vehicles, Guided Missiles, Ballistic Missiles, Rockets, Torpedoes, Bombs, and Mines
V	Explosives, Propellants, Incendiary Agents, and their Constituents
VI	Vessels of War and Special Naval Equipment
VII	Tanks and Military Vehicles
VIII	Aircraft and Associated Equipment
IX	Military Training Equipment
X	Protective Personnel Equipment
XI	Military Electronics
XII	Fire Control, Range Finder, Optical, and Guidance and Control Equipment
XIII	Auxiliary Military Equipment
XIV	Toxicological Agents and Equipment and Radiological Equipment
XV	Space Systems and Associated Equipment
XVI	Nuclear Weapons Design and Test Equipment
XVII	Classified Articles, Technical Data and Defense Services Not Otherwise Enumerated
XVIII	[Reserved]
XIX	[Reserved]
XX	Submersible Vessels, Oceanographic and Associated Equipment
XXI	Miscellaneous Articles

Source: Department of State (current as of 4 June 2002)

Appendix 2.5
Defense Trade Controls: Embargo Reference Chart

Country	Date	Federal Regulation	Comments
Afghanistan	27 June 1996	61 FR 33313	Amendment to ITAR 126.1
	8 May 2001	66 FR 23310	Denial policy to territory of Afghanistan under Taliban control and all of Afghanistan
Angola	2 July 1993	58 FR 35864	License reviews on case-by-case basis, with a presumption of denial for lethal articles
	4 April 1994	59 FR 15624	Amendment to ITAR 126.1 (An arms embargo exists with respect to UNITA)
Armenia	22 July 1993	58 FR 39280	Amendment to ITAR 126.1
Azerbaijan	22 July 1993	58 FR 39280	Amendment to ITAR 126.1
Burma	16 June 1993	58 FR 33293	Department of State suspension notice
	22 July 1993	58 FR 39280	Amendment to ITAR 126.1
Belarus	22 July 1993	58 FR 39280	Amendment to ITAR 126.1
China	7 June 1989	54 FR 24539	Department of State suspension notice
	22 July 1993	58 FR 39280	Amendment to ITAR 126.1
Cuba	6 Dec. 1984	49 FR 47682	Amendment to ITAR 126.1
Cyprus	18 Dec. 1992	57 FR 60265	Department of State denial notice; does not affect exports for U.N. forces in Cyprus or for civilian end-users
Haiti	9 Oct. 1991	56 FR 50968	Department of State suspension notice
	4 April 1994	59 FR 15624	Amendment to ITAR 126.1
India	20 May 1998	63 FR 27781	Department of State revocation notice
Indonesia	14 Oct. 1999	64 FR 55805	Department of State suspension notice
	25 Jan. 2001	66 FR 7836	Requests for export and re-transfer of C-130 aircraft spare parts considered on a case-by-case basis
	22 March 2001	66 FR 16085	Exception for defense articles and defense services to Indonesia for ultimate end-use by a third country considered on a case-by-case basis
	18 Dec. 2001	66 FR 65235	Exception for non-lethal defense articles and spare parts considered on a case-by-case basis
Iran	23 Jan. 1984	49 FR 2836	Department of State notice designating Iran as a terrorist country
	29 Oct. 1991	56 FR 55630	Amendment to ITAR 126.1

Appendix 2.5 (continued)
Defense Trade Controls: Embargo Reference Chart

Country	Date	Federal Regulation	Comments
Iraq	3 Aug. 1990	55 FR 31808	Department of State revocation notice
	13 Sept. 1990	55 FR 37793	Department of State notice designating Iraq as a terrorist country
	29 Oct 1991	56 FR 55630	Amendment to ITAR 126.1
Liberia	18 Dec. 1992	57 FR 60265	Department of State suspension notice
	22 July 1993	58 FR 39280	Amendment to ITAR 126.1
	5 Sept. 2001	66 FR 46491	
Libya	29 Oct. 1991	56 FR 55630	Amendment to ITAR 126.1
North Korea	6 Dec. 1984	49 FR 47682	Amendment to ITAR 126.1
Pakistan	17 June 1998	63 FR 33122	Department of State revocation notice
Rwanda	2 June 1994	59 FR 28583	Department of State suspension notice; licenses and approvals suspended until further notice; current applications to be denied
	17 Aug. 1994	59 FR 42158	Amendment to ITAR 126.1
Somalia	16 Dec. 1992	57 FR 59851	Department of State suspension notice
	22 July 1993	58 FR 39280	Amendment to ITAR 126.1
Sudan	3 Nov 1992	58 FR 49741	Department of State suspension notice
	8 Oct. 1993	58 FR 52523	Department of State notice designating Sudan as a country supporting terrorism
	4 April 1994	59 FR 15624	Amendment to ITAR 126.1
Syria	29 Oct. 1991	56 FR 55630	Amendment to ITAR 126.1
Vietnam	6 Dec 1984	49 FR 47682	Amendment to ITAR 126.1
Yemen	16 Dec. 1992	57 FR 59852	Department of State notice; presumption of denial for lethal articles or items supporting such articles or services
Zaire	29 April 1993	58 FR 26024	
	22 July 1993	58 FR 39280	
Zimbabwe	17 April 2002	67 FR 18978	Department of State suspension notice

Source: Department of State. This chart does not include all policies toward foreign countries for the export of defense articles and defense services. The informal listing represents certain policies published in the Federal Register, an official U.S. government publication that should be consulted regularly to ensure up-to-date awareness of country policies.

Appendix 2.6
U.S. Direct Investment Abroad: Country Detail for Capital Outflows, 2001 (Amounts in $ Millions; Shares in %)

Destination	Amount	Share
All countries, all industries	141,203	100.00
Canada	20,023	14.18
Europe	68,243	48.33
Austria	−754	−0.53
Belgium	537	0.38
Denmark	−468	−0.33
Finland	120	0.08
France	2,373	1.68
Germany	11,964	8.47
Greece	41	0.03
Ireland	444	0.31
Italy	2,836	2.01
Luxembourg	3,296	2.33
Netherlands	13,102	9.28
Norway	623	0.44
Portugal	152	0.11
Spain	1,078	0.76
Sweden	1,144	0.81
Switzerland	5,674	4.02
Turkey	−29	−0.02
United Kingdom	23,523	16.66
Other	2,588	1.83
Latin America and Other Western Hemisphere	31,544	22.34
South America	3,273	2.32
Argentina	−264	−0.19
Brazil	487	0.34
Chile	1,434	1.02
Colombia	173	0.12
Ecuador	−70	−0.05
Peru	153	0.11
Venezuela	1,020	0.72
Other	340	0.24
Central America	18,090	12.81
Costa Rica	162	0.11
Guatemala	−268	−0.19
Honduras	69	0.05
Mexico	17,505	12.40
Panama	682	0.48
Other	−60	−0.04
Other Western Hemisphere	10,180	7.21
Bahamas	−140	−0.10
Barbados	728	0.52
Bermuda	6,819	4.83
Dominican Republic	149	0.11
Jamaica	86	0.06
Netherlands Antilles	128	0.09
Trinidad and Tobago	205	0.15
U.K. Islands, Caribbean	1,906	1.35
Other	299	0.21

Appendix 2.6 (continued)
U.S. Direct Investment Abroad: Country Detail for Capital Outflows, 2001 (Amounts in $ Millions; Shares in %)

Destination	Amount	Share
Africa	1,295	0.92
Egypt	654	0.46
Nigeria	281	0.20
South Africa	22	0.02
Other	337	0.24
Middle East	1,019	0.72
Israel	195	0.14
Saudi Arabia	60	0.04
United Arab Emirates	175	0.12
Other	588	0.42
Asia and Pacific	19,561	13.85
Australia	−46	−0.03
China	1,481	1.05
Hong Kong	2,888	2.05
India	338	0.24
Indonesia	735	0.52
Japan	7,212	5.11
Korea, Republic of	1,067	0.76
Malaysia	300	0.21
New Zealand	143	0.10
Philippines	50	0.04
Singapore	3,506	2.48
Taiwan	840	0.59
Thailand	1,154	0.82
Other	−108	−0.08
International[1]	−482	−0.34
Addenda:		
Eastern Europe[2]	2,287	1.62
European Union[3]	59,387	42.06
OPEC[4]	3,220	2.28

Notes: [1]"International" consists of affiliates that have operations spanning more than one country and that are engaged in petroleum shipping, other water transportation, or offshore oil and gas drilling.

[2]"Eastern Europe" comprises Albania, Armenia, Azerbaijan, Belarus, Bulgaria, Czech Republic, Estonia, Georgia, Hungary, Kazakhstan, Latvia, Lithuania, Moldova, Poland, Romania, Russia, Slovakia, Tajikistan, Turkmenistan, Ukraine, and Uzbekistan.

[3]The European Union comprises Austria, Belgium, Denmark, Finland, France, Germany, Greece, Ireland, Italy, Luxembourg, Netherlands, Portugal, Spain, Sweden, and the United Kingdom.

[4]As of 1995, OPEC (the Organization of Petroleum Exporting Countries) comprised Algeria, Indonesia, Iran, Iraq, Kuwait, Libya, Nigeria, Qatar, Saudi Arabia, the United Arab Emirates, and Venezuela. Prior to 1995, Gabon was also a member.

Source: Department of Commerce (2002a).

Appendix 2.7
U.S. Direct Investment Position Abroad on a Historical-Cost Basis, 2000 (Amounts in $ Millions; shares in %)

Destination	Amount	Share
All countries	1,244,654	100.00
Canada	126,421	10.16
Europe	648,731	52.12
Austria	3,676	0.30
Belgium	16,409	1.32
Denmark	5,618	0.45
Finland	1,279	0.10
France	39,087	3.14
Germany	53,610	4.31
Greece	672	0.05
Ireland	33,369	2.68
Italy	23,622	1.90
Luxembourg	19,470	1.56
Netherlands	115,506	9.28
Norway	6,303	0.51
Portugal	1,784	0.14
Spain	14,561	1.17
Sweden	11,371	0.91
Switzerland	54,873	4.41
Turkey	1,378	0.11
United Kingdom	233,384	18.75
Other	12,760	1.03
Latin America and Other Western Hemisphere	239,388	19.23
South America	79,354	6.38
Argentina	14,489	1.16
Brazil	35,560	2.86
Chile	10,846	0.87
Colombia	4,423	0.36
Ecuador	838	0.07
Peru	3,317	0.27
Venezuela	8,423	0.68
Other	1,456	0.12
Central America	74,754	6.01
Costa Rica	1,983	0.16
Guatemala	904	0.07
Honduras	115	0.01
Mexico	35,414	2.85
Panama	35,407	2.84
Other	931	0.07
Other Western Hemisphere	85,280	6.85
Bahamas	668	0.05
Barbados	1,227	0.10
Bermuda	54,114	4.35
Dominican Republic	1,126	0.09
Jamaica	2,596	0.21
Netherlands Antilles	3,725	0.30
Trinidad and Tobago	1,331	0.11
UK Islands, Caribbean	20,165	1.62
Other	329	0.03

Appendix 2.7 (continued)
U.S. Direct Investment Position Abroad on a Historical-Cost Basis, 2000 (Amounts in $ Millions; shares in %)

Destination	Amount	Share
Africa	15,813	1.27
Egypt	2,735	0.22
Nigeria	1,283	0.10
South Africa	2,826	0.23
Other	8,969	0.72
Middle East	11,851	0.95
Israel	3,426	0.28
Saudi Arabia	4,784	0.38
United Arab Emirates	573	0.05
Other	3,069	0.25
Asia and Pacific	199,599	16.04
Australia	35,324	2.84
China	9,577	0.77
Hong Kong	23,308	1.87
India	1,258	0.10
Indonesia	11,605	0.93
Japan	55,606	4.47
Korea, Republic of	9,432	0.76
Malaysia	5,995	0.48
New Zealand	5,340	0.43
Singapore	23,245	1.87
Taiwan	7,737	0.62
Thailand	7,124	0.57
Other	1,138	0.09
International[1]	2,851	0.23
Addenda:		
Eastern Europe[2]	11,009	0.88
European Union[3]	573,416	46.07
OPEC[4]	32,401	2.60

Notes: [1]"International" consists of affiliates that have operations spanning more than one country and that are engaged in petroleum shipping, other water transportation, or offshore oil and gas drilling.

[2]"Easter Europe" comprises Albania, Armenia, Azerbaijan, Belarus, Bulgaria, Czech Republic, Estonia, Georgia, Hungary, Kazakhstan, Latvia, Lithuania, Moldova, Poland, Romania, Russia, Slovakia, Tajikistan, Turkmenistan, Ukraine, and Uzbekistan.

[3]The European Union comprises Austria, Belgium, Denmark, Finland, France, Germany, Greece, Ireland, Italy, Luxembourg, Netherlands, Portugal, Spain, Sweden, and the United Kingdom.

[4]As of 1995, OPEC (the Organization of Petroleum Exporting Countries) comprises Algeria, Indonesia, Iran, Iraq, Kuwait, Libya, Nigeria, Qatar, Saudi Arabia, the United Arab Emirates, and Venezuela. Prior to 1995, Gabon was also a member.

Source: Department of Commerce (2002a).

CHAPTER 3

U.S. Economic Sanctions Against Cuba

INTRODUCTION

An island nation in the Caribbean Sea, Cuba historically has been linked both commercially and politically to its mainland neighbor 90 miles to the north, the United States. Cuba has provided the United States with commodities such as sugar and nickel, while its small but growing local market has offered export opportunities to U.S. producers in a variety of sectors. Meanwhile, the United States, with its relative abundance of capital, was the largest investor in Cuba prior to 1960.

But despite the obvious economic arguments in favor of close and sustained relations between the two nations, a chasm in political ideologies divides them. This chasm was precipitated by the 1959 overthrow of the Batista regime by revolutionaries led by Fidel Castro and his cohorts, who advocated the creation of a socialist-style republic. A concomitant strengthening of commercial and political relations between Cuba and the Soviet Union caused the United States to initiate a series of policies effecting a near-total economic embargo against Cuba. Many Cubans left the island and emigrated, especially to South Florida, where a Cuban diaspora flourishes.

Economic sanctions imposed by the United States on Cuba are broad-reaching in scope and duration, with a track record of more than four decades. As such, the case of Cuba is particularly instructive concerning the staying power of the United States in unilaterally maintaining pressure on another nation via economic sanctions[1] and in terms of the ability of sanctions to effect policy changes in a target nation.

The impetus for these sanctions and the resulting economic and social impacts on Cuba are best understood by dividing the sanctions history into two periods, with 1990—the year of the Soviet collapse—at the fulcrum. The first period's sanctions were motivated largely by a desire to contain the threat of communism globally and in the Western Hemisphere in particular. The subsequent period's sanctions have been motivated by desires to effect a transition to a democratically elected government and to protect various human rights for Cuban citizens. This period's sanctions reflect, in large part, the lobbying efforts of the Cuban exile community, a group motivated morally and politically by concerns for democracy in their homeland and economically by restitution claims for properties expropriated by the Castro government and/or abandoned on the island.

In terms of achieving its goals, the policy of containing the spread of communism in the Western Hemisphere was largely met, though whether this result was due to the imposition of U.S. sanctions is difficult to prove (or disprove).[2] The geopolitical result, however, is undeniable: today, democracy abounds in one form or another throughout the Americas. Most observers of Cuba-U.S. relations will concede this policy "victory" for sanctions. Since the Soviet collapse, however, criticism has emerged concerning the appropriateness and efficacy of U.S. sanctions against Cuba.

The Cuban economy has not performed well in recent years, although the nation did have many years of notable economic growth after sanctions were first imposed by the United States in 1960. We argue, however, that sanctions alone are not to blame for the country's current economic weakness. A largely inefficient centralized system and related policy shortfalls are at the core of Cuba's economic problems. For example, a reliance on monocrop exports with little added value has subjected the nation to swings in world commodity prices and, at times, unfavorable climatic conditions. Failure to accept membership terms set by multilateral institutions such as the International Monetary Fund (IMF) and World Bank have prevented Cuba from gaining access to development assistance that provided many of its neighbors in the region with the impetus needed for enhanced growth and development. And similarities in natural endowments with other Caribbean nations have made Cuba an easy target for the diversion of product exports to, and service exports from, the United States, mostly in the form of tourism to the other Caribbean countries.

The enormous size disparity between the United States and Cuba has made U.S. economic losses fairly trivial. Losses by Cuba have been much more significant, though they were largely offset until 1990 by intensive Soviet engagement and assistance. In 1988, some 85 percent of Cuba's trade was with the Soviet bloc; by 1992, these levels were down nearly two-thirds. Economic and military aid from the Soviet Union represented one-fifth of Cuban GDP in the pre-1990 period (Rich Kaplowitz 1998).

Another important moderator of the impact of U.S. sanctions is the Cuban diaspora, which remits significant sums of money (in dollars) to family and friends on the island. Remittances from abroad are believed to be the single largest contributor of external resources to the Cuban economy (Perez-Lopez 2000). These remittances, coupled with recent Cuban moves toward liberalizing the economy, have allowed the Castro regime to weather the economic storm and avoid renouncing its socialist system. The diaspora's contributions to the Cuban economy, in tandem with selective economic liberalizations, have resulted in a dual economy—one in dollars and one in pesos[3]—with resulting inequities between sectors of society. Although most Cubans have suffered somewhat under the imposition of U.S. economic sanctions, those outside the "dollar economy" have shouldered the heaviest burden.

Even though the overall economic impact of sanctions on the United States has been minimal, we feel they have exacted great costs in terms of lost and foreclosed international business opportunities. They also have compromised U.S. global leadership on trade and social policy issues and caused potentially irreparable damage for humanity in key areas such as advances in biotechnology and avoidance of environmental degradation.

In this chapter we analyze U.S. unilateral economic sanctions against Cuba. We review the history of relations between the countries, discuss the sanctions and their precipitating policy rationales, assess the impact of U.S. sanctions on Cuba economically and socially, and identify (and, where possible, measure) the impact of sanctions on the United States as well as on third countries most affected by the U.S.–Cuban relationship. We conclude by assessing the efficacy of U.S. sanctions on Cuba and offer projections for their future relationship and recommendations for improving the likelihood of meeting current U.S. policy goals toward Cuba.

CUBA'S ECONOMIC RECORD

Cuba's economy historically has depended on linkages with other countries. Resources from abroad have always been required to finance the nation's development—before the revolution, during the Soviet support phase, and since 1990. Unfortunately, reliable economic data on Cuba have not been widely available since the Castro regime took power. Official Cuban reporting of economic activity has been sporadic, and typical conventions in reporting are not universally observed (Perez-Lopez 2000). Cuba is not a member of the International Monetary Fund or other multilateral agencies that can provide or vouch for the veracity of national economic data. The primary sources of what little data exist on the Cuban economy are the Cuban National Statistics Office (Oficina Nacional de Estadisticas, or ONE), the Central Bank of Cuba (Banco Central de Cuba, or BCC), and the United Nations Economic Commission for Latin America and the Caribbean (ECLAC in English and CEPAL in Spanish). ECLAC figures for the main Cuban economic indicators are found in Table 3.1.

Macroeconomic Picture

Carmelo Mesa-Lago (2001) provides the most comprehensive compendium and assessment of economic statistics for Cuba. Table 3.2 contains his aggregated macroeconomic indicators for the period 1989–2000. The base year of 1989 corresponds to the final year of Soviet support; in 1990, Soviet subsidies for Cuba were withdrawn. In the following paragraphs, we summarize his key economic reporting and findings and include data and assessments from other scholars and analysts where appropriate.

In the period immediately after the withdrawal of Soviet assistance, the Cuban economy suffered a stark contraction, with GDP declining by nearly 50 percent from 1989 to 1993. Despite gains in the latter half of the 1990s, overall growth for Cuba lagged that of its regional counterparts throughout the period (ECLAC 2000). According to Mesa-Lago (2001), at its average growth rate from 1994 to 2000, Cuba's GDP would recover its 1989 level in six years and its per-capita GDP in eight.

Gross capital formation in 2000 was only half its 1989 level of 26.7 percent of GDP, and future growth will require GDP to expand more quickly since consumption is already being held as low as possible in the economy (Triana Cordovi 2001). Cuba's reports of deflation in 1999 and 2000 are suspect due to the official use of a base year of 1981 (when inflation was particularly and uncharacteristically high relative to prior years), a lack of reporting on the composition of the CPI basket, and conflicting data on the GDP deflator and cumulative monetary liquidity (Mesa-Lago 2001). Further concerns regarding official inflation statistics stem from the existence of the dual economy. Prices within the dollar economy are largely outside government influence while prices within

Table 3.1
Main Cuban Economic Indicators, 1991–99

	1991	1992	1993	1994	1995	1996	1997	1998	1999[a]
Annual Growth Rates[b] (%)									
Growth and investment									
Gross domestic product	−9.5	−9.9	−13.6	0.6	2.5	7.6	2.5	1.3	6.2
Per capita GDP	−10.4	−10.6	−14.2	0.2	2.2	7.2	2.1	0.9	5.7
Gross domestic product, by sector									
Goods	−16.2	−19.2	−16.7	4.2	7.1	11.8	6.0	1.9	7.8
Basic services	−10.4	−13.2	−17.2	−0.9	7.0	7.0	4.6	1.2	4.5
Other services	−4.4	−3.3	−11.5	−1.1	−0.5	5.3	0	1.0	5.4
Consumption	−9.9	−11.1	−5.1	0.7	1.6	3.6	2.1	2.2	2.7
Government	−10.4	−5.2	−1.1	−1.9	−0.6	4.0	1.3	2.0	0.7
Private	−9.6	−14.4	−7.7	2.5	3.0	3.3	2.6	2.3	4.0
Gross domestic investment	−45.9	−58.3	−39.7	1.9	35.2	22.8	13.7	7.3	9.4
Exports (goods/services)	−3.5	−5.9	−24.9	9.1	4.3	24.6	5.8	2.0	11.0
Imports (goods/services)	−37.0	−45.3	−5.4	19.2	11.5	24.3	11.0	8.0	3.0
Employment									
Rate of unemployment (%)	—	—	—	—	7.9	7.6	7.0	6.6	6.0
Currency									
Consumer prices (% change)	—	—	—	—	−11.5	−4.9	1.9	2.9	−3.0
Terms of trade (1935 = 100)	69.9	51.5	54.4	65.9	73.9	66.7	68.5	66.8	57.4
Official exchange rate (pesos/dollar)	1.0	1.0	1.0	1.0	1.0	1.0	1.0	1.0	1.0
Informal exchange rate (pesos/dollar)[c]	20.0	35.0	78.0	95.0	32.1	19.2	23.0	21.0	20.0

Table 3.1 (continued)
Main Cuban Economic Indicators, 1991–99

	1991	1992	1993	1994	1995	1996	1997	1998	1999[a]
Balance of payments ($ millions)									
Current account	1,454	−420	−372	−260	−518	−167	−437	−396	−176
Trade balance (goods and services)	−1,138	−215	−371	−308	−639	−419	−746	−617	−426
Exports	3,563	2,522	1,968	2,542	2,926	3,707	3,882	4,182	4,521
Imports	4,702	2,737	2,339	2,849	3,565	4,125	4,628	4,800	4,947
Capital and financial accounts	1,421	419	356	262	596	174	458	413	200
External debt									
Gross debt (as % of GDP)[d]	37.0	39.1	52.9	44.6	45.6	42.7	41.1	43.3	39.9
Percentages of GDP									
State revenues and expenditures									
Total revenues	62.4	56.5	57.3	62.6	56.6	50.0	49.5	48.3	48.6
Total expenditures	83.8	86.3	87.7	69.6	60.0	52.3	51.3	50.5	50.8
Financial balance	−21.4	−29.7	−30.4	−7.0	−3.3	−2.3	−1.9	−2.2	−2.2
Money									
Liquidity	37.4	51.0	66.5	48.8	40.2	38.9	38.3	37.5	35.4
Currency outside banks	18.9	24.9	27.4	17.7	15.4	16.3	16.3	16.6	16.1
Savings deposits	18.5	26.1	39.0	31.1	24.8	22.7	22.0	21.0	19.3

[a]Preliminary figures.
[b]Based on series at constant 1981 prices.
[c]Average exchange rate.
[d]Calculated on the basis of the official rate of one peso to the dollar.
Source: ECLAC (2001a), on the basis of official figures and own estimates.

Table 3.2

Cuban Macroeconcmic Indicators, 1989–2000 (Percentages Except GDP per Capita)

Indicators	1989	1993	1994	1995	1996	1997	1998	1999	2000	% change 1989–2000
GDP growth rate[a]	1.2	−14.9	0.7	2.5	7.8	2.5	1.2	6.2	5.6	−21[b]
GDP per capita (pesos)[a]	1,976	1,172	1,175	1,201	1,290	1,317	1,327	1,405	1,478	−25
Gross capital formaticn/GDP[a]	26.7	5.4	5.5	7.2	8.2	9.5	9.4	10.3	13.2	−51
Inflation rate[c]	N.A.	19.7	25.7	−11.5	−4.9	1.9	2.9	−2.9	−2.3	N.A.
Monetary liquidity/GDP[d]	21.6	73.2	51.8	42.6	42.0	41.1	40.1	38.8	37.9	75
Fiscal balance/GDP[d]	−7.2	−33.5	−7.4	−3.5	−2.5	−2.0	−2.3	−2.4	−2.5	−65

[a]At constant 1981 prices.

[b]Percent change in GDP level based on GDP at constant 1981 prices, in million pesos: 20,960 in 1989 and 16,552 in 2000.

[c]Annual variation in the Consumer Price Index.

[d]At current prices.

Source: Mesa-Lago (2001).

the official peso economy are controlled, yet inflation reporting is stated solely in terms of the peso economy. Although the fiscal deficit shrank in the years immediately following the Soviet withdrawal, an increase to 2.5 percent was reported in 2000, owing largely to subsidies to the inefficient state-owned agriculture sector (Mesa-Lago 2001).

External Sector

Because of its small size and limited natural resources, Cuba relies more than many countries on commercial relations with other nations. Prior to 1990, barter-like trade with socialist countries under favorable terms and subsidies from the Soviet Union dominated Cuba's commercial relations. A hard-currency component of trade did exist during this period, corresponding to about 15 percent of merchandise trade turnover (Perez-Lopez 1991). With the Soviet withdrawal, the external picture changed dramatically. All international transactions must now be conducted using hard currency, and trade credits, besides being scarce for Cuba, are no longer available at favorable interest rates.[4] As of 2000, only two G-7 countries had official export credit agencies active in Cuba; in 1999 there were none, indicating a general lack of global optimism about Cuba's ability to pay its debts (Ex-Im Bank 2002a).

Although the official balance of payment (BOP) statistics produced by the National Statistical Office (ONE) purportedly follow IMF methodology in their computation, observers have questioned the validity and comparability of these data (Morris 2000; Perez-Lopez 2000). The broad conclusion is that the sector has shrunk since 1990 (Perez-Lopez 2000). The trade deficit expanded sharply from 1989 to 2000 and was financed at costly market rates (Mesa-Lago 2001). Debt service and profit remittances further pressured the nation's balance of payments position. Gains in tourism receipts offset some of the merchandise deficit, though remittances from Cubans living abroad provided the largest inflow of funds into Cuba during the period (Perez-Lopez 2000).

Table 3.3 provides a summary of relevant external sector data from Mesa-Lago (2001). Appendix 3.1 provides contemporary composition-of-trade figures, Appendix 3.2 provides contemporary export values by destination country, and Appendix 3.3 provides contemporary import values by sending country (CIA 1999).

A reliance on monocrop and natural resource exports (sugar and nickel, respectively), coupled with a dependence on external energy supplies, have boded ill for Cuba's trade balance since 1989, when sugar prices were down by one-third and oil prices were 2.5

Table 3.3
Cuban External Sector Indicators, 1989–2000

Indicators	1989	1993	1994	1995	1996	1997	1998	1999	2000	% Change 1989–2000
Exports (billion pesos)	5.4	1.1	1.3	1.5	1.9	1.8	1.5	1.4	1.7	−68
Imports (billion pesos)	8.1	2.0	2.1	2.8	3.6	4.1	4.2	4.3	4.9	−40
Trade balance (billion pesos)	−2.7	−0.9	−0.8	−1.3	−1.7	−2.3	−2.7	−2.9	−3.2	+18
Terms of trade (1989 = 100)	100.0	54.4	65.9	73.9	66.7	68.5	57.3	55.9	49.9	−50
External debt ($ billions)	6.2	8.8	9.1	10.5	10.5	10.1	11.2	11.1	11.0	+77
Foreign investment[a] ($ billions)	n.a.	n.a.	n.a.	2.1	n.a.	n.a.	n.a.	2.2	4.3b	n.a.
Exchange rate[c] (pesos/$)	7	78	95	32	19	23	21	20	21	+200

[a]According to Cuban Central Bank data from 2001, foreign direct investment in Cuba (in $ millions) was as follows: 1993-54.0; 1995-4.7; 1996-82.1; 1997-442.0; 1998-206.6; 1999-178.2; 2000-399.9; and 2001-1,876.9.

[b]"Committed investment" rather than actual.

[c]Unofficial rate, annual average.

Source: Mesa-Lago (2001).

times their previous level (Mesa-Lago 2001). The Castro government negotiated a petroleum deal with Venezuela in 2000 to provide some relief from fluctuating oil prices and the need for immediate cash payments, but recent reneging by Cuba on payments for petroleum delivered has been met with calls in Venezuela to disregard this accord (*Wall Street Journal* 2002a).

Trade composition figures point to decreasing food self-sufficiency and de-industrialization in the nation (Mesa-Lago 2001). Cuba explicitly trades with a diverse set of countries to avoid depending on a single dominant trading partner (Jatar-Hausmann 1999). In 2000, these countries included Venezuela (13.9 percent of trade), Spain (13.4 percent), Canada (9 percent), the Netherlands (8.3 percent), China (7.6 percent), Russia (6.7 percent, versus 65 percent with the Soviet Union in 1989), Mexico (5.1 percent), France (5.1 percent), and Italy (4.8 percent) (BCC 2001).

Cuba's external debt increased during the 1989–2000 period, but since suspending debt repayments in 1986 (Perez-Lopez 2000), the Castro regime has not resumed new borrowing, despite negotiations with the Paris Club concerning government debt (Mesa-Lago 2001). Current trading is financed with short-term, high-cost borrowing (BCC 2000). Few, if any, official lenders are willing to extend loans to Cuba at this time (Frank 2001).

Reliable statistics on foreign investment are not available. Estimates of committed investment range as high as $5 billion (Mesa-Lago 2001), but anecdotal reports indicate that a weak domestic economy coupled with investments in key sectors (such as tourism) that have failed to achieve expected results have curtailed delivered foreign investment (Jatar-Hausmann 1999). According to the U.S. Department of State, foreign investment funds committed and/or delivered to Cuba during 1990–1999 totaled some $1.8 billion, as contrasted with official Cuban announcements of $6.1 billion for the same period. The sectors receiving the largest foreign investment in 2001 were telecommunications, mining, and tourism, with $650 million, $350 million, and $200 million, respectively. The Cuban government reports the largest investors, in terms of committed or delivered investment, are Canada, Mexico, and Italy, with $600 million, $450 million, and $387 million, respectively (USCTEC 2001a).

Morris (2000) asserts that official statistics on capital investment in Cuba are problematic because all figures are shown as net flows, there is a large "other" category, and official data on hard currency debt do not mesh with capital accounts flow figures. The total net capital inflows she reports, based on official Cuban statistics, vary from a low of $22 million in 1994 to a high of $612 million in 1995 (Morris 2000).

Despite the 1:1 par value exchange rate between the U.S. dollar and the Cuban peso, the rate fluctuated from official estimates of 1:95 in 1996 to 1:21 in 2000. Market convertibility is restricted, although the holding of dollars has been decriminalized in Cuba.

The tourism sector has earned the most hard currency and attracted the most overall foreign investment since the Soviet collapse. Arrivals increased sevenfold from 1989 to 2000, with gross revenues increasing by a factor of 10 (Mesa-Lago 2001). To meet standards of service demanded by foreign tourists, however, the import burden to support the sector is estimated at more than 50 percent of revenues (Gutierrez Castillo 2000). Occupancy rates, although growing, are low by international standards (59.7 percent in 1999, according to ECLAC 2000), and average expenditures and stay length have declined since 1995 (Espino 2001, reported in Mesa-Lago 2001). Current policy to guarantee profit remittances for foreign-owned tourism facilities, a necessary inducement for attracting investment in this sector, serves as a significant drain on hard currency, with negative balance-of-payments implications for the island.

Manufactures and Productive Output

Other than oil and nickel, natural resource production in Cuba has declined since 1989 (Mesa-Lago 2001). Sugar, historically the most significant source of product export revenues, has suffered greatly due to lack of investment, low world prices, and poor weather conditions. A recent announcement of the closure of seventy-plus sugar mills (of the approximately 170 in the country) is indicative of the sad state of this key industry (*Wall Street Journal* 2002a; Alvarez and Pena Castellanos 2001).

Social and Labor Indicators

Unemployment is high in Cuba. Official unemployment dropped from 7.9 percent of the economically active population in 1989 to 5.8 percent in 2000, but these statistics are questionable, particularly when coupled with increased restrictions on self-employment (primarily through licensing requirements and special taxation) during this period (Mesa-Lago 2001). ECLAC estimates of unemployment point to a 35.2 percent level in 1993 and a 25.1 percent level in 1998—much higher than official Cuban statistics would indicate.

Real wages are estimated to have declined around 40 percent from 1989 to 2000 (Togores, 1999). Wages in Cuba are largely decoupled from prices due to a necessary reliance by Cuban citizens on black market purchases in dollars (Jatar-Hausmann 1999). Discontent among workers has resulted (Garve 2001).

Social security expenditures, naturally high in a socialist economy, rose 31 percent from 1989 to 2000 (Mesa-Lago 2001). An aging population largely explains this increase, and pension reforms are being considered to increase the retirement age and incorporate the growing private sector (Gutierrez and Penate 2000).

Infant mortality fell by more than a third during 1989 to 2000, placing Cuba first in the region for this health indicator (Mesa-Lago 2001). At the same time, however, overall morbidity rates and illness increased, despite a surplus of (underemployed) medical professionals (Mesa-Lago 2001). Caloric intake is estimated by the United Nations Development Program (2000) to have dropped in the period, due largely to decreases in protein and fat intake.

University enrollment dropped by more than half in the period, owing largely to limited professional opportunities upon graduation, restrictions on self-employment in university-trained professions, and reduced university quotas (Mesa-Lago 2001).

A housing scarcity and deterioration of the housing stock are key social ills facing Cuba. The situation is particularly grave in Havana, where only half of city dwellers receive water daily (Perez Villanueva 2001) and power blackouts are common (Jatar-Hausmann 1999).

Cuba's Economic Problems: Cuban Scholars' Assessments

Mesa-Lago (2001) provides a succinct summary of key economic problems facing Cuba as identified by several Cuban scholars (Carranza, 2001; Gonzalez, 2001; Marquetti, 2000; Monreal, 2001; Triana, 2000). It is important to note that despite their acknowledgment of widespread economic problems on the island, all of these scholars argue for the continuation of a socialist framework for the Cuban economy. While their motivation for adhering to a socialist model may be normative in nature, it may simply reflect the need for consistency with the calls of a regime rigidly beholden to such economic organization. Their main arguments, as summarized by Mesa-Lago (2001), are as follows:

1. Macroeconomic adjustment is difficult and produces tensions between economic and political objectives.
2. Increased domestic efficiency and enterprise competitiveness are required to make up for lost investment formerly provided by the Soviet Union.
3. Multiplier effects from tourism, current foreign investment, and remittances are limited.

4. The depressed sugar industry is retarding growth in the rest of the economy.
5. The economy is dominated by production that adds little value to goods.
6. Growing dependence on food and energy imports reduces capital and hinders purchases of intermediate goods needed for growth.
7. Hard-currency earners such as tourism are too dependent on imports.
8. An overvalued peso limits export opportunities.
9. Access to, and the high cost of, credit limit growth and trading prospects.
10. The dual exchange rate must be corrected (i.e., there must be a unification of official and unofficial exchange rates between pesos and dollars).
11. Agricultural market prices are fueling inflation.
12. Wages are disconnected from prices.
13. Centralized physical planning is not viable, yet no consensus exists on an alternative.
14. There is a trend toward enterprise concentration.
15. There is an increasing stratification of society along economic lines (correlated with dollar access).

The Cuban economy clearly is under significant pressure from internal forces (growing public discontent, an aging population, and economic inefficiencies) as well as from abroad (lack of credit, declining terms of trade, and competition in key sectors). We turn our attention now to summarizing key domestic considerations in Cuba.

DOMESTIC CONSIDERATIONS IN CUBA: KEY POLICIES AND PRESSURES

The 1980s: Before the Soviet Fall

The 1980s in Cuba were characterized by a unique mix of socialist ideals and policies (e.g., centralized planning for production and near-universal higher education and health care) with initial moves toward economic liberalization. Under the System of Economic Management and Planning, state-owned enterprises allowed managers limited discretion in terms of buying and selling at set prices, reporting profit (with concomitant resource reallocations within firms), and providing incentives for productivity increases (Jatar-Hausmann 1999). Goods were in fairly ample supply, owing largely to the patronage of the Soviet Union but also to efficiency gains and high investment in the late 1970s.

In 1980, in response to food shortages, the government legalized free farmers' markets (mercados libres campesinos, or MLCs), where farmers could directly sell their produce to customers. By 1985, some 250 MLCs were in existence, corresponding to roughly 7 percent of arable land in private hands. These markets were successful in providing a wide variety of agricultural products to the populace but could not effect overall productivity gains in the agriculture sector. The involvement of intermediaries (illegal under the MLC provision) and upward pressure on prices caused subsequent stiff taxation on these markets. Taxation alone was insufficient, though, to close the markets (Jatar-Hausmann 1999).

Self-employment was made legal in 1978, but with strict limits. Individuals engaging in self-employment activities were first required to agree to mandatory production commitments, and those with university educations were prohibited from plying their professions for their own gain. No non-family members were to be employed in these ventures. Strict licensing was utilized to keep the self-employed sector "in check" (Jatar-Hausmann 1999).

In 1982, Law-Decree 50 was issued, allowing limited foreign ownership of local business (to a threshold of 49 percent). Despite this move, however, little in the way of non-Soviet investment materialized. Ownership laws were further liberalized for Cuban citizens, who were now able to buy their homes through lease conversions or build homes through a state mortgage scheme.

By the mid-1980s, however, many within the Castro regime were questioning the results of these actions. Growing social inequities, coupled with resource allocation beyond the control of the state (owing to liberalized agriculture, foreign investment, and housing), prompted a reassessment of these policies. By 1986, the regime had put on the brakes and rescinded these decisions, with painful economic ramifications for Cuban citizens (Jatar-Hausmann 1999).

Although the backtracking of liberalization can be blamed for much economic dislocation in the late 1980s, the fall of the Soviet Union in 1989 seemed to sound the death knell of the Cuban economy. At the time, trade with the Soviet Union accounted for 84 percent of external commerce, and the Cuban economy was being kept afloat only through the immense subsidies provided by the Soviets (Spadoni 2001). The "successes" of the 1980s owed largely to Cuba's continued focus on producing sugar for a captive Soviet market[5] in exchange for cheap energy from the communist bloc. With the Soviet withdrawal and the loss of an estimated $4.3 billion in annual subsidies (Hernandez-Cata 2001), the Cuban situation appeared desperate—prompting the declaration of a "Special Period" for the nation.

The 1990s: The Special Period and Beyond

The loss of the sweetheart trading arrangement with the Soviet Union created clear and broad-reaching difficulties for Cuba. Productivity was down in the public sector, and by 1993 the "informal" market was seven times larger than it had been in 1989 (Jatar-Hausmann 1999). Consumer goods were in particularly short supply (Canadian Department of Foreign Affairs and International Trade 1999). GDP plunged 40 percent in the early 1990s owing to a lack of inputs for production (most notably in agriculture), the elimination of trade subsidies from the (former) Soviet Union and its allied countries, domestic policies promoting overly aggressive economic diversification at the microeconomic level (Jatar-Hausmann 1999; CDFAIT 1999), and new trading pressures imposed by the United States under the Cuban Democracy Act. Cuba's resistance to joining multilateral institutions such as the IMF and the World Bank denied the nation a natural escape route for financing an economic transition.

In response, the regime initiated a series of policies intended to lift Cuba from this predicament. Internally, these efforts took the form of extreme austerity measures, including rationing food and other necessities, substituting human- and animal-powered processes for oil-consuming machinery and vehicles, and forcing migration from the cities to the countryside in the form of agricultural worker brigades (Perez-Lopez 1995). Externally, the Cuban government introduced further reforms through an expansion of Law-Decree 50 to make investment in the nation more attractive (particularly in tourism) and to promote enhanced external trade while still excluding Cuban society from the "ills" of capitalism, including earning dollars. These moves exempted foreign investors from taxes and provided for unlimited profit repatriation and the hiring of foreign executives (Jatar-Hausmann 1999). The foreign investment market responded by forming 110 new joint ventures from 1990 to 1993 (Perez 1997).

Perhaps most notable during this period, however, was the implementation of a policy of exchange controls entailing the reallocation/rationing of foreign exchange (dollars) in lieu of devaluing the peso. Non-tourism sectors subsequently found scarce resources unavailable to them, as these were diverted to the hard-currency-denominated tourism sector. Reforms eventually allowed for foreign investment in other areas—even in the "Holy Grail" sector, sugar—bringing much-needed technology and dollars. The rising liquidity spurred by dollar infusions into the economy did not, however, comport well with a centrally planned system for production and consumption allocation. Extreme shortages in the official peso-based economy spurred the development of dollar-based black markets (Jatar-Hausmann 1999), creating irresistible pressures on citizens to enter the informal (dollar-based) sector for survival. By the economic low point of 1993–1994, the Cuban regime realized that more profound economic reforms would be required to satisfy the growing needs of Cubans whose ration cards could not provide them with even a basic subsistence.

These reforms took place across a variety of fronts: the legalization of hard currency (U.S. dollars) and the concomitant opening of "dollar stores" where such money could be spent, thereby enticing remittances from abroad; the establishment of agricultural cooperatives, monetary incentives for productivity, and free markets for farmers and artisans; the allowance of full ownership by foreigners of firms in Cuba (with guarantees against future nationalization); an increase in the number of approved self-employment professions to 157 (although the government quickly imposed taxes on these new activities to tap into this income stream for socialistic redistribution); and the creation of free zones for production and re-export (Jatar-Hausmann 1999).

Following these reforms, remittances from abroad flowed in to provide Cubans the funds needed to survive via black market transactions. These remittances are estimated at some $800 million annually (ECLAC 2001).[6] The reforms also succeeded in producing growth in Cuba from 1993 to 1996, when the economy became less dependent on sugar exports. The peso gained value relative to the dollar, though the economic escape valve provided by the influx of tourism and remittance dollars created a social division between those with access to dollars and those locked into the formal peso economy. The regime now contends with four primary stakeholders: foreign investors (primarily in tourism but also in tobacco, citrus, nickel and other resource mining, oil, coal, and telecommunications); the Cuban diaspora (most notably in South Florida); foreign tourists; and the self-employed in Cuba (Jatar-Hausmann 1999).

The current policy is best described as state capitalism, whereby efficiency gains are sought through the decentralization of state-owned industries and foreign investment is encouraged through joint ventures with the government (Jatar-Hausmann 1999). Law-Decree 50, pertaining to the involvement of foreigners in the economy, was replaced in 1995 with Law-Decree 77, which opens more sectors to foreign investment (all but education, public health, and the military), expands legal protections for firms doing business in the nation, and allows foreigners to hold real estate geared toward tourism or non-Cubans. All non-executive hiring of Cubans, however, must still go through the state, which pays wages in pesos but charges investing firms dollar wages for these employees—a very hefty implicit wage tax.

Mexico is now the largest investor in Cuba. Altogether, more than 300 planned investments are on the books, according to the Agence France Presse, but reliable figures on the size and nature of foreign direct investment in Cuba are scarce, owing to a reluctance by Cuban officials to identify foreign investors and possibly subject them to the extraterritorial reach of U.S. sanctions.

All in all, Cuba has made the transition from subsidies and guaranteed markets under the Soviet umbrella to a unique form of state capitalism with surprising (in the view of many observers) success. The regime has maintained control over the economy and society, and the economic losses of the early 1990s have been offset through the implementation of important economic reforms. These reforms have come at a cost, however—the erosion of social equality and solidarity that are the cornerstones of traditional socialism. Domestic economic policies, coupled with previous development decisions and falling world market prices for important commodities (especially sugar and oil), largely explain Cuba's difficult economic—and thus, to a great extent, social—situation today (Suchlicki 2000). Nonetheless, the unilateral economic sanctions imposed by the United States have had direct and indirect effects on Cuba, as we explain in the following section.

OVERVIEW OF U.S. UNILATERAL ECONOMIC SANCTIONS AGAINST CUBA

U.S. sanctions have been in force against Cuba since 1917 but most notably since 1960, after the Batista regime was overthrown. In this section we briefly summarize the primary sanctions against Cuba as delineated by the International Trade Commission (2001) in chronological order of their imposition. We also note key historical events that precipitated the imposition of these sanctions.

1917: Passage of Trading with the Enemy Act

This act provides the legislative basis for U.S. financial sanctions against Cuba. Initially focused on U.S. entry into World War I, it authorizes the president to "prohibit, limit, or regulate trade with hostile countries in time of war." An amendment in 1933 expanded presidential authority to invoke this act during times of national emergency. Although another amendment in 1977 nullified the national emergency option, it allowed the president to provide annual justification for any existing sanctions. Since 1977, all U.S. presidents have issued annual determinations extending the "state of emergency" and, hence, the embargo against Cuba.

1960: Imposition of Sanctions Under Export Control Act

In 1960, President Eisenhower imposed export sanctions against Cuba under the 1949 Export Control Act after Castro's government began expropriating U.S. property on the island, namely petroleum processing facilities owned by Texaco. Only unsubsidized foodstuffs and medical supplies were exempted from export controls.

1961: Passage of Foreign Assistance Act

This act authorized President Kennedy to impose a total trade embargo against Cuba. In 1962, during the annual recertification of the act, subsection 602(e) was added, disallowing U.S. assistance to communist countries and reinforcing sanctions against any countries expropriating U.S. property.

The Foreign Assistance Act was passed on the heels of the CIA-backed Bay of Pigs invasion, wherein some 1,200 Cuban exiles landed in Cuba with the goal of ousting the Castro regime. Cuban military forces quickly defeated this exile contingent, killing 80 and imprisoning the remainder. Some of those captured were executed for allegedly committing brutal crimes during the Batista period; most of the others were freed in December 1962 (National Bipartisan Commission on Cuba 2000).

Soon after the passage of the Foreign Assistance Act, Castro declared, "I am a Marxist-Leninist, and I shall be a Marxist-Leninist to the end of my life." Almost a year later, Kennedy announced that the Soviet Union had placed nuclear missiles in Cuba, initiating the five-day Cuban Missile Crisis, which brought the United States and the Soviet Union to the brink of nuclear war. This incident, coupled with Castro's declaration of allegiance to socialism, forged the political and economic relationship between Cuba and the Soviet Union (National Bipartisan Commission on Cuba 2000).

1962: Passage of Tariff Classification Act

This act suspended Cuba from receiving reduced and most-favored-nation (MFN) duty rates. Under the act, suspension of reduced duties is required when the United States concludes a country "is dominated or controlled by the foreign government or foreign organization controlling the world communist movement." It is important to note that this was in many ways a symbolic declaration (at least with respect to Cuba), as imports from the island had ceased arriving in the United States earlier that year as a result of actions pursuant to the Foreign Assistance Act. Later in 1962, the Cuban Missile Crisis took place, solidifying U.S. sentiment against the communist world.

1963: Imposition of Cuban Assets Control Regulations

These regulations were published by the U.S. Treasury Department's Office of Assets of Foreign Control, which issues, interprets, and applies economic sanctions. The regulations effectively froze all private and public Cuban assets in the United States, prohibited all unlicensed American financial and commercial transactions with Cuba or Cuban citizens (including those by U.S. subsidiaries overseas, the first extraterritorial provision of U.S. sanctions policy against Cuba), and prohibited direct and indirect U.S. exports to and imports from Cuba. Explicit exceptions to these sanctions included publications, telecommunications services, informational materials, and up to $100 of Cuban merchandise in possession of authorized travelers. The Treasury Department is required to approve all transactions and transfers with Cuba.

1973: Establishment of Bilateral Anti-Hijacking Agreement

In keeping with the détente between the United States and the Soviet Union during the mid-1970s, the United States and Cuba took small actions to normalize relations. One such action was the negotiation of an anti-hijacking agreement, which allows for the sharing of information to promote mutual interests in thwarting hijacking in Cuba or the United States.

1975: Amendment to Cuban Assets Control Regulations

In 1975, the Treasury Department issued an amendment loosening the regulation that restricts subsidiaries of U.S. companies operating in third countries from conducting business with Cuba. Later that year the Treasury Department revoked the regulation altogether and replaced it with a specific trade license.

1977: Lapse of Travel Restrictions/Agreement on Maritime Issues/Bilateral Opening of "Interest Sections"

Under President Carter, some restrictions on U.S. citizens traveling to Cuba were allowed to lapse (e.g., U.S. citizens were now allowed to spend up to $100 on Cuban goods) and an accord on fishing rights and maritime boundaries between the United States and Cuba was signed. "Interest sections" were opened in Havana and Washington, D.C., in lieu of official embassies. Each interest section is "attributed" to the respective Swiss embassy, but physically located on the site of each country's former embassy.

1982: Reinstatement of Travel Restrictions

In the late 1970s, Cuba sent military forces to Africa, effectively halting further normalization with the United States. In 1982, President Reagan reinstated restrictions on U.S. citizens traveling to Cuba, reversing the easing of these sanctions under President Carter.

1992: Passage of the Cuban Democracy Act ("Toricelli Act")

This act codified and expanded many of the existing U.S. sanctions against Cuba and added new ones, effectively ending all steps toward normalization. The act does the following:

- Prohibits subsidiaries of U.S. companies from conducting business with Cuba, thus reinstating the 1963 regulation that was rescinded in 1975
- Restricts the movements of any trade "vessels" between the United States and Cuba. Any vessel loading/unloading freight in Cuba cannot enter a U.S. port or place within 180 days of leaving Cuba. In addition, U.S. ports are closed to vessels carrying goods or passengers directly to/from Cuba, and no goods are to be transported in vessels in which Cuba or a Cuban national has "any interest."
- Subjects medical supplies, equipment, and so on to inspection to make sure they are only to be used for their intended purposes and for the direct benefit of the Cuban people (i.e., humanitarian medical supplies cannot be resold for profit or used by the Cuban government)
- Grants the president the authority to prohibit economic assistance, military assistance or sales, debt forgiveness, or reductions of monies owed to the United States to any country providing assistance to Cuba
- Requires the president to maintain "strict limits" on remittances to Cuba by people in the United States
- Allows the Treasury Department to levy civil fines and property forfeitures on those found to be violating U.S. sanctions against Cuba
- Allows (with some limitations) telecommunications and postal services to be operated between the United States and Cuba and provides for payments to the Cuban government for these services

International response to the Cuban Democracy Act (CDA) was relatively mild. Some observers expected the application of the sanctions against U.S. subsidiaries operating abroad to raise the ire of important trading partners and political allies, such as the European Union. Leaders in those countries apparently were willing to "sacrifice" U.S. subsidiaries in favor of their domestic firms, which benefited from reduced competition for Cuban business under the act (Preeg 1999b).

1996: Passage of the Cuban Liberty and Democratic Solidarity Act ("Helms-Burton Act")

This act corresponded with a stark expansion of U.S. sanctions against Cuba prompted by the downing of a Cuban exile group's airplane over international waters by Cuban military aircraft. The act is organized into four titles, as follows:

- Title I requires U.S. representatives of international financial institutions to oppose Cuban membership within their respective organizations and restricts U.S. payments to institutions that provide assistance to Cuba over U.S. objections.
- Title II makes removal of sanctions dependent ("contingent") on the settlement of all outstanding claims on U.S. property expropriated in Cuba (property rights provisions are extended to Cuban exiles who have become U.S. citizens). The president must determine that a "Transition Government" is in place in Cuba prior to removing sanctions. Fidel Castro and his brother Raul are explicitly excluded, by name, from any legitimate "Transition Government."
- Title III permits U.S. nationals to sue Cuban government entities and third-party foreign investors over profits earned from the use of confiscated properties previously owned by U.S. nationals.
- Title IV denies individuals who "traffic in" U.S.-claimed properties in Cuba both visas to enter the United States and entry into the United States.

The Helms-Burton Act generated controversy among many U.S. allies due to its extraterritorial nature. U.S. sanctions imposed on Cuba were now, in essence, extended to other countries trading with or conducting business with Cuba and the United States. Canada and Mexico quickly passed "antidote" legislation in response to Helms-Burton, while the European Union requested dispute-settlement consultations with the United States through the World Trade Organization.[7]

Canada added an amendment to its 1992 Foreign Extraterritorial Measures Act (FEMA), which requires Canadian companies (including U.S. subsidiaries) to ignore any instructions not to trade with Cuba. The amendment strengthened protections for Canadian companies doing business with Cuba, making any Helms-Burton legal judgments unenforceable in Canada and enabling Canadians sued in the United States to recover settlements from their opposing party's Canadian assets. Thus, the 1996 amendment to FEMA made actions taken against Canadian companies under Helms-Burton illegal in Canada.

Mexico joined Canada in responding to Helms-Burton by passing the Law to Protect Trade and Investment from Foreign Laws that Contravene International Law. This measure provides for the levying of fines on Mexican companies that comply with Helms-Burton and other similar laws. As with the Canadian statute, the Mexican law refuses to recognize or enforce foreign judgments based on laws like Helms-Burton.

The European Union's WTO dispute-resolution request resulted in the "EU-U.S. Understanding of May 18, 1998." The EU agreed to develop "rules regarding investment projects dealing with illegally expropriated properties," while the Clinton administration agreed to ask Congress for authority to waive restrictions under Titles III and IV.

Cuba, recognizing the potential chill the act could have on valuable foreign investment, developed its own legislation to counteract the extraterritoriality of Helms-Burton. Law 80, the Reaffirmation of Cuban Dignity and Sovereignty Law, requires the Cuban government to do what is necessary to protect all current and potential foreign investment in Cuba, including legitimate interests threatened under Helms-Burton (Spadoni 2001). One such action deemed necessary by the Cuban government pertains to limiting the release of data on foreign involvement in the Cuban economy. Data on foreign direct investment, for instance, is viewed as potentially harmful to investors given the extraterritoriality of U.S. sanctions law, and thus the Cuban government does not reliably or regularly provide it (Spadoni 2001).

1998: Passage of the Omnibus Appropriations Act

Under Section 211 of this law, all trademarks that previously had been abandoned by their original owners as a result of Cuban property confiscation cannot be registered or renewed in the United States, and U.S. courts cannot recognize or enforce rights associated with these trademarks. In July 1999, the European Union filed a WTO complaint contending that this act does not conform to "U.S. obligations" under the WTO Agreement on Trade Related Aspects of Intellectual Property Rights.

1998: Implementation of Humanitarian Policies

The Department of Commerce and other federal agencies implemented policies in 1998 to make it easier to acquire humanitarian medical licenses and export medical supplies and equipment for donation or nongovernmental sales.

2000: Passage of the Trade Sanctions Reform and Export Enhancement Act

Signed by President Clinton, this law relaxed unilateral sanctions imposed on several countries (including Cuba) to allow conditional sales of food, medicine, and some medical equipment. Direct or private export financing for this trade is prohibited, however, effectively nullifying the act's impact due to Cuba's hard currency shortages and abysmal debt rating.

Potential Legislation and Activities Concerning Sanctions Against Cuba

The Cuba Working Group

On 21 March 2002, a bipartisan group of members of the House of Representatives led by Jeff Flake, R-Arizona, and William Delahunt, D-Massachusetts, announced the creation of the Cuba Working Group, comprising 17 members each from the Republican and Democratic parties, largely from agricultural states (but none from Florida[8]). The group's stated goals are to ease or eliminate travel restrictions and increase U.S. exports of agricultural products.[9] The group is conducting its own review of U.S. policy toward Cuba and is interested in winning House approval to prohibit the use of funds to enforce restrictions on travel to Cuba—a backdoor approach to limiting the impact of sanctions (Willis 2002).

The Cuban Diaspora and the Cuban American National Foundation

It is important to recognize the critical role played by the Cuban diaspora,[10] particularly that located in South Florida, in U.S. economic sanctions policy toward Cuba (Ratliff and Fontaine 2000). Despite opposition to U.S. sanctions by politicians as well as key business groups, a well-organized and politically savvy Cuban exile group has proven successful at persuading lawmakers to maintain pressure on Cuba in the form of sanctions (Erickson

2002). The Cuban American National Foundation is the most vocal and best-known group representing the proembargo interests of the exile community, and it supports research and lobbies lawmakers to that end. Dennis Hays, executive vice president of the foundation, said in a meeting of the InterAmerican Dialogue (Hays 2002) in Washington, D.C., that his organization supports continued sanctions against Cuba in order to restore democracy and protect human rights.[11] At the heart of the foundation's concerns is compensation for property confiscated by the state in the revolution.

Notwithstanding the group's calls for continued pressure on Cuba via sanctions, its members, according to Hays, privately send remittances to friends and family within Cuba, actions that effectively weaken the impact of sanctions. The foundation's monolithicism has been called into question recently—a rift apparently has emerged between the founders of the group, who espouse a strong anti-Castro stance, and younger Cuban-Americans (Erickson 2002).

During former President Carter's humanitarian visit to Cuba in 2002, the Castro regime demonstrated unprecedented openness in allowing public discussion of sensitive topics such as the Varela Project, a dissident group pressuring the regime for political and social reforms. Carter called for closer U.S.–Cuba ties in terms of travel and other exchanges as the best policy for ensuring a stable transition to a new government (Carter 2002). Observers note, however, that Castro likely will remain in power throughout his lifetime (Dominguez 2002).

On the heels of Carter's visit, President Bush announced a commitment to current U.S. sanctions policy toward Cuba until democracy and full protection of human rights are restored—a reiteration of the requirements under Helms-Burton. The fact that the president's brother is facing reelection as governor of Florida, where support from the Cuban diaspora is considered crucial, has not gone unnoticed by observers of U.S. sanctions policy (Coughenour 2002). Once the election has passed, perhaps the Bush administration will consider normalizing relations with Cuba.[12]

THE DIRECT IMPACT OF SANCTIONS ON CUBA AND THE UNITED STATES

Historically, trade between the United States and Cuba consisted primarily of exchanges of Cuban agricultural products (sugar and tobacco) for American grains, timber, and manufactures. The United States also was a leading destination for Cuban tourists. Prior to the revolution, the United States dominated Cuba's trade, supplying and receiving more than two-thirds of its imports and exports, and it provided the lion's share of public and private capital to the island. Cuba, on the other hand, represented only a fraction of U.S. trade in the preembargo period—less than 5 percent of U.S. exports and imports (ITC 2001). This trade and investment relationship changed sharply after the revolution, owing initially to political risk and its impact on potential investors and later to sanctions imposed by the United States on Cuba.

Econometric Analyses and Estimates of the Direct Impact of Sanctions on U.S.–Cuban Trade

The most comprehensive and up-to-date empirical study of the economic impact of U.S. sanctions on Cuba was conducted by the ITC under the direction of the House Ways and Means Committee. The time period for the study is 1960 through the implementation of the Helms-Burton Act, with a historical examination of the period 1960–1995 and an economic impact assessment for 1996–2000 (assuming no policy changes in Cuba). Average trade data from 1996–1998 were used in creating estimates of sanctions' impact on trade.

The ITC used a gravity model to estimate the quantitative impacts of sanctions on bilateral trade and investment, a common practice in such analyses. The study explicitly incorporated other previous econometric analyses of sanctions. Scarce official data on Cuba's economy and its external trading relationships were augmented for this study with primary research by ITC staff, testimony from a public hearing in September 2000, written submissions from the public, an informal telephone survey of more than 200 U.S. companies and associations, and a review of the relevant economic literature. The analysis excluded trade in military goods and goods subject to U.S. export controls.

The findings of the study, published in 2001, are summarized in Tables 3.4, 3.5, and 3.6. Table 3.6 reports actual trade between the United States and Cuba. Tables 3.4 and 3.5 report estimated trade (imports and exports, respectively) in the absence of sanctions, broken out by sector.

As Table 3.6 shows, U.S. exports to Cuba in 1999 totaled $4.7 million. Donated goods—$2.4 million in medical/pharmaceutical products, $1.6 million of relief/charity items, and just under $200,000 in clothing—comprised 90 percent of this amount. The 1997 figure includes $7.4 million in medical goods, while the higher figure for 2000 (compared to 1999) is due to increased relief/charity exports. Imports from Cuba are almost 100 percent artwork (ITC 2001).

Table 3.4
Estimated Annual U.S. Imports from Cuba in the Absence of U.S. Sanctions (Based on Average 1996–98 Trade Data)

Sector	All Cuban Exports, 1996–98 average ($ millions)	Estimated U.S. Share of Cuban Exports (%)	Estimated U.S. Imports from Cuba ($ millions)	Estimated Cuban Share of All U.S. Imports, 1996–98 average (%)
Selected agricultural products				
Winter vegetables	(a)	45-90	(a)	(b)
Tropical fruit	(a)	25-45	(a)	(b)
Citrus fruit	46	20-50	9-23	2-6
Sugar	860	(c)	(c)	(c)
Distilled spirits	100	15-25	15-25	1
Cigars	99	15-30	15-30	5-10
Seafood	109	5-10	5-11	(b)
Subtotal[d]	1,214	13-25[e]	45-89[e]	(b)
Selected intermediate and manufactured goods				
Pharmaceuticals	36	0-5	0-2	(b)
Textiles and apparel	5	10-15	0-1	(b)
Steel	44	0-25	0-11	(b)
Nickel and cobalt	391	0	0	(b)
Cement	25	75-95	19-24	2-3
Subtotal[f]	501	4-7	19-37	(b)
Other products[g]	101	5-20	5-20	(b)
Total	1,817	7-15[e]	69-146[e]	(b)

[a]Less than $500,000.
[b]Less than 0.5%.
[c]Not available.
[d]Represents more than 95% of total Cuban exports of agricultural products.
[e]Estimate excludes sugar.
[f]Represents more than 85% of total Cuban exports of intermediate and manufactured goods.
[g]"Other products" consists of miscellaneous Cuban exports for which the ITC has not made separate determinations of potential U.S. imports. These include, but are not limited to, coffee, tobacco products other than cigars, miscellaneous chemical products, non-ferrous metals, manufactured metal products, miscellaneous machinery, travel goods, and other miscellaneous manufactures.
Note: Totals may not add due to rounding.
Sources: 1996–98 average annual base value of Cuban trade data from various sources. Estimated U.S. share of Cuban trade and estimated U.S.-Cuban trade data are derived from International Trade Commission estimates and the ITC gravity model (ITC 2001).

Based on average trade data from 1996–98, the ITC estimates annual U.S. exports to Cuba in the absence of sanctions at between $658 million and $1 billion. This equates to at least 17 percent and as much as 27 percent of total Cuban imports, though less than 0.5 percent of total U.S. exports. Using the same trade data (1996–98), the ITC estimates that U.S. imports from Cuba without sanctions

Table 3.5
Estimated Annual U.S. Exports to Cuba in the Absence of U.S. Sanctions (Based on Average 1996–98 Trade Data)

Sector	Total Cuban Imports, 1996–98 Average ($ millions)	Estimated U.S. Share of Cuban Imports (%)	Estimated U.S. Exports to Cuba ($ millions)	Estimated Cuban Share of U.S. Imports, 1996–98 Average (%)
Selected agricultural products				
Meat	95	65-80	62-76	1
Dairy	82	5-15	4-12	1-3
Wheat	86	40-60	34-52	1
Rice	99	40-60	40-59	4-6
Feed grains	10	90-100	9-10	(a)
Animal feed	53	80-90	42-48	1
Fats and oils	37	80-90	29-33	1
Dry beans	64	20-40	13-26	4-8
Cotton	12	50-70	6-8	(a)
Winter vegetables	(b)	(b)	(c)	(a)
Tropical fruit	(b)	(b)	(c)	(a)
Seafood	21	5-10	1-2	(a)
Subtotal[d]	559	43-58	241-327	1
Selected intermediate and manufactured goods				
Fertilizer	75	10-20	8-15	(a)
Pesticide	41	0-10	0-4	(a)
Pharmaceuticals	26	0-5	0-1	(a)
Textiles and apparel	60	10-15	6-9	(a)
Steel	121	(a)	(c)	(a)
Machinery	342	35-45	120-154	(a)
Transportation equipment	123	35-45	43-55	(a)
Power generation machinery	78	(a)	(c)	(a)
Electronics goods	169	0-10	0-17	(a)
Medical equipment	12	50-70	6-8	(a)
Plastics	42	0-10	0-4	(a)
Tires	33	65-75	21-25	1
Sporting goods	5	20-30	1-2	(a)
Subtotal[e]	1,127	18-26	204-294	(a)
Other products[f]	2,129	10-20	213-426	(a)
Total	3,815	17-27	658-1,047	(a)

[a]Less than 0.5%.
[b]Not available.
[c]Less than $500,000.
[d]Represents more than 90% of total Cuban imports of agricultural products.
[e]Represents about one-third of total Cuban imports of intermediate and manufactured goods.
[f]"Other products" consists of miscellaneous Cuban imports, mostly of intermediate and manufactured goods, for which the United States International Trade Commission has not made separate determinations of potential U.S. exports.
Source: 1996–98 average annual base value of Cuban trade data from various sources. Estimated U.S. share of Cuban trade and estimated U.S.–Cuban trade data are derived from ITC estimates and the ITC gravity model (ITC 2001).

Table 3.6
U.S.–Cuba Trade, 1995–2000 ($ Hundred Thousands)

	U.S. exports to Cuba	U.S. imports from Cuba
1995	5,846	0
1996	5,457	0
1997	9,315	0
1998	3,455	0
1999	4,662	649
1999 (Jan.–Oct.)	4,056	644
2000 (Jan.–Oct.)	6,260	323

Source: ITC (2001).

(excluding sugar[13]) would be between $69 million and $146 million per year. These amounts represent 7 percent to 15 percent of total Cuban exports, but less than 0.5 percent of total U.S. imports. When contrasted with pre-sanctions bilateral trade figures, it becomes clear that both Cuba and the United States have diversified and diverted their trade and that the impact of lifting sanctions in net trade terms would be far smaller than historic bilateral trade statistics would indicate.

The ITC study also estimates that in the absence of sanctions, tourism and travel receipts generated by Cuba would total $100–350 million, a potentially important addition to the nation's foreign exchange earnings. Currently, tourism is the nation's largest earner of foreign exchange, larger even than sugar. The other important service sector likely to be affected by a lifting of sanctions is telecommunications; the ITC estimates that some $15–30 million in additional net foreign exchange could be earned by Cuba (ITC 2001).

A gravity model study by Hufbauer, Schott, and Elliot (1990) indicates that in the absence of sanctions, U.S. exports to Cuba in 1987 would have totaled $432 million as opposed to the actual $1 million figure. This figure was derived by using actual OECD exports to Cuba, then assuming the 49 percent U.S. share of OECD exports to "non-OECD America." Another analysis estimated the value of lost U.S. exports to Cuba at $1 billion in 1995 (Hufbauer, Elliot, Cyrus, and Winston 1997). Preeg (1999b) estimates annual losses at around $1 billion. Despite differences in data sources and assumptions among the analyses, estimates of the impact of sanctions are consistent: in dollar terms, the effect on the U.S. economy is negligible, but relatively strong on the Cuban economy.

The ITC study points to four main barriers to potential trade between the United States and Cuba. First, investments in productive capacity in Cuba have not kept pace with equipment depreciation, much less increased capacity on the island (Dominguez 2002). As a result, any increases in production geared for export to the United States would come at the expense of domestic consumption or be diverted from trade with other nations. This situation is exacerbated by the second barrier, continued restrictions on foreign investment in Cuba. Despite significant liberalization over the past decade to attract foreign investment, the political risk of "doing business with Castro" (Fisk 1999), and concerns about weaknesses in domestic demand and the supply of inputs and trained labor have limited foreign investment, which has not been sufficient to boost productive capacity in Cuba to warrant expanded exporting. Third, the island is constrained in terms of foreign exchange and is considered an unworthy credit risk in global lending markets because it suspended debt servicing on foreign loans. This situation makes import expansion difficult if not impossible.[14] Finally, the Cuban government, having twice suffered the consequences of over-reliance on a single trading partner,[15] made an explicit decision to diversify trade among a variety of trading partners, despite potentially negative short-term economic consequences (ITC 2001).

Thus, even if the United States dropped its sanctions on Cuba, little impact on bilateral trade would result. Any impact would come, at least in the short and perhaps medium term, at the expense of domestic consumption—which Triana (2001) notes is already at a bare minimum—or, more likely, at the expense of trade with other nations.

The overall impact of sanctions as calculated by the ITC (and others as reported previously) is overshadowed by the $67 billion Cuban government estimate of the cumulative impact since the imposition of U.S. sanctions four decades ago (ITC 2001). That estimate includes losses from reduced trade and tourism, higher shipping costs due to the limitation on vessels traveling between Cuba and the United States, the inability to access spare parts, foreign debt considerations, assets frozen in U.S. banks, and the "brain drain" from Cuban exiles living in the United States. This loss estimate, however, excludes economic benefits to Cuba provided via Soviet assistance during much of the sanctions period. The political significance of the disparity between Cuban estimates of the costs of sanctions and those of the United States lies in the Cuban stance that any U.S. claims for reparations for expropriated property in Cuba must include compensation to Cuba for costs exacted under sanctions. The economic validity of these additional sanction cost claims by Cuba are discussed next.

Cuban Estimates of Impacts

Claims by the Cuban government of losses due to reduced trade and tourism rely on the difficult-to-measure yet anecdotally supported notion that when an economic superpower (such as the United States) sanctions a country, it has a chilling effect on firms and citizens of other nations. Given the extraterritorial reach of U.S. sanctions on Cuba, this claim is not unfounded.[16] Empirically assessing the impact of any such effect would require establishing an accepted baseline of trade with the United States in the absence of sanctions, as is routinely done in gravity model estimations of sanctions' impact. Once such a baseline is established, second-stage gravity models for other Cuban trading partners could be performed to gauge the level of trade diverted away from Cuba by U.S. sanctions.

Reduced trade with other countries may have further negative effects on the Cuban economy due to multipliers from upstream and downstream industry associated with foregone investments in the nation. Multipliers in the tourism sector are believed to be relatively weak (Carranza Valdez 2001; Marquetti Nodarse 2000), so any chilling effect on tourists from outside the United States would likely be limited to that sector.

The Caribbean region is dominated by well-established shipping networks (DuBois 2002). Most shipments traverse the Caribbean basin prior to arrival in the United States (the dominant trading partner in the region) or vice versa in order to enjoy economies of scale or scope in freight. Even when goods are bound to or from other markets, such as the EU, the United States may be transited en route. Cuban imports and exports are effectively denied participation in these shipping networks due to the 180-day restriction on vessel landings between Cuban and U.S. ports. Thus, Cuban goods must travel via dedicated shipments that forego stops in the United States—a costly proposition for Cuban traders.

A significant portion of the productive capacity in Cuba—in terms of plants and equipment, machinery, and vehicles—is of U.S. origin. Some of this capacity was purchased from the United States prior to the embargo; goods procured after the embargo took effect (which, by definition, were produced outside the United States) often hailed from U.S. subsidiaries abroad. Recall that these subsidiaries were not denied the right to trade with Cuba until the first extraterritorial extension of U.S. sanctions law in 1963. This restriction on subsidiaries was significantly loosened in 1975, then replaced with a specific trade license later that year. Not until 1992 (with the passage of the Toricelli Act) was the extraterritorial restriction on U.S. subsidiaries operating abroad reinstated. Thus, during the embargo period, U.S. subsidiaries abroad were entitled to supply productive capacity to Cuba for some two decades altogether.[17]

By denying the Cuban economy access to spare parts to refurbish and maintain its plants and equipment, the embargo effectively hastened the rate and scope of depreciation of Cuba's productive capacity. To measure this depreciation would require an understanding of the uniqueness of U.S. plants and machinery in Cuba and the extent to which parts from non-U.S. sources could substitute directly or be adapted to suit the repair and maintenance needs of Cuban productive assets. A fair and thorough assessment of this impact of U.S. sanctions would naturally require consideration of U.S. spare parts smuggled into Cuba through third countries. Such an analysis is beyond the scope of this presentation.

A nation's creditworthiness owes directly to a lender's assessment of the country's ability to generate the revenues needed to service debt obligations. For Cuba, denial of access to the United States clearly limits its ability to generate revenues efficiently. Concerns about political risk in Cuba are voiced publicly in policy circles in Washington, D.C., further eroding lenders' confidence in the creditworthiness of the Cuban government. Since U.S. commercial lenders are the most active and important throughout the Caribbean basin area, denial of access to these sources of credit limits Cuba's ability to leverage funding to grow.

A frank assessment of Cuba's ability to secure credit would likely conclude, however, that the country's largely anti-market policies create bureaucratic inefficiencies that limit the growth of many sectors of the economy. The Cuban government's repudiation of external debts during the 1990s, coupled with its disinclination to submit to the financial discipline required for membership in multilateral institutions such as the World Bank and IMF, likely have done much more than U.S. sanctions to deny Cuba access to credit from abroad.

The U.S. government has frozen assets linked to Cuba and holds $178.2 million (including accrued interest) as of January 1998 (OFAC 1998). Although these assets are accruing interest, they cannot be put to productive uses by Cuba. The overall impact on the Cuban economy from denied use of these funds is not large, however.

The Cuban exile community in the United States is sizeable, representing nearly 5 percent of the electorate in Florida alone, and many of these individuals benefited from investments by the Cuban government in their education. They are recognized as an entrepreneurial group with significant drive, though whether their temperament would have served a socialist Cuba well is debatable.

Although they took their educations with them to the United States, they often left productive assets and real estate behind. The quantifiable impact of this "brain drain" on Cuba is difficult to ascertain but must be weighed against the productive assets abandoned in Cuba and tempered by questions about what sort of environment best allows an individual to achieve his or her potential.

Direct Trade Impact of Sanctions on Specific Sectors

Although the net trade impact of sanctions is small (Suchlicki 2000),[18] the ITC study notes that certain sectors are particularly affected by sanctions. U.S. producers of agricultural products such as dairy goods, rice, and dry beans could benefit from a lifting of sanctions against Cuba, as could providers of transportation services to support increased tourism in Cuba. U.S. communications exports would likely be constrained due to foreign investment that has already taken place in Cuba (ITC 2001).

As for Cuban agricultural and manufacturing products, citrus, tobacco, and cement would all find the United States to be an important export market. Lifting sanctions would not appreciably increase prospects for Cuban services with the possible exceptions of entertainment- and health-related exports. Tourism, the sector targeted by the regime for priority development, paints a mixed picture. Although significant short-term demand exists for travel to Cuba—on the order of a million tourists annually—many expect those numbers to fall once pent-up demand for visits to Cuba has been satisfied. Other than visits by friends and family in the exile community, gains in this sector would come at the expense of tourism to other countries within the region, particularly nations such as Mexico and the Dominican Republic that depend heavily on tourists from the United States (Crespo and Suddaby 2000). Cultural, hunting, medical/health, and other specialized travel packages represent important opportunities to market to a yet-untapped U.S. client base (ITC 2001).

Most observers believe that U.S. sanctions have not significantly dampened the growth of tourism in Cuba (Crespo and Suddaby, 2000). Growth in the sector averaged 23 percent in the 1990s, with revenues of $2 billion in 2000 (Canadian Trade and Economic Section 2001). Current economic prospects do not appear to support such robust growth for the future. Portela (2002) reports that 2001 tourism figures for Cuba were flat over 2000 and arrivals in the first quarter of 2002 are down 14.4 percent.

Resistance to lifting sanctions by Sen. Jesse Helms of North Carolina (an important tobacco-growing state) and Florida politicians (given their state's dependence on citrus exports and tourism) is not surprising. As noted by the 2000 legislation relaxing sanctions on exports of food and medical supplies to Cuba, these sectors hold great promise for normalized relations because of their importance to the U.S. economy and their political sway—no side in the debate on sanctions against Cuba wants to be accused of denying food or medicine to a needy Cuban public.

"Special" Sectors: Food and Medicine

In light of the unique importance of food and medicine, the Stern Group conducted a study to assess the impact of lifting sanctions on these sectors under three scenarios (Stern Group 2000). One scenario projected U.S. sales to Cuba in the first year following passage of the then-pending Trade Sanctions Reform and Export Enhancement Act, which partially lifted restrictions on U.S. food and medical sales to Cuba. The second scenario projected sales to Cuba after five years of partial liberalization, which would be the likely time frame for U.S. suppliers to gain market share in

Table 3.7
Potential U.S. Exports of Food and Agricultural Products to Cuba and Associated U.S. Job Gains (Three Scenarios)

	First Year of Partial Liberalization	After Five Years of Partial Liberalization	Unrestricted Trade
Export value ($ millions)	105	420	1,000
U.S. job gains	1,418	5,670	13,500

Source: Stern (2000).

Table 3.8
Potential U.S. Exports of Medical Products to Cuba and Associated U.S. Job Gains (Three Scenarios)

	First Year of Partial Liberalization	After Five Years of Partial Liberalization	Unrestricted Trade
Export value ($ millions)	6	24	600
U.S. job gains	81	324	8,100

Source: Stern (2000).

Table 3.9
Potential U.S. Exports of Food and Medical Products to Cuba and Associated U.S. Job Gains (Three Scenarios)

	First Year of Partial Liberalization	After Five Years of Partial Liberalization	Unrestricted Trade
Export value ($ millions)	111	$444	1,600
U.S. job gains	1,499	5,994	21,600

Source: Stern (2000).

Cuba. Market share estimates were based on average market shares of 60 to 70 percent for U.S. exports to other Caribbean countries.[19] The third scenario assumed unrestricted trade in both sectors, including the removal of credit and financing prohibitions, the use of approved intermediaries in both sectors, and the opening of all related sectors. This scenario explicitly recognized positive spillover potential from related industries, such as tourism.

As shown in Tables 3.7, 3.8, and 3.9, the estimated trade impacts in these sectors range from $400 million to $1 billion annually in agricultural exports and $20 million to $600 million in medical exports. In aggregate, this study finds that trading in these two sectors alone would generate as much as $444 million in U.S. exports and create as many as 6,000 U.S. jobs under partial liberalization, rising to highs of $1.6 billion in aggregate exports and 20,000 jobs under a complete lifting of restrictions.[20]

Even in these sectors, where significant gains (or losses) could be expected from the lifting of sanctions, the trade picture pales in comparison to some of the more important indirect impacts of sanctions on Cuba. We will discuss these effects next.

THE INDIRECT TRADE IMPACTS OF SANCTIONS ON CUBA AND THE UNITED STATES

Assessing the indirect trade impacts of U.S. sanctions on Cuba again involves analyzing two time periods: the era of Soviet support and the period after withdrawal of that support. We first address the contemporary period, then note the indirect trade impacts in the period under Soviet support.

Higher Costs of Trade and Consumption for Cuba

Sanctions on Cuba clearly have increased the costs of exports to the island since the Soviet withdrawal. One source of increased costs stems from removing the competition provided by U.S. suppliers, resulting in higher prices charged by alternative suppliers. Transportation costs are higher due to restrictions on shipping between Cuba and the United States within a 180-day window, effectively disrupting normal shipping patterns and requiring that special shipments be made solely to Cuba.[21] Borrowing costs also are higher because of the lack of access to U.S. financial institutions for funding. Nonmonetary costs to Cuban consumers take two forms: fewer goods and services from which to choose and frustration caused by lack of access to U.S. goods (identified in communications between the Cuban exile community in the United States and their friends and family on the island).

On the export side, Cuba is denied access to its natural market, the United States, the largest market in the world for many goods and services and the largest in the region for nearly all sectors of the economy. By denying Cuba the ability to sell to this large and wealthy market, U.S. sanctions effectively limit the ability of Cuban producers to operate at the efficient scale that only access to a large market like the United States can justify. Thus, the cost of goods produced for export by Cuba are higher than those produced elsewhere in the region by firms that can enjoy scale economies by selling to the United States. Similarly, since U.S. consumers are not competing to purchase Cuban-made goods, there is likely a dampening of prices for Cuban exports to other markets.

Diversion of Cuban Trade from the United States

During the period of Soviet support, the Soviet bloc and member countries of the Council for Mutual Economic Assistance (mostly Soviet-bloc nations, but also Mongolia and, until 1961, Albania) became Cuba's major trading partners, largely replacing all preembargo trade with the United States. Commerce in sugar and oil—Cuba's predominant export and import—was diverted to the Soviet bloc, with little or no loss in volume in either direction. Thanks to subsidies and preferential trading treatment, Cuba earned as much or more income from sugar exports to the Soviets as it had under the U.S. quota system.[22] Energy was procured at favorable rates as well, generally less than the market-based prices paid prior to 1960.

Despite assistance from the Soviet Union during the years 1960 to 1990, the Cuban economy remained small relative to its Latin American neighbors. Its economy depended directly on aid from, and subsidized trade with, the Soviet Union and its satellite states.

The one sector in which Cuba experienced net trade losses during the period of Soviet support was tourism, where lower-end Soviet tourists replaced premium-service travelers from the United States. In the late 1950s, some 300,000 U.S. tourists visited Cuba annually, but during the 1960–1990 period fewer than 30,000 Soviet-bloc tourists visited Cuba each year (ITC 2001). The withdrawal of U.S. tourism firms (and the reputed involvement of U.S.- based organized crime in the tourism and related entertainment trade) shifted the nature of Cuban tourism after the imposition of the U.S. embargo to a more basic, budget-conscious fare. Although some tourists from non-Soviet bloc countries continued to visit Cuba, the incomes generated in the sector declined in this period.

After the Soviet withdrawal in 1990, the Cuban government explicitly liberalized the tourism sector with the intention of attracting foreign investment to rejuvenate and upgrade tourism offerings. Like many nations in the region, Cuba boasts a tropical climate, lovely beaches, and marine resources for diving and fishing. However, given the fiercely competitive nature of tourism in the Caribbean basin region, particularly in better-developed, upscale tourist destinations such as Mexico and the Dominican Republic, Cuba has found itself severely disadvantaged in terms of its tourist infrastructure. Although the liberalization measures have had a positive impact on investment in the sector, producing growth in tourism receipts in the 1990s,[23] many observers note that Cuba's infrastructure and staff quality still are not on a par with better-known tourist destinations in the region. Statistics on return visits, length of stay, money spent during stays, and occupancy rates in Cuba all trail averages for the region as a whole (Crespo and Suddaby 2000).

Cuba has adopted an explicit trade policy of avoiding dependence on a particular trading partner (ITC 2001). As such, the country knowingly engages in trading relationships that may not be the most economically efficient (Jatar-Hausmann 1999). On the import side, Cuba has instituted policies aimed at promoting economic self-sufficiency, but these policies generally have been unsuccessful. Cuba remains dependent on external sources for most goods, although declining financial resources and limited access to credit produced a decline in merchandise imports from a 1990 level of $4.6 billion to a 1999 level of $3.99 billion (World Bank 2001). An oil pact with Venezuela fell apart in June 2002 (*Wall Street Journal* 2002a), leaving the island in the difficult position of having to further reduce domestic energy consumption (with obvious hardships for citizens) and thus dampen local production, particularly in energy-intensive sectors such as sugar refining.

Nor is the island self-sufficient in food production (Canadian Department of Foreign Affairs and International Trade 1999). Imports of basic grains, meat, and dairy products are required to satisfy even the meager caloric intake of Cuban citizens, and declines in agricultural output and productivity over the past decade point to a likely need for such imports well into the future.[24] Although Cuba's agricultural imports from the European Union were down in every category in 1998–99, they still were higher than 1990 levels (FAS 2000). Some agricultural imports take the form of donor aid from other countries, while the remainder use scarce foreign exchange resources.

Cuba is thought to be successful in trading with foreign firms to fill gaps in its domestic production that previously were filled by U.S. firms (Hufbauer et al. 1997). It is believed that there are few capital or other goods that Cuba is unable to acquire from sources outside the United States (Hamilton 1999).

In terms of exports, key sectors in Cuba have suffered from input scarcity (especially energy[25] and raw materials), depreciated and/or inefficient production processes, and climatic conditions (e.g., droughts and hurricanes), so overall production levels are down. Declines in production are borne largely by rationing domestic consumption (Trianis 2001) but are also reflected in falling export levels. From 1990 to 1999, Cuban merchandise exports dropped from $5.1 billion to $1.6 billion,[26] contributing to an overall trade deficit of more than $2.3 billion in 1999 (World Bank 2001).[27] Exports that would be targeted to the United States in the absence of sanctions are being diverted to other markets (albeit on potentially less favorable terms) and are not boosting local consumption.

The overall trade cost of sanctions to Cuba as estimated by the Institute for International Economics, including both direct and indirect impacts, is presented in Table 3.10. As Table 3.10 shows, Cuba's exports and imports are both down. Most imports that would be purchased from the United States are acquired elsewhere, not produced locally, but financial hardship and a general lack of access to credit make import purchases difficult for Cuba.

Displacement of U.S. Exports by Cuban Exports

The most compelling potential indirect trade consequences for the United States of sanctions against Cuba stem from the displacement of U.S. exports by Cuban exports in third-country markets. In sectors such as sugar, citrus, and possibly tourism, Cuba may be crowding out otherwise competitive U.S. producers.

Table 3.10
Estimated Economic Impact of U.S. Sanctions on Cuba (Annual Cost to Cuba in $)

1961–1973[a]	
Increased freight costs caused by ship blacklist policy	$50 million
Diversion of trade (welfare loss estimated at 10% of average annual value of trade with non-socialist economies) Reduction in purchasing power associated with shift in trade to countries with nonconvertible currencies (welfare loss estimated at 30% of total trade with those countries)	$400 million
Compensatory aid flows from U.S.S.R. (welfare gain estimated at 70% of transfers)	($270 million)
Average annual total, 1960–1973	$180 million
1975–1989	
Reduction in purchasing power associated with shift in trade to countries with nonconvertible currencies (welfare loss estimated at 30% of total trade)	$2,850 million
Compensatory aid flows from U.S.S.R. (welfare gain estimated at 70% of transfers)	($2,715 million)
Average annual total, 1975–1989	$135 million
Average annual total, 1961–1989	$150 million
1990–95	
Loss of trade due to U.S. embargo and Soviet collapse (welfare loss estimated at 30% drop in average annual value of trade in 1992–95 compared to 1985–87)	$3,200 million
Remittances from Cubans living abroad[b]	($350 million)
Average annual total, 1990–1995	$2,850 million

[a]Data for 1974 are excluded because a sudden increase in the world price for sugar sharply and temporarily increased the value of Cuban trade.
[b]Most remittances from the United States to Cuba are transferred illegally, and estimates of the total value range widely. The estimate used here is an average of "current transfers" for 1993–95 as reported by the National Bank of Cuba and could well include hard currency inflows from many other sources (for example, unrecorded loans or receipts from drug trafficking or money laundering). Assuming no offsetting dollar flows would raise the estimated cost as a percentage of Cuba's GNP to 15.8 percent but would not change the order of magnitude of the cost, which is well above the average for other cases.

INDIRECT NON-TRADE IMPACTS OF SANCTIONS ON CUBA

As we noted previously, the direct trade impact of sanctions on Cuba, although somewhat large relative to the size of the Cuban economy, is not as great as might be expected from such a sweeping embargo. This impact, however, is compounded by other factors inhibiting trade by, and investment in, the island nation. These inhibitors include productive capacity constraints, limited foreign investment, a lack of hard currency, and an explicit Cuban trade policy that favors dealing with a host of trading partners (Falcoff 2000; Seiglie 2001).

In sum, the loss of Cuba's "natural trading partner"[28] (Preeg 1999b) has repercussions beyond the direct trade impact estimated previously. Although the economic consequences of these indirect effects are hard to quantify, we shall outline the additional areas in which sanctions have affected Cuba.

Negative Impacts on Investment

While actual cases under Helms-Burton have been rare, the act does provide for extraterritorial sanctions against firms and individuals doing business in Cuba. Antidote laws in Canada, Mexico, and Cuba itself, along with EU moves in multilateral trading fora such as the WTO, have dampened the impact of Helms-Burton on foreign investments in Cuba.[29] Nonetheless, Helms-Burton undoubtedly has had somewhat of a chilling effect on foreign investment in Cuba by high-profile firms seeking favorable treatment in the United States (or in venues where the United States wields important influence, such as the World Bank).[30]

The Cuban domestic market is not very large, by world or even regional standards. Foreign direct investment in a country typically is influenced by (among other factors) access to a large domestic market or export markets easily serviced from that nation. In the absence of sanctions, Cuba could represent an obvious production platform for entering the U.S. market. Caribbean basin countries have used this argument successfully to promote foreign investment in key sectors such as textiles and data processing.

Furthermore, firms are recognizing the opportunities provided by enhanced regional integration for specialization and rationalization of production across the Americas. Tourism alone represents an important missed opportunity within this context, given high disposable incomes in Europe and geographic proximity that would allow a coupling of travel between Cuba and the United States for travelers from Europe and elsewhere if direct flights were available. Sanctions limiting trade and shipping between the United States and Cuba have thus taken Cuba out of contention for many investments in the region.

Even where investments have taken place in Cuba, lack of access to the U.S. market has deprived the island of offering the value-added activities that serve as an engine for enhanced economic growth. An illustrative example is the case of nickel. Canadian interests have invested heavily in nickel extraction in Cuba. The raw materials are exported to Canada, where they are processed for re-export to other countries as intermediate and finished goods. The United States imports nickel-based products from Canada, effectively diverting trade and thus value-added production from Cuba to Canada.

It is likely that these extra indirect costs to Cuban consumers will persist well into the future, since Cuba explicitly avoids relying on a single (or a few) trading partners. The Castro regime has made it clear that it is willing to pay a higher price for imports (and/or earn a lower price for exports) in pursuit of this trade diversification dictum.[31]

Strategic Costs: Denying Cuba Full Advantage from Its Investments in Development

Perhaps the greatest cost of sanctions borne by Cuba stems from the vast investments the nation has made in higher education and health care. In keeping with its socialist philosophy, the country has allocated scarce funds to encourage advances in medicine and train professionals in a variety of sectors, particularly medicine. Given the market potential presented by rising health care costs in the United States, sanctions have eliminated opportunities for Cuba to reap direct commercial rewards for its cumulative investments. Ironically, areas in which Cuba has demonstrated a global competitive advantage through investment prioritization are also areas with significant market needs in the United States—a trading opportunity that sanctions preclude.

In a related vein, Cuban enterprises (state-owned or otherwise) are denied access to resources from potential commercial/strategic partners in the United States. Since all firms possess unique complements of resources, technologies, and talents, many optimum partners for Cuban enterprises likely reside within the United States. Sanctions deny firms in both countries the fruits of collaboration among enterprises with synergistic resources.

Benefits to Cuba of U.S. Sanctions

It is wrong to conclude that U.S. sanctions work only to the detriment of Cuba and, in particular, the political needs of the Castro regime. For a government facing an increasingly discontented public, the opportunity to point to U.S. economic sanctions as the root of all problems is a welcome benefit. Many observers in the United States as well as representatives of dissident groups within Cuba claim that the ability of the Castro regime to blame society's ills on U.S. sanctions causes far more harm to the United States than the direct or other indirect impacts of sanctions.

Furthermore, by inciting feelings of sorrow and familial obligation, U.S. sanctions have prompted the diaspora to send a considerable amount of money, denominated in dollars, to Cuba. Some have estimated that annual remittances exceed $1 billion per year (Jatar-Hausmann 1999), an important amount of funding for the Cuban economy that has an obvious dampening effect on sanctions (the direct trade loss effects are roughly equivalent in size).[32] Without the economic hardship suffered under sanctions, it is likely that these funds from abroad would diminish—remittances were a fraction of today's levels during the Soviet subsidy period, when the Cuban economy was growing. Remittances are viewed by the diaspora as charitable acts in support of beleaguered family members and friends in the homeland (Council on Foreign Relations 1999). Such charity could be replaced by direct investment in a non-sanctioned Cuba. More immediately, though, if the lifting of sanctions allows for economic prosperity on the island, remittances from the diaspora will not be needed.

INDIRECT EFFECTS OF SANCTIONS ON THE UNITED STATES

In addition to the direct trade impacts of sanctions on the U.S. economy, there are additional effects that warrant discussion. We summarize these effects in this chapter.

Market Lockout

Sanctions clearly have directly curtailed U.S. private investment in Cuba and likely will dampen investment prospects for U.S. firms long after they are lifted. As we noted previously, economic problems in Cuba, particularly in the post-Soviet period, reduced investments in infrastructure and productive capacity. Physical infrastructure, power generation, and telecommunications are hungry for investment in Cuba and are areas in which U.S. firms have demonstrated a competitive advantage. However, strategic windows exist for investment in these sectors. Once foreign firms have entered the Cuban market, U.S. firms will be effectively closed out from current opportunities (Preeg 1998). The impact will linger in the form of exclusion from participating in follow-up projects, supplying replacement parts, and so on.

A similar phenomenon can be expected in the tourism sector. Once premium locations are purchased by foreign firms, U.S. businesses will be playing a catch-up game that will be very challenging given the correlation between choice location and occupancy/profitability. Concerns also may arise due to U.S. firms being characterized as potentially unreliable suppliers, with long-lasting implications (Kittredge 1999).

U.S. firms' business opportunities in Cuba after sanctions are lifted will also be limited by lost learning opportunities. Foreign firms currently active in Cuba are helping to shape the economic environment through their dealings with upstream and downstream enterprises and relations with key players in the market. These foreign firms are taking risks that will be repaid through customer and supplier loyalty in the future. They are also learning what makes for a successful endeavor in the unique market that is Cuba—learning how to deal with heavy state participation, an inadequate infrastructure, scarce resources, and the psyche of the Cuban consumer. This intimate yet tacit knowledge of a market's conditions requires firms to make significant investments in time and other resources. It is difficult at best (and often impossible) to jump this learning curve upon entering a market, despite the resources or other strengths a U.S. firm might bring to the table. Thus, U.S. firms likely will suffer the consequences of nonengagement in Cuba well beyond their initial forays into the market.

U.S. firms are also locked out of opportunities in other markets as a result of sanctions against doing business with Cuba. Preeg (1999b) points to the example of U.S. firms not being able to bid on projects for airline maintenance that require pan-regional service coverage to qualify for bidding. In this case, U.S. firms must walk away from potentially significant non-Cuban business since they cannot legally provide seamless service coverage to the tendering organization. A similar case involves Florida-based Gruman Worldwide Limited, which cannot service its clients abroad that are seeking assistance in collecting commercial debts in Cuba (USCTEC 2000).

Another aspect of sanctions that has a negative effect on U.S. firms concerns research and development (R&D) trajectories. In many industries, global research consortia have been created to allow for economies of scale and scope as well as specialization in innovation. Global R&D teams within and across organizations are becoming the norm for a wide range of product and process innovations. In certain industries, perhaps most notably biotechnology,[33] pharmaceuticals, organic agriculture, and food production, comparative R&D advantages exist in both the United States and Cuba for a whole range of treatments and other innovations. By restricting collaboration among organizations actively pursuing these innovations, U.S. sanctions may be preventing U.S. firms from developing important new products. At the most extreme level, prohibiting such collaboration among Cuban and U.S. firms may jeopardize human (or animal or plant) health on a global scale by reducing the likelihood of treatment discovery.

Piracy and Other Intellectual Property Rights Violations

The United States produces products (such as software) that are recognized global leaders in their sectors (e.g., Microsoft's Windows operating system). It is in the best interests of the United States to ensure the continuity of such leadership by U.S. firms. However, given the embargo on sales of such products to Cuba, U.S. policy effectively promotes the illegal copying of protected goods. Cuba refuses to support intellectual property violation claims for these goods in light of the embargo.[34]

Subsidiary Fire Sales

From 1963 to 1975 and again since 1992, U.S. sanctions against Cuba have applied as well to U.S. subsidiaries located overseas. Many subsidiaries were actively doing business with Cuba prior to the imposition of sanctions, putting their parent companies in a difficult situation when the sanctions took effect. Their holdings of these subsidiaries suddenly were illegal, forcing them to conduct a sort of "fire sale." Many foreign competitors were able to purchase the subsidiaries at prices well below their fair market value.

Loss of Prestige and Global Leadership

The United States has suffered politically on the world stage as a result of sanctions imposed against Cuba. Of particular note in this regard is the extraterritoriality provision of Helms-Burton, which runs counter to well-established international law. In international venues such as the United Nations and the World Trade Organization, the United States has consistently received little or no support for its sanctions policy, even from traditional allies. What makes the extraterritorial application of sanctions (or the threat of same) by the United States particularly egregious is the fact that the United States has argued against such actions by other states, as in the case of the Arab League's boycott of Israel (Bergsten 1998).

Global leadership by the United States is further strained by its unilateral stance on Cuba. The National Association of

Manufacturers' position on the imposition of unilateral economic sanctions echoes this concern: "[The United States's] resort to unilateral sanctions can only be explained in terms of a failure of leadership and a subsequent decision—in light of that failure—to go it alone" (NAM 1999).

Another inconsistency in U.S. sanctions policy is the continued listing of Cuba as a state-sponsored terrorist nation, despite no evidence of such acts by Cuba in recent years. By retaining Cuba on this list, the United States provides no incentive for active state sponsors of terrorism to mend their ways (Haass and O'Sullivan 2000). Critics point out that the United States has granted normalized trading status to Vietnam and China despite claims and/or records of limits on democracy and restricted human rights (Erickson 2002). Proponents of normalized relations with those nations argued that closer engagement was needed to demonstrate the benefits of democracy and human rights protection to citizens and leaders in those countries. One wonders why such arguments are not employed more effectively in the case of Cuba.[35] As Richard Haass of the Brookings Institution argues, "American dollars, tourists and ideas constitute a greater threat to Fidel Castro and communism in Cuba than the embargo" (Haass 1998).

A further apparent inconsistency in U.S. policy concerns the requirement that democracy be restored in Cuba as a condition of normalizing relations. It is commonly understood in a democracy that each citizen has a political voice through the right to vote in local, regional, and national elections. However, arcane districting rules as well as voting systems in effect at state and national levels have created a situation in the United States whereby organized and vocal minorities can effect policy choices that support their interests at the expense of majority opinion. Such is the case with the Cuban diaspora, composed largely of (aging) exiles with significant confiscation claims from property abandoned in Cuba or nationalized prior to their departure. This group, concentrated in South Florida, uses districting and voting rules to its advantage to press for retention of the embargo against Cuba. Despite its relatively small numbers and the fact that its stance runs counter to majority opinion in the nation (and, for that matter, in the state of Florida),[36] the diaspora has been successful in countering the basic tenets of democracy in promoting its self-interest.[37] The political leaders of the United States, by allowing this breach of basic democratic principles, have created a credibility deficit with respect to demanding democracy for Cuba.

Despite public statements by the Castro regime rejecting any retrenchment of socialist ideals and principles for Cuba (*Wall*

Street Journal 2002b; Sandza and Remy 2002), most observers believe that some form of political and economic transition will occur in Cuba—either under Castro or, more likely, upon his death or cession of power. Countries like Canada (Boehm 2002) have recognized the importance of working with Cuba now to plan for transition by providing assistance and training to shape the Cuban state administratively (and, potentially, politically and economically). Canada has long provided such training and aid with the objective of forging an enduring partnership with, if not playing a future leadership role in, Cuba. The United States, on the other hand, lacks such leverage. In summary we quote William Ratliff and Roger Fontaine (2000), who argue that "[U.S. sanctions policy toward Cuba is] so cluttered with contradictions and inconsistencies it has become a dishonest, embarrassing and pernicious policy unworthy of the United States."

Avoiding Bad Loans: A Small Blessing for U.S. Firms

One clear, positive impact of sanctions for U.S. firms stems from restrictions on lending by U.S. financial institutions to Cuba. Given the suspension of debt payments by Cuba in 1986 and the country's inability to fully reschedule or renegotiate with the Paris Club, the likelihood of satisfactory resolution of claims by financial institutions against Cuba is low. U.S. sanctions thus insulated U.S. financial institutions from what likely would have been a large-scale loss on bad debts in Cuba.

THIRD-COUNTRY IMPACTS OF U.S. SANCTIONS AGAINST CUBA

Many of the impacts of U.S. sanctions against Cuba are felt beyond the confines of the bilateral relationship. Threats (and, occasionally, actual cases) of extraterritorial application of sanctions under Helms-Burton are perhaps the most prominent of these third-country impacts. We now highlight some of the more important impacts for particular countries.

Caribbean Basin Countries

The Caribbean basin countries are both blessed and cursed with sunshine and proximity to the United States. Although favorable climates produce ideal conditions for growing tropical products (e.g., sugar, citrus, bananas, coffee, and tobacco) and attracting tourists, geography dictates that these nations are endowed with largely similar resources. Other similarities, especially in cultural and political legacies, have resulted in common development paths focused on a reliance on monocrop exports (and, in countries like Cuba, Jamaica, and Trinidad & Tobago, mineral extraction). The imposition of trade sanctions on Cuba, a relatively large nation in the region, lessened competition for U.S. markets (and U.S. aid dollars) among Cuba's neighbors. Should sanctions on Cuba be lifted, its Caribbean neighbors have the most to lose—especially in tourism and agriculture. Of particular importance to many of these countries would be the redistribution of the U.S. sugar import quota, which would directly and immediately curtail their export earnings in this already beleaguered sector (Council on Foreign Relations 1999).

Major Trade Partners

Major exporters to Cuba that might be displaced by the United States if sanctions are lifted include Spain, Venezuela, Canada, France, and China. Meanwhile, chief importers of Cuban goods—Russia, Canada, the Netherlands, Spain, France, China, and Japan—might have to pay higher costs for these products or find alternative suppliers (CIA 1999). An assessment of potential market share/value shifts is beyond the scope of this exposition, however.

Investor Nations

Nations that have made investments in Cuba in sectors geared toward exports to the United States—including big investors in tourism, agriculture, and cement production, such as Mexico, Canada, Australia, South Africa, Italy, Spain, and the Netherlands—stand to gain the most from the lifting of sanctions against Cuba. Secondary benefits would be enjoyed by firms in sectors benefiting from spillovers from U.S. export sectors (upstream and downstream industries).

Exile Community Linkages

An open question concerns the potential role of the Cuban exile community in trading relations should sanctions be lifted. Other than the United States, Venezuela and Spain have the largest Cuban diaspora communities. It is possible that with further involvement by the U.S.-based exile community in the Cuban economy, heritage links could benefit Venezuela and Spain as well.

We now turn our attention to conclusions we have drawn regarding the effectiveness of U.S. sanctions against Cuba.

THE EFFECTIVENESS OF U.S. SANCTIONS AGAINST CUBA

In our introduction, we argued for a disjunction of sanctions history in 1990 to reflect the involvement of the Soviet Union in the Cuban economy and Cuban affairs and, later, its withdrawal. This disjunction is particularly important when assessing the effectiveness of sanctions. For our purposes here, we argue that an effective sanction is one that, at a minimum, produces the intended result.

In the 1960–1990 period, the stated objective of U.S. sanctions policy toward Cuba was to contain the threat and spread of communism in the Western Hemisphere. Given the fact that every country in the Americas practices some form of democratic rule, the pre-1990 sanctions appear to have accomplished their objective (Council on Foreign Relations 1999). Furthermore, the Soviet Union was believed to be spending half its foreign aid on Cuba, and this resource drain may have precipitated its fall and helped usher in democracy in the Soviet bloc.

Once the Soviet Union collapsed, many (if not most) observers believed that a socialist Cuba's days were numbered. But national solidarity, coupled with policy flexibility, allowed Cuba to weather the storm in the "Special Period" following the fall of the Soviet Union. The survival of the Castro regime and a socialist economic model in Cuba in the absence of Soviet support required a reassessment of U.S. sanctions policy. U.S. policymakers shifted gears, calling for a return to democracy in Cuba and, subsequently, protection of human rights as the "new" objectives of sanctions against Cuba. An emerging form of "state capitalism" in Cuba, whereby limited economic activity is permitted to ensure the populace's (and the Castro regime's) survival, appears to be holding its own. As recently as June 2002, Castro publicly declared, "Today we are taking another oath . . . that we shall be unshakably faithful to the homeland, the revolution and to socialism, that imperialist domination and the capitalist system shall never return to Cuba" (*Wall Street Journal* 2002b).

Most Americans believe the embargo against Cuba to have failed in reaching its stated objectives. The debate over the effectiveness of post-1990 sanctions on Cuba hinges on perceptions of whether sanctions, normalized relations, or enhanced engagement is most likely to produce a smooth, nonviolent transition to democracy in Cuba. U.S. policy elsewhere in the world, such as in China and Vietnam, favors enhanced engagement for achieving democratic ends. Canada (among other countries) has chosen engagement with Cuba and is providing training and assistance to help shape and promote a transition to a democratic Cuba. Former U.S. President Jimmy Carter, along with many business, academic, and political observers, has called for the United States to adopt similar measures. The success of the Cuban exile lobby in promoting a continued embargo has ensured that U.S. policy toward Cuba is unique in its insistence on a full return to democracy prior to lifting sanctions.

Remittances, provided largely by the Cuban exile community to friends and family in Cuba, help explain the Cuban economy's staying power. Partly as a result, however, a dual economy has emerged in Cuba, creating extreme social tensions that are likely to produce one of two results. The first scenario envisions a crackdown on economic liberalization to reduce disparities; the second involves some sort of violent overthrow pitting dollarized "haves" against peso-strapped "have nots." Given these scenarios, it appears that some sort of normalized relationship is in the best interest of the United States.

Possible Areas for Normalization

Property Claims

Normalizing relations with Cuba will necessitate resolving a significant sticking point: claims by U.S. corporations and citizens for properties nationalized or confiscated after the 1959 revolution. The Cuban government estimates these claims to amount to roughly 50 years' worth of exports by Cuba (Jatar-Hausmann 1999), while the United States Foreign Claims Settlement Commission values the 5,911 certified claims at $1.85 billion, which includes a permitted interest accrual of 6 percent per annum (USCTEC 2001c). The Cuban government has settled claims raised in other countries[38] but argues that the negative economic effects of sanctions (which it estimates at $67 billion) must be offset against U.S. property claims. The Cuban American National Foundation (the pro-embargo lobby representing Cuban exiles) has stated publicly that private claims of houses can be released, but all commercial claims must be resolved (Hays 2002). An informal market reportedly is emerging in South Florida for buying claim rights of aging Cuban exiles at steep discounts, effectively monetizing these claims (Sanguinetty 2002).

The situation appears ripe for some sort of brokering of key interests between the exile community, which seeks compensation for confiscated property, and the Cuban government, which wants to attract foreign investment and technology. A mechanism whereby joint enterprise rights to former commercial holdings would be granted to former property owners might provide the currency needed to effect a workable solution on the property claims question.

The joint enterprise rights would provide partial ownership of former commercial holdings that would become effective only upon rights holders investing a stipulated amount of capital, technology, or other valuable resources to the venture controlling the property. Claimants could sell their joint enterprise rights to the highest bidder in an open market. Cuba would gain infusions of capital and other important resources needed to reinvigorate lagging industry as well as create opportunities for new enterprise development. As a nod to the need for human rights protection, a further stipulation might be the incorporation of some level of privatization for these joint enterprises, with potential entrepreneurial promotion within Cuba.[39] This sort of policy initiative to normalize economic relations with Cuba may be sufficient to satisfy the lingering concerns of the Cuban exile community in the United States.

Travel and Tourism

Cuba welcomes visitors from the United States who spend dollars in the country. An inevitable result of travel by U.S. citizens in Cuba is an exchange of ideas and experiences. Travel by professionals could promote the exchange of important information in areas such as biotechnology and organic agriculture, to the benefit of both nations. By allowing for greater interaction between Americans and Cubans, a fuller understanding of each other's economy and society is likely to result. Common middle ground might be discovered—for example, the U.S. position could be modified to allow for an economic model in Cuba that arguably is capitalistic and perhaps, to a certain extent, democratic while relying heavily on socialist principles. Such hybrid models already exist in Scandinavian countries allied with the United States.

We conclude that although the direct trade impact of sanctions on the United States and Cuba is small, many indirect effects will likely stay with both countries for a long time to come. For the United States, Cuba will always remain a fairly insignificant trading partner in absolute terms, though certain sectors (such as agriculture) could stand to gain significantly from access to the Cuban market. Despite the limited importance of trade considerations, the costs to U.S. political leadership in the region and beyond as well as the potential security interests in the region would indicate a need for the United States to consider normalizing relations with Cuba.

The Cuban people clearly have a lot to gain from normalized trading relations with the United States. Cheaper, more varied, and higher-quality imported products would enhance the public welfare. Export sales to a lucrative market such as the United States would provide Cuba with more resources to fund economic development. Given the current regime's adherence to an economic model that has not succeeded in producing economic prosperity and a stated policy of avoiding dependence on a single trading partner (even when such a partner represents the most viable and economically advantageous trading opportunities), it is questionable whether the potential economic gains from lifting sanctions would in fact be enjoyed by Cuba.

Despite rhetoric and some actions to the contrary, Cuba is creeping toward market-based economic organization. Whether the island is successful in fleshing out its emerging form of state capitalism in terms of providing prosperity and growth remains to be seen. In the interim, economic hardships suffered by its citizens are conveniently attributed to U.S. sanctions, easing the regime's ability to maintain control over the economy and society (Haass 1999).

NOTES

The authors wish to acknowledge the capable research assistance of Anne Ruppel in preparing this chapter.

1. From 1964 to 1975, the Organization of American States membership also imposed economic sanctions against Cuba. Other than this limited period of multilateral involvement, the United States has been alone in imposing sanctions against Cuba.

2. Preeg (1999b) notes that the Reagan administration's policy pressured the Soviet Union by "forcing higher levels of Soviet defense, foreign aid, and counterinsurgency expenditures to the point of internal and external financial crisis."

3. The International Trade Commission (2001) describes the dual economy as "the two Cuban pesos." The domestic peso floats at a value of roughly 20 to the dollar (versus 150 to the dollar in 1993 during the "Special Period"). Domestic pesos may not be legally exported from Cuba and are not convertible. The official peso is convertible at a fixed 1:1 exchange rate with the dollar and is used for government accounting and transactions, insulating Cuba from external shocks. Cubans are now legally permitted to own and use foreign currencies, including the preferred U.S. dollar, which circulates alongside the peso for most transactions and can be used to denominate bank accounts. The only sources of

foreign currency in the economy are remittances from abroad and transactions by self-employed individuals who are licensed (and specifically taxed) to transact with foreigners.

4. Cuba is estimated to have paid between 18 percent and 22 percent interest for six- to twelve-month trade financing of imports in 2000, in addition to pledging collateral of Cuban assets in Cuba and abroad (USCTEC 2000).

5. Prior to the period of Soviet support, Cuba specialized in sugar production as the holder of the lion's share of the U.S. sugar import quota. This quota allowed protected sales of sugar into the United States at prices well above the world standard at the time.

6. Although beyond the scope of this chapter, observers have noted inconsistencies in official Cuban statistics on the capital account (cf. Morris, 2000). Betancourt (2000) provides a cogent and potentially convincing analysis of the level of ECLAC-reported data on remittances and concludes that such a figure is unreasonably high given the number and incomes of Cuban exiles living abroad. He credits the discrepancy to a concerted effort by Cuban officials (and Fidel Castro individually) to plug the balance-of-payment gap in Cuba with funds received through drug trafficking and subsequent money laundering. Morris (2000) provides an alternative (or potentially compatible) conclusion on the discrepancy—individuals earning funds illegally in the informal tourist trade cite remittances from friends and family abroad as the source of said funds. Betancourt (2000) cites a well-documented demographic study of Cuban exiles by Sergio Diaz-Briquets (1994) that posits remittances at an annual high of $300–400 million and indicates that since the total number of immigrants has not changed significantly since 1994, these estimates should be roughly accurate today. Given that level of remittances, a disparity of between $400 million and $500 million remains. Whether such a large sum could be attributed to informal tourist sector receipts when official tourism receipts totaled $1.9 billion in 1999 is open to debate and will require further empirical work to substantiate.

7. The European Union is also reported to be considering targeted tariffs on exports from the state of Florida—a form of "smart sanction" against the home state of the Cuban exile community that supports Helms-Burton.

8. The number of members of the Cuba Working Group had grown to 44 by June 2002, as follows: Neil Abercrombie (Hawaii), Tammy Baldwin (Wis.), Howard Berman (Calif.), Marion Berry (Ark.), John Boozman (Ark.), Kevin Brady (Texas), Dave Camp (Mich.), William Clay (Mo.), Peter DeFazio (Ore.), William Delahunt (Mass.), Cal Dooley (Calif.), Jo Ann Emerson (Mo.), Sam Farr (Calif.), Jeff Flake (Ariz.), Sam Graves (Mo.), Wally Herger (Calif.), Tim Johnson (Ill.), Ray LaHood (Ill.), Nick Lampson (Texas), Jim Leach (Iowa), Stephen Lynch (Mass.), Jim McGovern (Mass.), Jerry Moran (Kan.), George Nethercutt (Wash.), Tom Osborne (Neb.), Butch Otter (Idaho), Ron Paul (Texas), Collin Peterson (Minn.), Jim Ramstad (Minn.), Charles Rangel (N.Y.), Dennis Rehberg (Mont.), Tim Roemer (Ind.), Mike Ross (Ark.), Paul Ryan (Wis.), Chris Shays (Conn.), John Shimkus (Ill.), Nick Smith (Mich.), Vic Snyder (Ark.), Hilda Solis (Calif.),

Charlie Stenholm (Texas), John Tanner (Tenn.), Mike Thompson (Calif.), John Thune (S.D.), Edolphus Towns (N.Y.).

9. Erickson (2002) reports that the American Farm Bureau Federation estimates losses in agricultural exports to Cuba are equal to 14 percent of the export market for rice, 10 percent for wheat, 5 percent for vegetable oil and barley, and 4 percent for corn.

10. The Cuban expatriate community in the United States is estimated at 580,000 individuals over 15 years of age (Betancourt 2000).

11. Jose Miguel Vivanco, executive director of Human Rights Watch's Americas Division, has stated, "The embargo (against Cuba) has become counterproductive to the promotion of human rights" (Vivanco 2000).

12. According to the Cuba Policy Foundation, a nonpartisan group of former Foreign Service officials who served under Republican administrations, U.S. public opinion is decidedly in favor of easing or eliminating restrictions on Cuba. By a 63–33 margin, Americans interviewed in a 2001 independent poll said they believe lifting the embargo would best promote democratic transition in Cuba. A Florida International University poll in 2000 found that even a majority (84 percent) of Cuban-Americans in South Florida believe the U.S. embargo against Cuba has failed (Cuba Policy Foundation 2002).

13. Assessing the potential impact of lifting sanctions on sugar imports is difficult because the United States imports sugar under a strict quota system. Although Cuba held the lion's share of the pre-embargo U.S. sugar quota, it is uncertain whether existing quota commitments would be reallocated to Cuba from other trading partners.

14. The Trade Sanctions Reform and Export Enhancement Act of 2000 explicitly excludes extending credit for food and medicine purchases, effectively nullifying this relaxation of sanctions against Cuba.

15. Prior to 1960, Cuba's dominant trading partner was the United States. From 1960–90, it was the Soviet bloc.

16. A 1997 study by the European-American Business Council, based on a survey of 42 multinational corporations, pointed explicitly to Helms-Burton extraterritoriality provisions as limiting FDI in Cuba (EABC 1997). The Canada Trade and Economic Section of the Canadian Embassy in Cuba echoes this finding in its publication, *Cuba: A Guide for Canadian Business* (CTES 2001).

17. Toricelli (1998) argues that a fairer assessment of the effectiveness of the embargo against Cuba would utilize an effective sanctions start date of 1993, when the Cuban Democracy Act's restrictions against U.S. subsidiaries operating abroad took effect. He cites a figure of $500 million in annual trade with Cuba by American companies operating from their bases in Europe. The U.S. Treasury Department estimated an average of $260 million per year between 1982 and 1987 (*Journal of Commerce* 1990).

18. Toricelli (1998) refers to estimates of $15–20 billion in economic costs from all U.S. embargoes as somewhat insignificant given the $3 trillion spent by the United States to win the Cold War. "Frankly, in the Senate, we call that (cost level) a rounding error," he said.

19. The study uses the more conservative figure of 60 percent as contrasted with pre-embargo market share in agriculture of 70 percent or Cuban government estimates of between 33 percent and 50 percent. For medical products, the Caribbean average of 60 percent of import market share held by U.S. firms is deemed eventually attainable in Cuba as well (Stern 2000).

20. A recent Agriculture Department report speaks to opportunities for agricultural trade with Cuba. Given credit restrictions currently in place on such trade, coupled with Cuba's low purchasing power, scarce access to hard currency, and exclusion from many sources of credit, the United States may find itself at a competitive disadvantage compared to countries that provide credit and donor assistance to agricultural exporters to Cuba (Department of Agriculture 2000).

21. John Hamilton, principal deputy assistant secretary, Bureau of Western Hemisphere Affairs, U.S. Department of State, estimated in 1999 that shipping costs increases for Cuba resulting from the embargo were in the 5 to 10 percent range (Hamilton 1999).

22. The Soviet Union was reported to have paid five times the world price for Cuban sugar in 1983 (IIE 2001).

23. Gross tourism earnings have climbed steadily, from $204 million in 1989 to $1.9 billion in 1999. These figures are based on official statistics that grossly underestimate economic activity in the informal tourism sector. Disaggregating remittances from incomes earned in this informal sector is difficult at best (Morris 2000).

24. Compared to a base index of 100 for 1989–1991, Cuba's agricultural output and productivity experienced sharp declines in the 1998–2000 period as shown in the following indices: crop production index, 54.5; food production index, 58.2; livestock production index, 63.6 (World Bank 2001).

25. Hernandez-Cata (2000) notes a strong correlation between Cuban productive output and power consumption.

26. The Economist Intelligence Unit (2002) estimates total 1990 exports at $5.4 billion and 1999 exports at $1.47 billion.

27. The decline in Cuban exports during the 1990s is explained largely by severe drops in sugar receipts, from $3.9 billion in 1989 to $504 million in 1999. Exports of minerals (mainly nickel) also declined in this period, but tobacco and seafood both posted gains (Morris 2000).

28. References to the United States as Cuba's "natural trading partner" are echoed by most analyses and commentaries concerning sanctions (see also Weintraub 2000). This label is supported by the gravity model methodology most commonly employed to gauge the direct impact of sanctions on bilateral trade. Given the mere 90-mile distance between the United States and Cuba (geographic distance is a key predictor of bilateral trade in gravity models), large-scale trade between the two nations is to be expected. When coupled with widespread complements in productive capability between the two countries (as contrasted with productive capability redundancies between Cuba and many of its regional neighbors), the label "natural trading partner" is warranted.

29. The U.S.–Cuba Trade and Economic Council (2002) reports that 34 of the 50 companies on the PriceWaterhouseCoopers annual list of the "World's Most Respected Companies" have some sort of presence (defined as products/services directly or indirectly available or an office, representative, joint venture, economic association, administrative agreement, or other commercial activity) in Cuba. Half of the 34 companies cited are headquartered in the United States.

30. A 1997 study by the European-American Business council based on a survey of 42 multinational corporations explicitly pointed to Helms-Burton extraterritoriality as limiting FDI in Cuba (EABC 1997). The Canada Trade and Economic Section of the Canadian Embassy in Cuba echoes this finding in its publication, *Cuba: A Guide for Canadian Business* (CTES 2001).

31. A CNN (2000) report quoted Cuban Foreign Trade Minister Raul de la Nunez as saying, "It makes no sense for us to buy rice from Asia when we could buy it from the United States (but) . . . we hope to have diversified trade . . . I think there is room for everyone."

32. It is important to note that others have questioned this scale of remittances (based on ECLAC figures), as it would require each and every Cuban exile to remit more than $1,000 annually. Furthermore, based on a 20:1 exchange rate, this figure would be far greater than total government revenues and more than the Cuban government might allow. Observers have cautioned that perhaps remittances are being cited to cover funding from drug and money laundering operations in Cuba (Betancourt 2000).

33. Since 1981, Cuba has committed roughly 1 percent of GNP to its biotechnology initiative under the National Center for Scientific Research, or Centro Nacional de Investigacion Cientifica (Ramkissoon 2001).

34. As of 1 June 2001, approximately 4,000 U.S.-owned trademarks were registered in Cuba of a total of 60,000 trademarks registered in the island republic (USCTEC 2001b).

35. The Council on Foreign Relations notes areas of potentially valuable collaboration between the United States and Cuba, including fighting drug trafficking and money laundering and protecting the regional environmental protection (Council on Foreign Relations 1999).

36. See Note 12.

37. Rich Kaplowitz (1998) provides an informative account of the influence wielded by the Cuban American National Foundation in national electoral politics, based upon data provided by the Center for Responsive Politics.

38. In July 1997, the ITT Corporation, a U.S. firm, sold 10-year usage rights to STET International (a Netherlands-based subsidiary of Telecom Italia S.p.A.) for telecommunications infrastructure it owned in Cuba. This transaction, corresponding to a certified claim of $130.7 million, is evidence of the novel ways U.S. claimants are garnering some returns on confiscated properties. This case is currently more the exception than the rule in Cuba, however (USCTEC 2000).

39. The Arcos Principles that spell out the mechanisms for supporting human rights in labor practices might provide a blueprint for satisfying U.S. concerns over human rights protection (Council on Foreign Relations 1999).

Appendixes

Appendix 3.1
Cuba's Composition of Trade, 1993-98 ($ Millions)

	1993	1994	1995	1996	1997	1998
Exports						
Sugar, molasses, honey	820	785	855	1,095	920	720
Nickel	170	190	345	450	445	380
Fish	90	110	115	125	125	120
Tobacco	75	85	95	100	140	170
Medicinal products	20	110	45	55	50	30
Fruit	50	80	45	55	60	55
Other	100	110	135	120	130	250
Total	1,325	1,470	1,635	2,000	1,870	1,725
Imports						
Fuels	750	750	835	1,060	1,100	700
Foodstuffs	490	430	560	645	625	625
Machinery	235	245	410	500	580	710
Semi-finished goods	180	225	390	425	410	445
Chemicals	160	190	300	275	295	265
Consumer goods	50	85	135	170	190	245
Transport equipment	80	115	105	140	155	155
Raw materials	35	25	85	100	85	90
Other	20	20	25	40	50	45
Totals	2,000	2,085	2,845	3,355	3,490	3,280
Trade Deficit	675	615	1,210	1,355	1,620	1,555

Source: CIA (1999).

Appendix 3.2
Cuba's Exports by Country of Destination, 1993–98 ($ Millions)

	1993	1994	1995	1996	1997	1998
Algeria	49	31	50	19	4	—
Argentina	2	48	7	8	4	7
Australia	0	3	3	2	3	3
Austria	2	3	1	1	1	1
Bahrain	0	0	0	1		
Belgium/Luxembourg	5	7	7	8	5	5
Bolivia	0	0	0	2	2	1
Brazil	10	57	40	32	22	7
Canada	133	143	234	294	255	220
Chile	0	0	1	1	1	1
China	74	121	214	138	100	94
Colombia	3	14	23	21	28	19
Costa Rica	4	7	0	2	0	—
Croatia	0	6	11	5	0	2
Cyprus	1	0	1	0	1	9
Czech Republic	1	0	1	1	1	1
Denmark	1	1	1	1	0	1
Ecuador	0	1	9		1	2

Appendix 3.2 (continued)
Cuba's Exports by Country of Destination, 1993–98 ($ Millions)

	1993	1994	1995	1996	1997	1998
Egypt	1	83	41	16	76	—
El Salvador	0	1	3	0	0	—
Finland	18	21	5	0	0	7
France	39	44	57	50	48	53
Germany	14	25	31	22	26	25
Greece	0	0	0	0	1	0
Guatemala	1	1	1	2	4	1
Honduras	0	0	0	2	1	2
Hong Kong	1	1	2	2	8	9
India	4	3	5	6	6	—
Ireland	2	1	1	2	1	1
Italy	33	50	54	38	19	13
Jamaica	1	0	3	2	4	—
Japan	51	63	89	67	109	39
Latvia	—	14	0	11	4	—
Macau	0	0	0	0	1	—
Malaysia	0	7	0	0	0	0
Mexico	4	12	6	23	36	28
Morocco	1	1	0	0	0	—
Netherlands	89	101	172	230	264	253
New Zealand	0	0	0	0	0	1
Nicaragua	3	1	1	2	1	1
Norway	0	1	0	0	0	1
Peru	1	1	1	2	1	1
Poland	1	1	1	2	1	2
Portugal	35	48	24	12	30	17
Romania	8	17	37	63	18	10
Russia	436	301	225	406	352	430
Saudi Arabia	0	0	0	1	—	—
Serbia/Montenegro	—	—	—	34	1	—
Singapore	0	0	1	2	3	7
Slovakia	—	0	0	0	1	0
Slovenia	5	5	0	0	0	0
South Africa	0	4	0	0	0	1
Spain	65	78	96	132	124	134
Sweden	5	1	2	4	3	4
Switzerland	7	8	11	11	14	18
Syria	—	—	5	14	9	—
Taiwan	0	3	1	1	1	2
Thailand	0	0	0	0	1	1
Tunisia	10	8	11	13	11	17
Turkey	0	0	0	9	0	0
United Kingdom	13	16	13	30	25	26
Uruguay	0	6	5	1	0	1
Venezuela	3	5	2	2	5	2
Others	0	0	0	0	0	0
Total	1,325	1,470	1,635	2,000	1,870	1,725

Appendix 3.3
Cuba's Imports by Sending Country, 1993–98 ($ Millions)

	1993	1994	1995	1996	1997	1998
Algeria	1	0	1	0	0	—
Argentina	72	48	65	125	114	70
Australia	0	0	1	5	1	2
Austria	1	2	1	3	6	1
Belgium/Luxembourg	52	33	69	39	30	35
Brazil	19	25	42	43	50	60
Canada	108	84	200	197	260	308
Chile	5	15	18	18	17	17
China	177	147	146	101	156	127
Colombia	20	35	18	22	19	22
Costa Rica	0	0	0	1	2	—
Croatia	2	3	3	1	0	0
Cyprus	2	0	0	0	0	0
Czech Republic	4	2	4	6	7	18
Denmark	5	5	6	5	6	5
Ecuador	4	5	7	0	5	7
Egypt	0	0	0	0	1	—
El Salvador	0	0	0	0	0	1
Finland	2	1	2	1	1	2
France	127	133	148	193	216	259
Germany	40	41	70	70	60	76
Greece	0	0	1	1	1	1
Guatemala	0	0	1	3	5	2
Hong Kong	1	3	6	11	13	15
Hungary	3	2	0	1	0	0
India	0	0	0	1	1	—
Indonesia	14	14	1	1	6	1
Ireland	6	4	8	0	3	4
Italy	65	63	82	113	122	192
Jamaica	1	0	0	1	1	—
Japan	18	24	19	24	21	23
Lithuania		1	0	1	2	1
Malaysia	1	1	1	1	0	15
Mexico	188	269	394	369	327	250
Netherlands	55	50	71	54	50	33
New Zealand	5	8	16	20	26	23
Nicaragua	0	1	3	3	1	3
Norway	0	1	1	4	3	1
Panama	2	2	3	5	3	—
Peru	2	1	1	1	0	1
Philippines	0	1	1	0	1	1
Poland	3	2	3	4	2	4
Portugal	2	1	12	7	5	6

Appendix 3.3 (continued)
Cuba's Imports by Sending Country, 1993–98 ($ Millions)

	1993	1994	1995	1996	1997	1998
Romania	5	9	36	20	21	6
Russia	—	249	237	465	284	71
Saudi Arabia	0	0	0	1	—	—
Singapore	0	0	3	4	4	2
Slovakia	—	2	2	4	4	16
South Africa	11	12	17	17	38	50
Spain	191	289	396	464	474	549
Sweden	8	7	11	11	17	15
Switzerland	12	8	8	7	9	11
Taiwan	1	1	7	17	19	22
Thailand	0	0	27	37	3	38
Trinidad and Tobago	9	7	20	26	23	14
Tunisia	9	6	20	16	11	9
Turkey	1	2	6	1	0	1
United Kingdom	21	41	30	38	32	56
United States	3	4	6	6	9	4
Uruguay	1	0	0	0	1	4
Venezuela	120	90	112	119	22	433
Others	607	334	481	652	973	393
Total	2,000	2,085	2,845	3,355	3,490	3,280

Source: CIA (1999).

CHAPTER 4

U.S. Economic Sanctions Against Iran

INTRODUCTION

During and after the Iranian Revolution and the U.S. hostage crisis, U.S.–Iranian relations deteriorated quickly. In addition to trading tough rhetoric with Iran, the United States, over time, imposed various sanctions designed to punish Iran and encourage a change in Iranian government policies. These sanctions have varied in scope and have been the subject of very different assessments in the two countries.

In the United States, some politicians and "experts on Iran" have praised the sanctions for their effectiveness, presumably for inflicting tremendous pressures on Iran and thus reducing its ability to damage U.S. national interests.[1] Other U.S. politicians and experts have cast a great deal of doubt as to their effectiveness,[2] while U.S. business interests have broadly labeled the sanctions as ineffectual.[3] In Iran, politicians universally have claimed that the sanctions merely demonstrate U.S. vindictiveness and have caused little or no harm to Iran and its economy but heavy losses to U.S. business interests. The average Iranian, meanwhile, is more likely to complain that sanctions have reduced the availability and (especially) increased the price of U.S. goods and services. Thus, there seems to be little or no agreement among the different interested parties in the two countries.

Jahangir Amuzegar (1997) provides perhaps the most elegant discussion on the diverse views and conclusions regarding the impact of sanctions on Iran. While we do not endorse Amuzegar's conclusions, some of his words merit repeating here:

a. "Economic indicators in Iran are healthier than at any time since the early 1990s."
b. "American sanctions have not appreciably worsened any of these ills. And whatever their adverse effects, they have not been strong enough to induce a noticeable change in Tehran's behavior."
c. "Sanctions matter not because they can, in their present configuration, bring the Islamic Republic to its knees, but because they may handicap it in the race to rapid economic growth."
d. "For its part, Iran can live with U.S. sanctions for a long time with much less difficulty than Cuba or Vietnam, although it can not prosper without Washington's blessing."

Although Iran's economic performance over the last thirty years has been less than exemplary, the degree of harm of U.S. sanctions is highly contentious. While sanctions have had a limited direct impact on Iran, their indirect effects, coupled with other U.S. pressures such as restrictions on financing, may have been more significant. Sanctions have reduced U.S.–Iranian trade in goods and services, and this negative effect may be expected to continue for some time even if sanctions are repealed because of the long-term rupture in U.S.–Iranian business relations. At the same time, there is little evidence to indicate that sanctions have directly eroded popular support for the Iranian government or reduced the well-being of senior government officials, much less changed Iranian government policies to be more in line with U.S. national interests.

The Political Context of U.S. Sanctions Against Iran

Prior to the Iranian Revolution, Iran arguably was the United States's second closest ally in the Middle East, after Israel. Every U.S. president from Lyndon Johnson to Jimmy Carter confirmed this close relationship, and there were other indications as well: The United States sold Iran nearly every piece of military equipment the shah requested, did not oppose the construction of nuclear power plants in Iran, and acceded to the shah's wishes and cut off all contact with Iranian opposition groups. Yet today, hard-line U.S. politicians and even average Americans see Iran as global enemy number one. In Iran, a large segment of the population and the entire clerical leadership see the U.S. government, because of its past "interference" in Iranian internal affairs, as their greatest enemy, intent on their subjugation and destruction.

How did two such close allies become the worst of enemies? The Iranian Revolution was a popular uprising against the policies of the shah of Iran, Mohammad Reza Pahlavi. Given the United

States's strong support for the shah—in the early 1950s, the U.S. Central Intelligence Agency had instigated the overthrow of constitutionally elected Prime Minister Mohammad Mossadeq, brought the shah back to power, and trained his oppressive secret service, SAVAK—the revolution also was a revolt against the pervasive role of the United States in Iran's domestic affairs. The backlash against the United States was made evident when a group of Iranian students entered the U.S. embassy compound in November 1979 and took American diplomats hostage. This unlawful act was later supported by hard-line elements in Iran who saw the hostage-taking as helpful to their consolidation of power because of anti-U.S. sentiment among the populace at large. After it became clear that the Iranian government was not going to take action against the students to free the hostages, President Carter initiated economic sanctions against Iran.

The hostage crisis quickly turned the average U.S. citizen against Iran (although only one American died during the revolution, in an incident believed to have been unrelated to the revolution itself). The nightly appearance of U.S. hostages on network news reinforced Iran's negative image, and Iran soon replaced the Soviet Union as America's main nemesis. Under these circumstances, imposing economic sanctions was the least the United States could do.

During the hostage crisis, Iraq invaded Iran. While the U.S. government espoused neutrality during the conflict, it openly supported Iraq with crucial military intelligence. In the view of the average Iranian, U.S. support to Iraq went far beyond the provision of intelligence: The United States encouraged, or at least did not discourage, Iraqi aggression and looked the other way while Iraq acquired chemical and biological weapons capabilities to use against Iran. The United States did not support Iran's assertions before the United Nations regarding Iraq's use of chemical weapons, which in turn allowed Iraq to continue its slaughter of Iranian citizens. After 500,000-plus casualties and an even greater number of soldiers and civilians injured, Iranians increasingly took to the streets to vent their rage at U.S. policies.

Each side has demanded an apology from the other for past actions; neither has issued an unequivocal apology. The United States continues to accuse Iran of opposing the Middle East peace process, supporting Hezbollah and Hamas, attempting to acquire nuclear weapons and ballistic missiles, and supporting international terrorism. Iran denies all of the above and, in turn, accuses the United States of interfering in its internal affairs, not settling Iran's legitimate financial claims stemming from the impoundment of military equipment sold to Iran, and instigating policies to isolate Iran.

The average American has been so turned against Iran by the memory (and constant reminding by the media) of the hostage crisis and by negative pronouncements about Iranian policies that a U.S. president is unlikely to take a bold step in the direction of reconciliation. In Iran, meanwhile, past U.S. meddling in Iranian affairs and U.S. support of Iraq during its war against Iran provides hard-line Iranian politicians with fodder to continually stoke anti-U.S. sentiment and consolidate their power base. It is, therefore, hard to imagine how this deadlock can be broken and/or economic sanctions removed any time soon. The lifting of economic sanctions will likely occur through either a change in U.S. *and* Iranian leadership or through an external event that will give both sides sufficient motivation for reconciliation. Economic sanctions, however, make reconciliation even more remote.

IRAN'S BROAD ECONOMIC RECORD

Iran's overall economic record since the Iranian Revolution is depicted in Table 4.1. In 1998, gross national product (GNP) in current dollars was about 35 percent higher than in 1979, for an annual growth rate of 1.58 percent, while GNP in constant dollars was about 15 percent lower in 1998, for a negative annual growth rate of 0.84 percent. Per capita GNP declined in both constant as well as current dollars: In 1998, per capita GNP in current dollars was nearly 18 percent lower than in 1979 and 48 percent lower in constant dollars, for annual rates of decline of 1.03 percent and 3.39 percent, respectively. These figures suggest rapid population growth, and indeed Iran's population grew at an annual rate of 2.64 percent over the entire period and even more rapidly (3.59 percent) from 1979 to 1988.

Iran's overall export growth also was less than stellar. Total exports in current dollars declined at an annual rate of 2.49 percent, with fuel oil exports—on which Iran depends heavily—declining at an annual rate of 4.27 percent (nonfuel exports increased at an annual rate of 10.92 percent). Petroleum exports declined for most major oil exporters over the same period because of significantly lower oil prices, a factor outside their control (Askari and Jaber 1999). But in the case of Iran, two internal developments further exacerbated the decline in oil export revenues—a decline in oil output (and capacity) and a rapid increase in domestic petroleum consumption.

Table 4.1
Iran's Economic Record, 1979–98

	1979	1980	1981	1982	1983	1984	1985
Population (millions)	37.8	39.1	40.5	42.00	43.6	45.3	47.1
GNP (billions of current $)	82,383	88,029	98,917	119,767	139.945	150,334	165,792
GNP per capita (current $)	2,180	2,250	2,440	2,850	3,210	3,320	3,520
GNP (billions of constant $)	130,614	122,291	125,919	149,454	172.464	180,953	200,523
GNP per capita (current $)	3,458.30	3,125.70	3,106.00	3,556.40	3,955.90	3,996.20	4,257.40
Foreign Trade ($ billions)							
Value of exports, f.o.b.	24,011	12,258	11,831	20,452	21,507	17,087	14,175
Fuel	23,359	11,693	11,491	20,168	21,150	16,726	13,710
Non-Fuel	0.652	0.563	0.440	0.284	0.457	0.361	0.465
Fuel/total exports (%)	97.3	95.4	97.1	98.6	98.3	97.9	96.7
Value of Imports, c.i.f.	8,497	10,835	13,138	12,552	18,027	14,729	12.006
Total External Debt ($ billions)	n.a.	4.50	3.86	8.21	7.11	5.10	8.06

	1986	1987	1988	1989	1990	1991	1992
Population (millions)	48.8	50.4	51.9	53.2	54.4	55.3	56.2
GNP (billions of current $)	178,191	180,014	161,922	141,054	140.352	139.863	130.332
GNP per capita (current $)	3,650	3,570	3,120	2,650.00	2,580	2,530	2,320
GNP (billions of constant $)	221,938	218,447	188,899	156,784	150.635	149.777	138.787
GNP per capita (current $)	4,546.10	4,332.20	3,639.80	2,945.50	2,769	2,709.3	2,470
Foreign Trade ($ billions)							
Value of exports, f.o.b.	7,171	11,916	10,709	13,081	19.305	18.661	19.868
Fuel	6,255	10,800	9,700	12,037	17.993	16.661	16.88
Non-Fuel	0.816	1.116	1.009	1,044	1.312	2.549	2.988
Fuel/total exports (%)	87.2	90.6	90.6	92.00	93.2	85.8	85
Value of Imports, c.i.f.	10,585	12,005	10,608	13,448	18.33	25.19	23.274
Total External Debt ($ billions)	5.83	6.14	5.8	8.52	9.02	11	18

	1993	1994	1995	1996	1997	1998
Population (millions)	57.1	58	59	59.9	60.9	61.9
GNP (billions of current $)	109.039	84.12	81.357	89.894	109.672	110.884
GNP per capita (current $)	1,910	1,450	1,380	1,500	1,800	1,790
GNP (billions of constant $)	144.403	87.153	81.357	87.892	107.243	111.189
GNP per capita (current $)	2,004	1,502.3	1,380	1,466.6	1,760.1	1,794.9
Foreign Trade ($ billions)						
Value of exports, f.o.b.	18.08	19.435	18.36	22.496	18.375	14.863
Fuel	14.333	14.604	15.103	19.271	15.464	10.193
Non-Fuel	3.747	3.831	3.257	3.225	3.911	4.67
Fuel/total exports (%)	79.3	75.1	82.3	85.7	84.1	68.6
Value of imports, c.i.f.	19.287	12.617	12.774	14.882	14.598	13.035
Total External Debt ($ billions)	28.5	22.8	21.89	18.71	11.82	n.a.

Sources: International Monetary Fund (2000); World Bank (2000b).

The decline in production capacity was due largely to investment shortfalls in the oil sector. The increase in domestic consumption was due to high population growth and one of the world's highest (if not *the* highest) petroleum product subsidies. Even after a doubling of gasoline prices in the mid-1990s, regular gasoline prices in Iran were about $0.30 per liter or roughly $0.12 per U.S. gallon (IMF 2000), meaning prices for petroleum products were below production costs. For 2001, the International Monetary Fund (IMF) estimated the implicit subsidy (due to regulated prices) of petroleum products at about 11 percent of GDP. Explicit subsidies on wheat, bread, sugar, milk, cheese, rice, vegetable oil, fertilizer, pesticides, and tractors/combines constituted another 1.4 percent of GDP (IMF 2001b). In fact, at the aggregate or macro level, it is hard to point to any area of positive economic performance besides that of nonfuel exports.

Although the economy underperformed and total exports did not fare well, Iran did not resort to significant external borrowing until 1988, after the Iran–Iraq war. Between 1988 and 1993, Iran's external debt exploded from $5.8 billion to $28.5 billion because of the rapid increase in imports to meet pent-up demand in the aftermath of the war. The rise in imports resulted in large current account deficits—$973 million in 1990, $10.2 billion in 1991, $7.3 billion in 1992, and $4.5 million in 1993 (IMF 2001b). Unfortunately, the increased external borrowing did not finance productive investments and, as a result, Iran received little long-term benefit.

This period, however, was followed by several years of current account surpluses—$4.9 billion in 1994, $3.1 billion in 1995, $5.2 billion in 1996, $2.2 billion in 1997, and $6.6 billion in 1999—due to lower imports. These current account surpluses reduced the stock of external debt to $10.8 billion for 1999–2000 (IMF 2000), and Iranian authorities expected it to be around $7.9 billion by the end of 2001 (IMF 2001b). At the same time, gross official reserves increased from $5.3 billion in 1997 to $12.6 billion in 2000. Iran's debt/GDP ratio stood at around 9.5 percent in 2000 and its debt service ratio (excluding short-term debt) was about 18 percent. These are low figures by any standard and represent a significant accomplishment relative to most other developing countries.

In the educational and health arenas, Iran seems to have enjoyed more success (see Table 4.2). Iran's life expectancy has risen steadily; infant mortality rates have fallen; access to safe water, sanitation, and health care have shown significant improvement; the number of physicians, dentists, and nurses per person have increased; and immunization rates have risen. Literacy rates have

Table 4.2
Iran: Health and Education Indices

Area (square kilometers)	1,648,000
Population (1998)	61.95 million
Urban	37.51 million
Rural	24.43 million
Population growth rate (1998)	1.66%
Life expectancy at birth (1998)	70.7 years
Infant morality rate (per thousand, 1996)	26
Education enrollment rates (by percent of age group)	
Primary (1997)	90
Of which: Female	89.2
Secondary (1997)	81.2
Of which: Female	75.8
Literacy ratio (15 years and over, 1997)	73.4%
Literacy ratio (6–29 years, 1997)	92.6%
Population density (per sq. km. of agricultural land, 1989)	91.2
Population density (per sq. km., 1998)	37.6
Active population (1997)	21.2 million
Per capita income (1998)	U.S. $1,826.42
Population per physician (1996)	1,354
Per capita energy consumption (kg of oil equivalent, 1990)	1,026
Daily calorie supply per capita (1989)	3,181

Additional health indicators	1980–85	1986–90	1991–95	1996–97	1997–98
Infant mortality rate[1]	91.6	59	50	26	26
Maternal mortality rate[2]	140	91	40	40	37
Access to safe water	50	71	89	90	95
Access to sanitation	60	65	82	80	—
Access to health care	50	73	90	90	94
Hospital beds/100,000	148	150	154	156	—
Physicians/10,000	3.4	3.8	—	8.2	9.0
Dentists/10,000	—	0.6	—	1.5	1.7
Nurses/10,000	8.5	8.7	—	23.4	—
Immunization (DPT)	29	77	88	97	97
Immunization (measles)	69	80	84	95	96
Death rate, crude[3]	11	10	6	5	—
Life expectancy at birth					
Male	59	65	67	68	69.8
Female	63	65	68	70	71.5

increased, from about 50 percent in 1987 to around 80 percent in 1997; enrollment rates are nearly 100 percent in primary education and 70 percent in secondary education, compared to 87 percent and 42 percent, respectively, in 1980 (IMF 2000); and the number of students receiving higher education has simply exploded.

Table 4.2 (continued)
Iran: Health and Education Indices

Indices of educational quality	1988–93	1993–95	1995–96	1996–97	1997–98
Students per school	169.3	182.3	182.5	178.0	173.6
Students per class	31.1	30.4	30.3	30.1	29.34
Students per teacher	25.1	24.2	24.9	24.2	21.5
Classrooms per school	5.4	5.9	5.7	5.9	—
Students in public universities and higher education institutes	250,709	436,564	478,455	579.070	625,380
Female	71,822	124,350	145,353	—	338,687
Male	178,887	312,214	333,102	—	286,693
Islamic Azad University	—	368,200	431,025	611,443	659,278
Students in primary schools (in thousands)	8,262	9,863	9,746	9,238	8,938
Female	3,725	4,652	4,594	—	4,720
Male	4,537	5,211	5,152	—	4,218
Students in guidance schools (in thousands)	2,725	4,440	4,712	5,189	—
Female	1,086	1,943	2,090	—	—
Male	1,639	2,497	2,622	—	—
Students in secondary schools (in thousands)	1,363	2,343	2,781	3,401	5,283
Female	585	1,061	1,290	—	2,881
Male	778	1,282	1,491	—	2,402

[1]Per 1,000 live births.
[2]Per 100,000 live births.
[3]Per 1,000 population.
[4]Includes number of students and classes of the new system of education since 1996–97.
Source: International Monetary Fund (2000).

While these indicators point to significantly improved social conditions, they tell us nothing about changes in quality. Many public schools are run on two shifts due to a lack of facilities and qualified staff. Although university enrollment has expanded since 1979 (from 250,709 in 1988–89 to 625,380 in 1997–98, with an additional 659,278 in Islamic Azad University), the quality of higher education does not appear to have improved commensurately; anecdotal evidence and unscientific polls indicate that the quality of higher education has in fact declined significantly, with rote learning becoming the norm. At the same time, most public hospitals are badly equipped and maintained, and state-of-the-art medications are not generally available.[4]

At the same time, unemployment and underemployment are high. Although the official unemployment figure for 1999 was around 13 percent (IMF 2000), casual observation would indicate a figure closer to 20 percent. In conversation with different segments of society, a number of concerns are voiced frequently. The average Iranian is not satisfied with his or her overall economic well-being. A significant percentage of heads of Iranian households hold more than one job in order to make ends meet. The average person is dissatisfied with the quality of health care. The young, meanwhile, are not happy with the quality of their education.

DOMESTIC POLICY CONSIDERATIONS IN IRAN

The conclusion that Iran's economic performance has been singularly unimpressive over the last twenty-plus years is apparent. But what have been the reasons underlying such dismal performance?

The Iranian Revolution, as would be expected of any revolution, caused major disturbances. Many business leaders and highly educated individuals left Iran, and most took their capital with them. This migration of talent and capital left the private sector and the higher education system without a rudder for some time.

As a major oil exporter, Iran's economic performance is determined to a significant degree by conditions in the international oil market. Iran's dependence on oil is especially apparent when it comes to export and government revenues. Major oil exporters were adversely affected by oil market developments from the mid-1980s to 1999,[5] and Iran was not immune to these developments. But Iran generally relies less on oil revenues than oil exporters of the Gulf Cooperation Council (GCC). While the ratio of oil GDP to total GDP in 1998 for Saudi Arabia, Kuwait, the United Arab Emirates, and Qatar was in the range of 33.57 percent to 45.50 percent, for Iran it was only 13.51 percent.[6] Similarly, in 1996 the ratio of oil exports to total exports was 82.41 percent for Saudi Arabia, 94.54 percent for Kuwait, and 92.61 percent for Qatar (Askari and Jaber 1999), but only 70 percent for Iran in 1998.[7]

While Iran may depend less on oil than the GCC countries, international oil price developments still have a significant impact on Iran's export earnings, availability of foreign exchange, and balance of payments. Figures 4.1 and 4.2 illustrate oil prices, oil exports, and GNP figures for Iran.

The quantity of oil exports is the other important factor in determining Iran's oil export revenues. This, in turn, is affected by oil production capacity, oil output, and domestic oil consumption, which are shown in Figure 4.3.

Why has Iran's oil production capacity gone down so much, and why has domestic consumption gone up so much? In the case of

Figure 4.1
Oil Prices and GNP in Iran, 1979–98

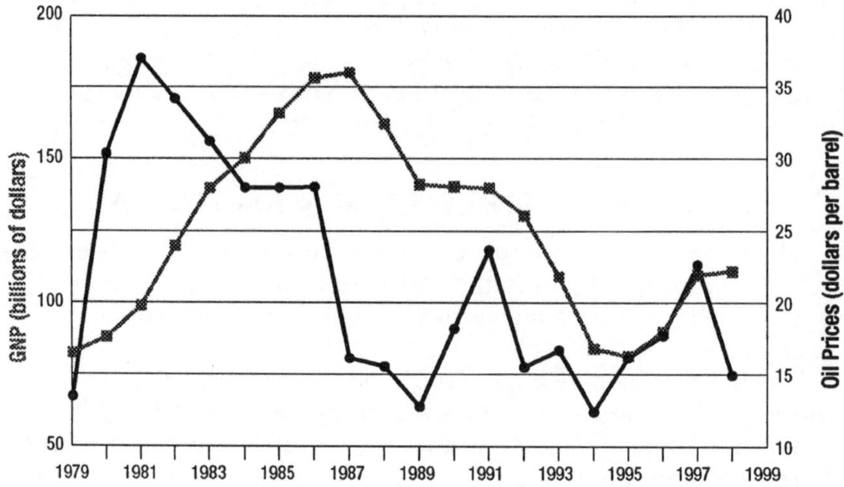

Source: Oil prices from U.S. Department of Energy; GNP figures from World Bank (2000).

the former, Iran's oil fields have not received the attention required. This is due to several factors: damage from the Iran-Iraq war; a shortage of foreign exchange (and, thus, investment in the fields); and government policies (Iran's postrevolutionary constitution) that strictly prohibit oil production-sharing agreements, thus reducing the attractiveness of foreign direct investment (FDI).[8] The rapid increase in domestic oil consumption, meanwhile, is due to massive domestic energy consumption subsidies (see Figure 4.4 for a comparison of gasoline prices in Iran and selected countries) and high population growth (see Figure 4.5 for changes in population and domestic oil consumption over time). While international oil prices are outside Iran's control, domestic production capacity (adversely affected by the war) and domestic consumption (ballooned by subsidies) are in large part determined by government policies.[9] The quality of government decisions has not lived up to expectations.

Besides changes in international oil prices, the other major factor outside government control that significantly affected Iran's economic performance was the Iran–Iraq war. This eight-year war (1980–88) resulted in heavy damage to Iran's oil fields, pipelines, refineries, and related oil facilities. Iran's basic non-oil infrastructure also took a heavy toll, as the war diverted badly needed resources away from industry and agriculture. While it is impossi-

Figure 4.2
Oil Prices and Oil Exports in Iran, 1979–98

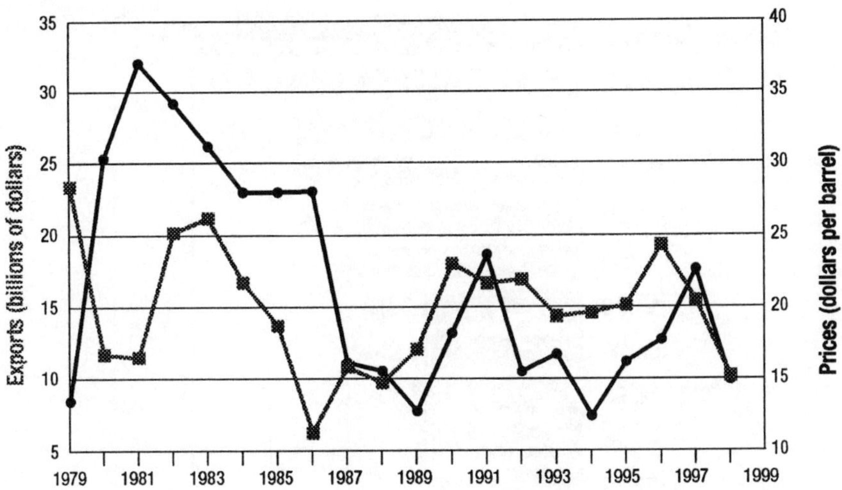

Source: Oil prices from U.S. Department of Energy; oil exports (f.o.b.) from World Bank (2000).

Figure 4.3
Oil Production, Domestic Oil Consumption, and Oil Production Capacity in Iran, 1979–99

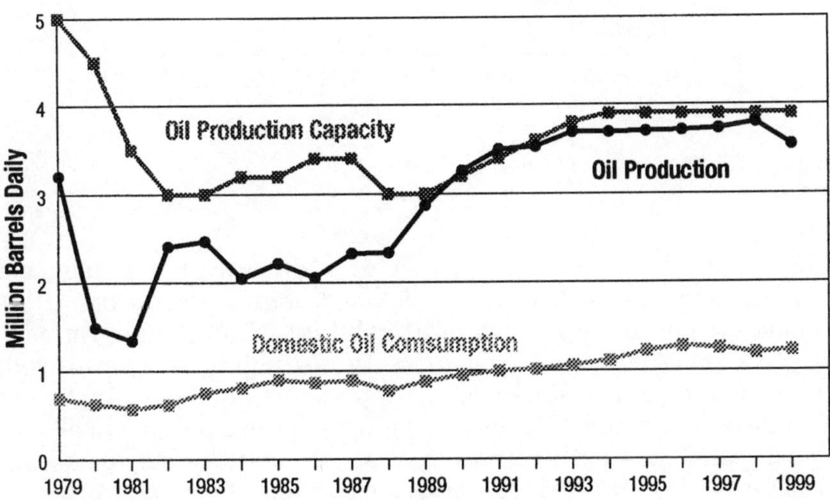

Source: Oil production and consumption figures from BP Amoco (1999); production capacity figures from U.S. Department of Energy.

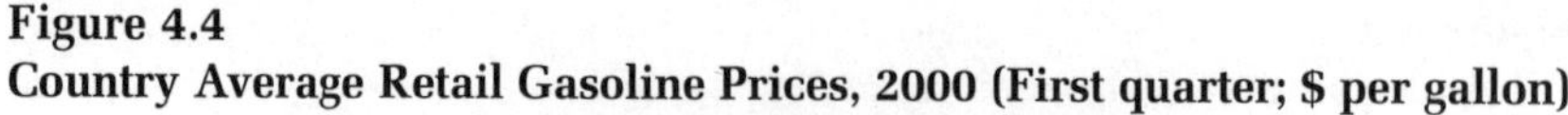

Figure 4.4
Country Average Retail Gasoline Prices, 2000 (First quarter; $ per gallon)

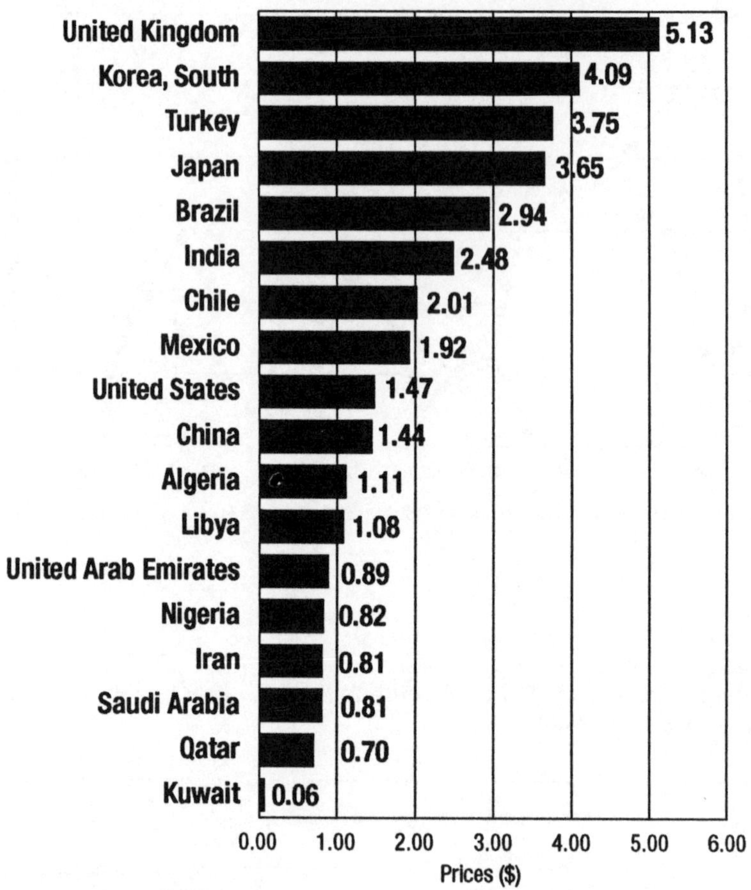

Source: U.S. Department of Energy.

ble to quantify the total economic cost of the war—the human cost was tremendous, with well over 500,000 Iranian dead—the direct damage is put in the vicinity of $150 billion.[10] During the war, productive investment was squeezed, infrastructure was destroyed, education programs declined in importance, and the number of disabled (more than 500,000) requiring prolonged medical and social assistance multiplied. The Iran of 2000 has yet to recover what it possessed in per-capita terms in 1980.

Another detrimental development outside government control was the influx of about 2 million Afghan and 1 million Iraqi

Figure 4.5
Population and Domestic Oil Consumption in Iran, 1979–98

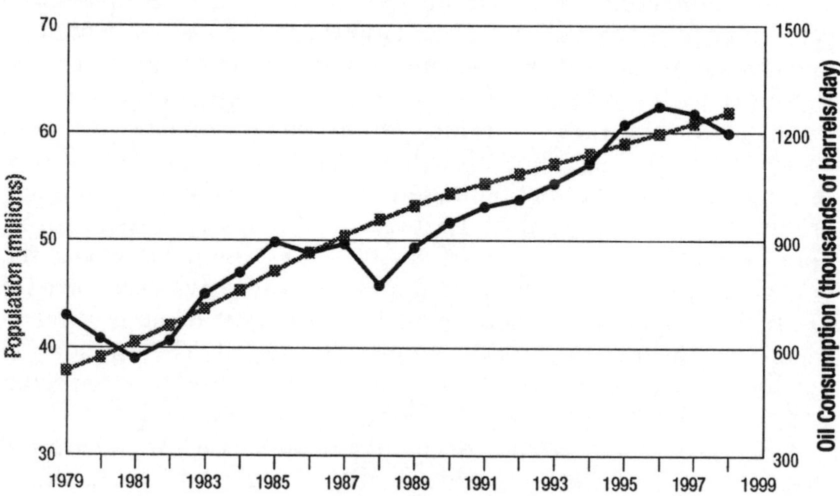

Source: Population figures from World Bank (2000); oil consumption from BP Amoco (1999).

refugees. Although Iran provided for their needs, it received very little international assistance to offset the financial burden. This large increase in Iran's temporary population imposed a significant economic demand on the country.

Thus, adverse developments largely outside government control—economic dislocations resulting from the revolution, falling oil prices, Iraq's invasion of Iran, and the influx of roughly 3 million refugees—have had a significant detrimental impact on Iran's economic performance over the last twenty years. The effects of government policies, however, have been equally detrimental. Indeed, the policy shortcomings and shortfalls of the Iranian government have been fundamental and numerous.

In the immediate aftermath of the revolution, the authorities created a number of state organizations and foundations and nationalized many industries. These actions reflected the regime's political and social philosophy and resulted in a massive reduction in the size of the private sector in favor of the public (although foundations are still included in the private sector for official statistical purposes). The new entities include the Foundation for the Oppressed and Injured, the Reconstruction Crusade, the Martyr Foundation, and three very large public-sector holding companies—the National Iranian Industrial Organization (NIIO), the

Industrial Development and Renovation Organization (IDRO), and the National Iranian Steel Corporation (NISC).

The Foundation for the Oppressed was formed with the confiscated assets of the Pahlavi Foundation and family. Its economic department manages its assets, and its nonprofit department uses its revenues to improve the lives of oppressed and disadvantaged Iranians. The holdings of this foundation can be seen everywhere in Iran—in industry, transportation, hotels and other tourism facilities, mining, construction, and commerce—and by some accounts they are the source of more than 1.5 percent of Iran's GDP, with direct employment well in excess of 70,000 (IMF 1995). Moreover, the contributions of this and other foundations to private-sector GDP are highly significant—their share in the output of large private-sector establishments could be around 20 percent. The Foundation for the Oppressed is above the laws applicable to the private sector, and its head is answerable only to the supreme leader.

The National Iranian Industrial Organization was formed around the confiscated assets of individuals connected to the Pahlavi regime, those who left Iran as a result of the revolution, and companies whose liabilities to banks exceeded their assets. The NIIO's goal is to promote Iran's industrial sector. The IDRO's goals, and the sources of its assets, are similar.

Nationalized industries include automobile manufacturing and assembly, shipbuilding, mining, metal production, and banking. In short, the lion's share of medium-size and large industrial establishments,[11] large-scale agricultural operations, and financial institutions have been nationalized. All of this came on top of previous nationalization in oil, gas, railroads, airways, utilities, and fisheries.

The Foundation for the Oppressed and other similar institutions function as an economy within the economy and are basically outside government control. These foundations, together with the three large government holding companies mentioned previously, dominate Iran's private sector. Thus, while the rest of the world is embracing privatization, Iran largely retains the nationalized economy it established twenty years ago. Although a process of privatization started in the 1990s, it has been slow to unfold. For 1996, the IMF estimates that the public sector (including all state enterprises) was directly responsible for about 70 percent of Iran's total employment (IMF 2000).

The structural changes brought about by nationalization have increased economic inefficiencies as opposed to the espoused goal of enhancing efficiency. This is not to say that Iran's industrial sector was efficient prior to the revolution; high tariffs and other explicit and implicit subsidies supported most of Iran's non-oil industrial and manufacturing production. But reliance on the private sector was the appropriate basis for gradual improvement, and this process might have accelerated with the emergence of the World Trade Organization (WTO) and attendant global trade agreements. Nationalization and the management and operation of nationalized enterprises represented a significant step backward in terms of efficiency.

Iran's foreign trade sector also is controlled heavily by the government. Iran requires import licenses for all imports and uses a multiple exchange rate system to discriminate among imports, in turn encouraging corruption. Additionally, Iran imposes both an ad valorem tax and customs duties on imported goods. In 1993, tariff rates (i.e., the combined effect of taxes and duties) were reduced from an average of 35 percent to 11 percent, then raised to 18 percent in 1994. The tariff structure was changed in 1995 as follows: 0 to 5 percent for essential goods and materials, 5 to 15 percent for intermediate goods and machinery, and 15 to 25 percent for nonessential and luxury goods (IMF 1995).

On top of these broad policy shortfalls, the Iranian government generally encouraged rapid population growth for political reasons in the aftermath of the revolution. The results are confirmed in Table 4.1. After the population increased dramatically in the 1980s (an average annual rise of 3.59 percent for the years 1979–88), this policy was reversed, with a significant reduction in the rate of population growth in the 1990s (1.53 percent annually from 1989 to 1998). The explosion in Iran's population—a doubling between 1979 and 2000—has placed a good deal of pressure on the Iranian economy. This pressure is evident on the infrastructure (with shortages of electricity, oil, water, and housing),[12] education, health, and the labor force, which suffers from an unemployment rate officially reported at 13 percent in 1995 (IMF 1995) but unofficially in the neighborhood of 20 percent (as well as significant underemployment). Creating gainful employment for the country's youth will be a problem for Iran in the first decade of the twenty-first century and beyond.

Iran's economic shortfalls have been further exacerbated by generous government subsidies. The single largest subsidy, for energy consumption (IMF 2000), amounted to an estimated 11 percent of GDP in 1997–98, 17 percent in 1999–2000 (because of sharp world price increases), and 11 percent in 2001.[13] In addition to the implicit energy consumption subsidies, most of the profits of the foundations, when distributed to the population, can be considered subsidies. Explicit (budgeted) consumer subsidies, meanwhile, amounted to more than 4 percent of GDP in 2001. Thus, implicit and explicit subsidies typically have accounted for more than 20 percent of Iranian GDP, even excluding the subsidy contributions of foundations.[14]

In sum, Iran's economy is in need of drastic and decisive structural reform. An excerpt from the IMF's 2000 report on Iran is an accurate summary of economic conditions:

> At the end of the war with Iraq in 1988, the Islamic Republic of Iran inherited a highly centralized economy. Most of the economic resources were administratively allocated through the vast public sector, widespread price controls, administratively mandated grid of financial rates of return and charges and credit allocations, extensive trade and exchange restrictions, heavily subsidized energy and petroleum products, multiple exchange rates, and restrictive labor and business practices. Furthermore, the state-owned enterprises had monopolies over large sectors of the economy, including the financial system.
>
> Over the past decade, the authorities have attempted to address these distortions and restore sustained economic growth. The First Five Year Development Plan (FFYDP), covering the period 1989/90–1993/94 (fiscal year ending March 20), initiated steps aimed at decontrolling a significant part of domestic prices, raising public utility rates, removing some nontariff trade barriers, lowering income tax rates, starting to privatize public enterprises, and liberalizing the exchange system. However, the main emphasis of the FFYDP was on infrastructure development and reconstruction programs, which were financed by expansionary policies.
>
> The broad liberalization direction of the FFYDP was reemphasized under the Second Five-Year Development Plan (SFYDP), covering the period 1994/95–1999/2000. However, opening of the economy continued to progress at a slow pace despite the recovery of oil prices during the first three years of the plan. The period of the SFYDP was characterized largely by macroeconomic instability and declining economic growth. As a result, the authorities' policy priorities were shifted to rectify the macroeconomic and external debt imbalances, while the much-needed structural reforms were delayed. (IMF 2000)

Essentially, over the last twenty years, while successful countries initiated programs of economic privatization and liberalization, Iran did the opposite, marching backward for about fifteen years, then slowly starting to reverse this process. As a result, in today's Iran the public sector's share of total employment is estimated at around 70 percent (IMF 2000), government controls abound, and subsidies hold back productive investment and growth. To our mind, these shortsighted policies—which are under government control—are the root cause of Iran's problems. The impact of developments outside government control (revolutionary dislocations, the Iran–Iraq war, the influx of refugees, oil price fluctuations, and U.S. sanctions), though significant, might have been overcome by better policies that encouraged domestic investment and induced European and Japanese multinationals to invest in Iran.

The government of Iran is aware of its economic policy shortfalls but is slow to move because of strong and conflicting internal political interests. In the Third Five-Year Development Plan (TFYDP), the government has again recognized at least the direction of needed policy changes. For example, the plan calls for the following:

- Limited reform of the multiple exchange rate system;
- Abolition of state monopolies in telecommunications, railways, tobacco, and tea;
- Privatization to proceed with the planned construction of the first private power plant (a foreign partner was earlier allowed to hold majority ownership in a joint-venture petrochemical plant);
- Private banks and increases in non-bank companies in the free trade zones (partial private ownership in other banks may be permitted); and
- Policies to attract foreign investors (Quest Economics 2000).

While policy shortfalls and factors outside government control have adversely affected Iran's economic performance, what has been the specific impact of U.S. sanctions on Iran? In the following sections, we outline the development of and changes in U.S. sanctions, examine their direct trade impact, and analyze their direct and indirect effects on Iran.

U.S. SANCTIONS AGAINST IRAN

U.S. sanctions against Iran have gone through a number of changes over the last twenty years. In Table 4.3 we list and briefly describe the most prominent sanctions affecting U.S.–Iranian economic relations. While the number of U.S. sanctions against Iran goes well beyond those in Table 4.3, a handful of U.S. actions have been especially significant and deserve mention.

Executive Order 12170 (14 November 1979)

Through this order, which froze Iranian assets in U.S. banks and their foreign subsidiaries, President Carter essentially severed relations between U.S. banks and Iran. Moreover, this action, coupled with the United States's predisposition to using economic sanctions, will likely prompt Iran to be very cautious in establishing

Table 4.3
U.S. Actions Significantly Affecting U.S.–Iran Economic Relations

Date	Action	Description	Status
8 Nov. 1979	Arms Export Control Act	Embargoes U.S. military exports to Iran	Active
12 Nov. 1979	Trade Expansion Act	Embargoes U.S. oil imports from Iran	Revoked by EO 12282 on 19 Nov. 1981
14 Nov. 1979	Executive Order 12170	Freezes Iranian assets in U.S. banks and their foreign subsidiaries	Active
7 April 1980	Executive Order 12205	Embargoes all U.S. exports to Iran, excluding food and medicine	Revoked by EO 12282
17 April 1980	Executive Order 12211	Prohibits all financial transactions between United States and Iran and their citizens; embargoes all U.S. imports from Iran; bans all U.S. travel to and from Iran; and impounds all U.S. military equipment already ordered and purchased by Iran	Revoked by EO 12282
19 Jan. 1981	Executive Order 12276	Directive relating to establishment of escrow accounts in London	Ratified by EO 12294 in 1981; active
19 Jan. 1981	Executive Order 12277	Directive to transfer frozen assets of Iranian government	Ratified by EO 12294 in 1981; active
19 Jan. 1981	Executive Order 12278	Directive to transfer frozen assets of Iranian government overseas	Ratified by EO 12294 in 1981; active
19 Jan. 1981	Executive Order 12279	Directive to transfer frozen assets of Iranian government held by domestic U.S. banks	Ratified by EO 12294 in 1981; active
19 Jan. 1981	Executive Order 12280	Directive to transfer Iranian financial assets held by non-banking institutions	Ratified by EO 12294 in 1981; active
19 Jan. 1981	Executive Order 12281	Directive to transfer certain assets of Iranian government	Ratified by EO 12294 in 1981; active
19 Jan. 1981	Executive Order 12282	Revokes prohibitions contained in EO 12205 and EO 12211	Ratified by EO 12294 in 1981

Table 4.3 (continued)
U.S. Actions Significantly Affecting U.S.–Iran Economic Relations

Date	Action	Description	Status
19 Jan. 1981	Executive Order 12283	Declines prosecution of claims of hostages for actions at U.S. embassy in Iran and elsewhere	Ratified by EO 12294 in 1981; active
23 Jan. 1984	State Department action	Adds Iran to list of governments supporting terrorism and thus places Iran under strict export controls	Active
28 Sept. 1984	Export Administration Act	Further restricts exports of U.S. military and dual-use equipment to Iran	Active
26 Oct. 1987	Executive Order 12613	Embargoes all U.S. imports from Iran but does not ban U.S. companies from buying Iranian crude; allows imports (from third countries) of refined products using Iranian crude; embargoes exports of 14 specific items considered dual-use goods	Active
7 Nov. 1989	State Department action	Transfers $567 million in frozen Iranian assets, leaving $900 million and all Iranian claims under the FMS program	NA
15 March 1995	Executive Order 12957	Bans all U.S. investment in Iran's petroleum sector	Active
6 May 1995	Executive Order 12959	Prohibits all trade (exports and imports) and investment between the United States and Iran. Ban includes refined products using Iranian crude	Active
4 August 1996	Iran–Libya Sanctions Act of 1996 (ILSA)	Imposes sanctions against non-U.S companies that invest more than $40 million during any twelve-month period in Iran's energy sector	Active
19 August 1997	Executive Order 13059	Expands sanctions against third countries that export to Iran	Active

full relations with U.S. banks and their subsidiaries if and when all sanctions are lifted.

Executive Order 12211 (17 April 1980)

This order prohibited all financial transactions with Iran, embargoed imports, banned all travel, and impounded Iranian military equipment in the United States. Before the revolution, the shah's government had purchased huge amounts of U.S. military equipment (through the Foreign Military Sales program, or FMS) but had not received delivery. President Carter's action resulted in the impounding of this equipment. Some was later used by U.S. forces, some was sold to third countries, and the rest was left to rust and rot in warehouses. Iran's claim against the United States (plus interest) is still being considered at the U.S.–Iran Tribunal at The Hague. In 1991 Iran claimed that the value of undelivered military equipment exceeded $12 billion; the United States countered that it was a fraction of that sum. The case will likely take another five to seven years if it goes through the tribunal process. Iran would like to reach a global settlement, while the United States wants to address one item at a time. Many observers feel these claims probably will be settled within the context of an overall political rapprochement between the two countries.

Executive Order 12613 (26 October 1987)

This order embargoed all imports from Iran and prohibited fourteen export items. Up to this point in time, the U.S. had imported Iranian crude oil. This action banned the importation of Iranian crude, which comprised the lion's share of Iran's total exports. There were, however, two major loopholes in this order. First, the order explicitly allowed the importation of petroleum products refined from Iranian crude oil by a third country. Second, the order was silent on the purchase (as opposed to the importation) of Iranian crude by U.S. oil companies.

Executive Order 12957 (15 March 1995)

This order banned all U.S. investment in Iran's petroleum sector.

Executive Order 12959 (6 May 1995)

This presidential order for the first time embargoed all U.S.–Iran trade (U.S. exports to and imports from Iran), prohibited imports of refined products from third countries using Iranian crude (allowed under Executive Order 12613), and effectively prohibited U.S. companies or citizens from buying Iranian crude. Moreover, this order prohibited any and all U.S. investment in Iran. These actions were designed to hurt the Iranian economy, as opposed to previous presidential orders that could better be categorized as conveying the *appearance* of a "get-tough policy" toward Iran.

The Iran–Libya Sanctions Act (August 1996) and Executive Order 13059 (19 August 1997)

The intent of the ILSA was to "reach" into third countries (a practice known as extraterritoriality) by essentially transforming a U.S. unilateral sanction into a multilateral sanction. The target of the ILSA was foreign investment in Iran's oil and gas industry (Iran's critical sector for earning foreign exchange), while the focus of the executive order was certain exports to Iran from third countries.

The European Union objected vehemently to these measures and threatened to take its dispute to the WTO. When a group of oil companies, lead by France's TotalFina, signed a $2 billion contract to develop two sections of Iran's South Pars gas field, the United States had no choice but to grant a waiver because in all likelihood it would have lost its case at the WTO and damaged its relations with the EU and Russia[15] (earlier, in 1995, TotalFina had agreed to develop the offshore Sirri oil field over U.S. objections). In 2000, ENI of Italy agreed to develop an additional two sections of South Pars, holding the majority in a 60–40 joint venture with Iran in a project with an estimated total investment of $3.8 billion.

These two U.S. attempts at secondary sanctions on Iran are unlikely to be effective with the European Union, Japan, Russia, or China given their economic, political, and military clout. They are also especially ironic, as during the latter part of the 1970s the United States vehemently opposed the secondary Arab boycott of Israel and condemned it as illegal under international law.

THE DIRECT TRADE IMPACT OF SANCTIONS

Empirical studies of the economic impact of sanctions have been few in number and narrowly focused. The work of Gary Hufbauer and his colleagues ranks among the most prominent empirical research in this area. In particular, their recent work has used a gravity model to investigate the impact of U.S. sanctions on U.S. merchandise exports, employment, and wages.

The gravity model, in its simplest form, predicts that the value of trade between the United States and the target country will be positively related to the size of their respective outputs and negatively related to the physical distance between them. In addition to output size and physical distance, the Hufbauer et al. research has included other variables and predicted that bilateral trade would increase if the target country shared a common border or language with the United States or belonged to the same trading bloc.

One study (Hufbauer et al. 1997) used a series of dummy variables to capture the effect of trade sanctions. The data set included bilateral trade (exports plus imports) among eighty-eight countries for 1985, 1990, and 1995 and exports alone for 1995. The broad result of the study is that U.S. economic sanctions in 1995 might have reduced U.S. exports to twenty-six target countries by as much as $19 billion. If there were no offsetting exports to other markets, that would mean a reduction of more than 200,000 jobs in the relatively high-wage export sector and nearly $1 billion annually in export-sector wage premiums. This was claimed to be a relatively high cost to the U.S. economy while sanctions were in place, but the study found only limited evidence that the negative impact of sanctions continued after they had been lifted.

The gravity model approach gives a very limited picture of what happens to bilateral merchandise trade as a result of sanctions. Specifically, U.S. direct trade with Iran may be down to almost zero, but some U.S. goods may be getting into Iran through third countries, albeit at a higher price (the situation is similar for U.S. imports from Iran). Moreover, goods from either country may be smuggled into the other country.

Even if U.S. exports to Iran (direct and through third countries) are down as a result of sanctions, does this necessarily represent a loss to the United States? Depending on the composition of the goods previously exported to Iran, it is possible that these same goods may be exported to other countries, albeit at a slightly lower price. If this is the case, the losses in export revenues, jobs, and wages may be minimal. Moreover, even if the loss in exports to Iran is not offset by exports to other countries, what is the nature of this loss for the United States? Surely this is only a loss in foreign exchange earnings, as the goods exported to Iran could be consumed domestically in the United States or the inputs redirected to produce other goods for U.S. markets.

On the import side, what does the loss of imports from Iran mean for the United States? If the United States can buy the same goods at the same price from other countries, there is no loss; if the price is higher, then there is a commensurate cost (the higher price

Table 4.4
Estimated Reduction in Direct U.S.–Iran Merchandise Trade as a Result of Sanctions ($ Billions)

Year	Estimated Reduction in U.S. Exports to Iran	Estimated Reduction in U.S. Imports from Iran
1980	1.5	0.8
1981	1.5	1.4
1982	1.9	1.1
1983	2.1	1.2
1984	2.3	2.4
1985	2.4	2.3
1986	2.2	2.8
1987	1.4	0.7
1988	1.3	1.6
1989	1.3	1.7
1990	1.2	1.6
1991	1.2	1.7
1992	0.7	1.6
1993	0.3	0.8
1994	0.5	0.8
1995	0.6	0.9
1996	1.0	1.3
1997	1.3	1.5
1998	1.4	2.0

minus the Iranian export price). If the Iranian goods cannot be secured from other sources, prices in the United States will increase, imposing a classical deadweight loss (from trade reduction) on the United States. The size and nature of this loss and its implications are very different from those of a loss in foreign exchange earnings associated with lower exports. (For Iran, similar considerations will determine the cost of U.S. sanctions on its merchandise exports and imports.)

Our estimated impact of sanctions on direct U.S.–Iran merchandise trade, using a gravity model, is shown in Table 4.4. Our results indicate sanctions reduced U.S. exports to Iran a minimum of $0.3 billion (in 1993) and a maximum of $2.4 billion (in 1985) and reduced U.S. imports from Iran a minimum of $0.7 billion (in 1987) and a maximum of $2.8 billion (in 1986).

Given that the focus of most studies is direct trade, analysis by and large stops with estimated reductions in foreign exchange earnings from exports to sanctioned countries and in foreign exchange expenditures on imports from sanctioned countries. Such estimates in no way represent the full impact of sanctions and the burden on both the sanctioning and sanctioned countries. We must look more deeply at Iran to get a measure of the impact of U.S. sanctions.

THE IMPACT OF U.S. SANCTIONS ON IRAN

Besides the initial freezing of Iranian bank deposits and FMS claims, the most prominent U.S. sanctions against Iran are the restriction on U.S. imports from and exports to Iran (imposed in 1995) and the prohibition on U.S. investment in Iran (imposed in 1995 and extended to third countries in 1996). While the direct (i.e., bilateral) impact of trade restrictions has been the most visible, noticed, studied (largely through gravity models), and debated aspect of U.S. sanctions, we believe that indirect restrictions on trade through third countries and especially non-trade and indirect policies may have had a more significant and longer-term impact on Iran. These non-trade sanctions and policies affect the following:

- The availability of export financing from the United States;
- The availability of export financing from third countries;
- The availability of IMF/World Bank financing;
- The cost and availability of commercial financing;
- Debt rescheduling efforts;
- Foreign direct investment (including that in the energy sector);
- The financing, construction, and operation of pipelines across Iran and oil swaps;
- Tourism receipts;
- The participation of U.S. companies and citizens in other Iranian-related business;
- The confidence of non-Iranians in Iran's economy; and
- Iranian economic policies.

Before tackling these issues, we will further examine direct, and especially indirect, U.S.–Iranian trade.

U.S.–Iran Trade: The Indirect Effects

While the focus of most studies of sanctions is reduced direct trade between the sender country and the target country, sanctions also affect the trade of both nations with third countries. For the sanctioned country, the cost is the loss in export revenues, the higher prices of imports, and, in extreme cases, the economic disruption due to the unavailability of imports from other sources. The trade impact of sanctions is by nature an empirical question that must be assessed on a case-by-case basis. But whether the trade effects of sanctions are larger or smaller than the non-trade effects depends on the economic, financial, and political characteristics of the target country and on the specifics of the target regime.

As is evident from our earlier discussions, petroleum (largely crude oil) comprises the lion's share of Iran's exports. This was especially the case in earlier years (see Table 4.1). Iran's non-fuel exports did not exceed $1 billion until 1987, climbing to $4.7 billion by 1998.

The United States was one of the major destinations for Iranian exports in the four years prior to the Iranian Revolution (see Appendices 4.1 through 4.4 for Iran's detailed trade data). Oil was the major export; non-oil exports to the United States totaled just $39 million in 1975–76, $31 million in 1976–77, and $63 million in 1977–78.

In the aftermath of the revolution, Iranian exports to the United States dropped dramatically but recovered later. The United States ranked tenth among export destinations in 1980, fell out of the top fifteen in 1981, climbed to twelfth in 1982 and seventh in 1983, dropped back to tenth in 1984 and 1985, then rose to fourth in 1986 and first in 1987. After falling out of the top fifteen during the years 1989–91, the United States surged to second in 1992, third in 1993, and second in 1994 before dropping to eleventh in 1995 and disappearing from the top fifteen thereafter.

This export pattern is indicative of a few simple conclusions. Iran's total exports to the United States were not affected dramatically by sanctions until 1995 and 1996; although exports to the United States declined in importance in the aftermath of the revolution and dramatically so in a few other years, they recovered significantly during the years 1992–94. This pattern may be more the result of changing U.S.–Iranian relations as opposed to sanctions per se. After the presidential order banning U.S. imports of Iranian crude was issued in 1987, U.S. companies continued to buy Iranian crude and refined it before bringing it into the United States or sold it to other countries as crude or refined products. Iran's non-oil exports to the United States were affected by the 1987 executive order, but the United States was not one of the twenty leading destinations of such exports in any year during the period 1980–88.

As an aside observation, Iran started to report sales of crude to U.S. companies as exports beginning in 1992. As a result, in 1992 Iran reported exports of $2.12 billion to the United States while the United States reported imports from Iran of only $1 million. In 1993, 1994, and 1995, Iran reported exports to the United States of

$1.41 billion, $2.21 billion, and $762 million, respectively. Iran's nonconventional definition of exports was intended to make a point.

What did Iran lose from the closing of the U.S. market for oil and non-oil exports as a result of U.S. sanctions?[16] In terms of oil export revenues, we believe Iran lost very little, if anything, as a result of U.S. sanctions. Up to 1987, there were no U.S. sanctions (except for the period 1980–81); between 1987 and 1995, buyers for Iranian crude did not decrease in number, although the number of primary destinations declined (i.e., Iranian crude could no longer be imported directly into the United States). Oil companies could shift Iranian crude to non-U.S. markets, with non-Iranian crude replacing it in the United States. After the 1995 presidential order was issued, Iran lost U.S. buyers for its crude, but it most likely got existing non-U.S. buyers to purchase the crude previously bought by U.S. companies (an amount representing roughly 10 percent of Iran's crude oil exports in the previous four years).

Patrick Clawson claims the 1995 ban cost Iran "$100–200 million during the first three months [it] took effect, May–July 1995. Even later, when Iran had found markets for all its oil, it had to sell at a discount" (Clawson 1996). We take exception to this view for a number of reasons.

First, the National Iranian Oil Company (NIOC) has close relations with most, if not all, major oil companies around the world. It could, therefore, quickly get others to purchase oil previously bought by U.S. companies (on average, roughly 10 percent of Iran's crude). Second, oil companies trade among themselves and could easily swap non-Iranian crude for Iranian crude with a U.S. company. Third, Iran has not always sold 10 percent of its crude to the United States—in fact, it sold very little oil to U.S. companies in 1981, 1988, 1989, 1990, and 1991.

Fourth, if Iran did incur some initial difficulties in selling some of its crude in 1995, the effect would have been temporary and quite small. Iran's storage costs may have increased slightly, and a very small discount (less than fifty cents per barrel) may have been necessary for a month or two. Given monthly exports of roughly $160 million to U.S. companies (the average over the previous three years), the reduction of $33 to $66 million per month estimated by Clawson would have represented a 20 percent to 40 percent discount per barrel of oil, or roughly four to eight dollars per barrel! A discount of fifty cents per barrel would have amounted to $3 to 4 million per month, and this may have lasted one to two months.[17]

Iran's non-oil exports became significant only after the 1987 embargo on U.S. imports from Iran (which contained the "oil import loophole"). To assess the impact of the loss of the U.S. market to Iran, it is essential to examine the composition of Iran's non-oil exports. Carpets and fresh and dry fruits were the two single largest items in the category of agricultural and traditional exports in most years. In 1998–99, these items amounted to $1.2 billion out of a total of $1.4 billion in this category; in previous years, the export of carpets was even more important, averaging about 50 percent of exports of agricultural and traditional goods. In the industrial category, which is roughly comparable in size to the agricultural and traditional goods category, no single product dominates. Chemicals, iron, steel, and gas comprise roughly 30 percent of these exports.

There is no doubt that the 1987 presidential order affected Iran's non-oil exports, but by how much? Before venturing a guess, a few points should be remembered. In the period 1980–88, the United States was not among the top 19 destinations for Iran's non-oil exports (see Appendix 4.2); however, the United States was the market for roughly 7 percent of Iran's non-oil exports in 1976–77, before the revolution. During the period 1973–77, Dubai (the United Arab Emirates) accounted for less than 2 percent of Iran's non-oil exports, but by 1986–87 its share was up to nearly 18 percent and in the period 1994–99 it averaged 10.7 percent. The point is that even before the 1987 executive order, Iranian goods were coming to the United States through Dubai, and this continues today (as well as through other third countries).

Still, demand for Iranian non-oil exports did shift somewhat due to the 1987 U.S. sanctions. The impact of this shift was most pronounced on carpets and dried fruits and nuts (pistachios), as Iran's industrial goods (chemicals, iron, steel, etc.) were relatively insignificant exports. Total exports of carpets and fresh and dried fruits for the period 1990–99 amounted to $14 billion. Assuming a scenario whereby U.S. sanctions had the greatest impact on Iranian exports—that is, because of U.S. sanctions no Iranian exports entered the United States through the UAE or other third countries and all of Iran's non-oil exports to the United States were withheld from world markets (i.e., consumed in Iran)—the total loss in Iran's non-oil exports would have been $980 million for the nine-year period 1990–99, for an average annual amount of roughly $110 million.

Given these extreme assumptions, this figure clearly is an upper bound. If we were to relax one of these assumptions—namely, that no non-oil exports to Dubai were destined for the United States—this figure would fall dramatically. It is inconceivable that in 1998–99 tiny Dubai could be the largest buyer of Iran's non-oil exports (for its own use) at $516 million, or 16.2 percent of Iran's total non-oil exports. If, over the same nine-year period, we assume that 25 percent of imports into the UAE were re-exported to the United States, the figure of $110 million per year would be reduced to $20 million per year! In short, we estimate that the U.S. sanctions of 1995 may have reduced non-oil exports from Iran by anywhere from $20 million to $110 million annually. To put this range of figures into some perspective, $110 million is equivalent to about three to five days' worth of oil exports, while $20 million is equivalent to less than one day's oil exports.

On Iran's import side, the 1987 sanctions essentially barred 14 categories of U.S. exports to Iran; the 1995 sanctions embargoed *all* exports. Prior to the revolution, the United States had been one of the two largest sources of imports into Iran. In 1980, U.S. exports to Iran were insignificant, but in 1981 the United States ranked tenth, with $330 million in exports to Iran. For the period 1982–85 the United States did not rank among the top fifteen sources of imports into Iran—its exports to Iran for the four years totaled $602 million, or an annual average of $150 million—and in 1986 and 1987 U.S. exports to Iran were insignificant and did not even register.

In short, Iran already had started to shift its imports to other sources two years before the 1987 executive order. This trend continued during 1988–90, as U.S. exports to Iran were insignificant. In 1991, U.S. exports to Iran totaled $140 million, then picked up in 1992 to $812 million and rose to $824 million in 1993. But they declined to $347 million in 1994 and $476 million in 1995 before becoming insignificant thereafter.

What did the 1995 sanctions banning all U.S. exports to Iran mean for Iran? Clearly, Iran could no longer buy U.S. goods directly from the United States, though it had already reduced its reliance on U.S. goods (at least directly) after the revolution. In response to economic sanctions, Iran shifted its imports to other sources and expanded imports of U.S. goods through the UAE. In fact, before the 1995 sanctions, Iran had started to import U.S. goods through the UAE. This was put in place for political reasons: Iran had reduced its direct imports from the United States because of deteriorating relations even before sanctions were put in place.

This assertion is supported by the fact that since 1986 the UAE has represented one of the top ten sources of imports into Iran. In Dubai, the infrastructure for the re-export of U.S. goods to Iran is everywhere to be seen: in the many companies owned by Iranians and registered in Dubai; in the number of UAE companies specializing in such trade; and in the volume of freight between Dubai and Iran. This fact is further confirmed by the high value of re-exports from the UAE. During the period 1993–97, re-exports from the UAE averaged $8.6 billion per year.[18]

The re-export of goods from Dubai to Iran increases the cost of imported goods to Iran as compared to direct imports from the source.[19] But not all UAE exports to Iran are U.S. goods, and such trade existed before 1995, before 1987, and even before 1980. Indeed, UAE trade has been a significant and stable component of Iranian imports for many years. To the extent such trade existed before 1995, it was Iran's choice and cannot be attributed to U.S. sanctions on Iran. Thus, any additional expense (except from the 14 categories barred in 1987) can be attributed to U.S. sanctions only after May 1995.

UAE exports to Iran totaled $441 million in 1995, $473 million in 1996, $562 million in 1997, and $551 million in 1998. Even if we assume that all of the increase in trade over 1995 was the result of additional re-exported U.S. goods, the extra trade costs in 1996, 1997, and 1998 were $32 million, $121 million, and $110 million, respectively. Assuming a 20 percent re-export mark-up on $32 million, $121 million, and $110 million, the extra burden to Iran

Table 4.5
U.S. Exports to and Imports from the UAE, 1975–97 ($ Millions)

Year	U.S. Exports	U.S. Imports
1975	372	781
1976	425	1,785
1977	515	2,278
1978	493	2,297
1979	667	2,522
1980	998	3,163
1981	1,077	2,102
1982	1,101	2,139
1983	864	542
1984	695	1,278
1985	597	722
1986	493	391
1987	619	723
1988	705	616
1989	1,204	737
1990	993	952
1991	1,456	769
1992	1,552	872
1993	1,811	775
1994	1,593	479
1995	1,994	486
1996	1,763	538
1997	2,606	965

Source: International Monetary Fund (1999).

Table 4.6
Estimated Direct Foreign Exchange Losses to Iran from Executive Order 12959 ($ Millions)

	1995	1996	1997	1998	1999
Loss in oil exports	21–28	36–48	36–48	36–48	36–48
Loss in non-oil exports	11.7–64.2	20–110	20–110	20–110	20–110
Loss in imports re-exported from the UAE to Iran*	—	5.3	20.2	18.3	12.3
Total losses	32.7–92.2	61.3–163.3	86.2–178.2	74.3–176.3	68.3–170.3

*For 1995, this figure would have been insignificant.

would have amounted to $5.3 million, $20.2 million, and $18.3 million, respectively.

In addition to officially reported exports to Iran from the UAE, there is also a great deal of smuggling (to avoid import duties), but on this activity we cannot even venture a guess. Official Iran–UAE trade may thus underestimate the amount of actual UAE exports to Iran. To get an idea of this, in Table 4.5 we present U.S. trade with the UAE. U.S. exports to the UAE have shown a dramatic increase since 1986, some of which represents higher official Iran–UAE trade and some of which represents smuggling.

In Table 4.6 we summarize our estimates of the trade effect (deterioration in Iran's balance of payments) of sanctions for the period 1995–99. Our estimates of the foreign exchange losses to Iran attributable to the sanctions—$32.7 million to $92.2 million in 1995 and $68.3 million to $170.3 million in 1999—represent roughly 5 percent of the figure, taking the second half of 1995 and the first half of 1996 (Clawson 1996). Even these losses to Iran are overestimated. As mentioned previously, we have assumed that lower non-oil exports to the United States were not offset by higher exports to other countries. It should also be remembered that these numbers represent foreign exchange losses rather than financial costs to Iran, because even if non-oil exports declined commensurately, these goods could have been consumed domestically or resources could have been reallocated to the production of other goods.

Reduced U.S. and Non-U.S. Export Financing

Most OECD countries promote their exports through a variety of political and economic initiatives. One of the major economic incentives they offer is low-cost export financing. There has been no U.S. export financing for Iran from the U.S. Export-Import Bank since 1990.

The absence of U.S. export financing has imposed several costs on Iran. First, Iran has incurred the differential cost between commercial trade financing and that afforded by U.S. export financing. Second, the absence of U.S. trade financing may have curtailed trade financing for Iran from other countries, for two reasons. One reason is that countries provide export financing in order to compete with other countries, and if the United States is not providing export financing for Iran, there is less pressure for other countries to do so. Moreover, U.S. sanctions may increase the perceived risk of Iranian financing and thus lower the availability (or increase the cost) of export financing from other countries.

To assess the impact on Iran of a reduction in export cover from the United States and other countries, we surveyed the export credit agencies of all OECD countries for data on the volume of export cover, its terms, and whether the volume or terms had been affected by U.S. sanctions. Unfortunately, we did not receive even one complete response, though we received nearly complete information from Switzerland. (In the case of the United States, we knew that no export cover had been available beginning in 1990.) As a result, we were forced to be less ambitious and make a number of assumptions in order to construct some estimates.

To get a rough idea of the reduction in export cover, we assumed the following: U.S. sanctions did not affect the volume or terms of export cover from other (i.e., non-U.S.) countries for Iran; none of the loss in U.S. export cover was replaced by other countries; the loss of export cover attributable to the United States was, on average, equivalent to 4.2 percent of Iran's export credits (this represents the highest percentage share of Iran's imports from the UAE during the period 1995–98 and is higher than the percentage share

Table 4.7
Estimated Foreign Exchange Losses by Iran Due to Absence of U.S. Trade Financing

	1995	1996	1997	1998
Total Export Credits for Iran ($ millions)	12,073	11,550	9,769	8,790
Estimated Loss in U.S. Export Credits for Iran (4.3% of total credits; figures in $ millions)	507	485	410	369
LC Confirmation Fees	7.0–10.0%	7.0–10.0%	4.0–4.75%	3.0–5.0%
Estimated Foreign Exchange Loss to Iran ($ millions)	36–51	34–48	16–19	11–18

Source: Export credit figures from World Bank (2000b). LC confirmation fees were obtained from a very large non-U.S. bank.

of imports from the United States during the period 1992–95); and the financial cost to Iran of the loss of U.S. export cover is approximated by the cost of confirming Iranian letters of credit (LCs).[20] The results of our assumptions are shown in Table 4.7. The losses are in the range of $11 million to $51 million, depending on the year in question.

We also tried to get an alternative and broader (including losses in non-U.S. export cover) idea of these losses by calculating the ratio of Iran's export credits to total imports and trying to identify a discernible pattern. There was not a pattern. We also compared Iran's ratio to those of Egypt, Indonesia, and Pakistan. Again, Iran's figures were not significantly different.

Reduced IMF/World Bank Financing

Severed U.S.–Iranian relations have essentially meant that since 1980 the United States has opposed any assistance for Iran from international organizations. In the case of the IMF, the United States has had no reason to take action, as Iran has so far decided not to apply for an IMF program (loan). During the late 1990s, Iran was seriously considering applying for a program but decided against such an initiative. It is possible, but highly unlikely, that potential U.S. opposition played a role in this decision. In any event, little damage has been inflicted on Iran at the IMF because of U.S. sanctions.

The story is somewhat different at the World Bank. Given that World Bank financing of projects is absent conditions that are attached to an IMF program, Iran has been much more interested in borrowing from the World Bank. Predictably, the United States has

Table 4.8
Iranian Projects Financed by the World Bank, 1980–2000

Date Approved	Project Description	Amount ($ millions)	Closing Date
14 March 1991	Earthquake Recovery	250.0	30 June 1996
28 May 1992	Teheran Drainage	77.0	31 Dec. 2000
28 May 1992	Sistan Flood Control	57.1	31 Dec. 2000
16 March 1993	Irrigation Improvement	157.0	30 June 2001
25 March 1993	Health and Family Planning	141.4	31 Dec. 2000
30 March 1993	Power Sector Inefficiency	165.0	31 Dec. 2000
18 May 2000	Teheran Sewerage	145.0	31 Dec. 2000
18 May 2000	Health Care	87.0	30 June 2000

Source: World Bank.

opposed World Bank financing of projects in Iran and has at times lobbied other members to oppose financing for Iran.

Under the shah's regime, Iran did not apply for any World Bank loans after September 1974. The dramatic increase in oil prices in the 1970s resulted in large current account surpluses, and Iran thus had little need for World Bank financing. In the post-revolutionary era, Iran did not borrow from the World Bank until March 1991 (see Table 4.8), but since then it has used World Bank financing with increasing frequency.

Some Iranian projects, however, were never finalized by the World Bank. These fall into three categories: (i) dropped without full executive board discussion; (ii) dropped with full executive board discussion; and (iii) reserved with full executive board discussion.

In the case of Iran, the most likely reason a project would be dropped or reserved is U.S. opposition. We have identified eight such dropped projects and one reserved project. Leaving the reserved project (totaling $387 million) aside, investment in the eight dropped projects would have amounted to $1.09 billion.[21] If Iran could have financed these projects through the World Bank, its interest rate would have been roughly 7 percent per annum; in the private markets, Iran's cost of capital in 1999 was 9.0 percent to 9.25 percent per annum.[22] Thus, the cost to Iran of U.S. opposition was roughly 2 percent × $1.09 billion for the term of the loans, or $21.7 million annually over the life of the projects.

Higher Cost and Reduced Availability of Commercial Financing

As mentioned earlier, Iran's substantial external borrowing in the aftermath of the Iran-Iraq war did little for its economy. The additional resources essentially financed consumption and dubious investment projects (it could, therefore, be argued that Iran was lucky not to have had better access to external financing). Granted, Iran is not alone in this regard: The world is full of countries that have enjoyed access to commercial financing but now have little to show for it except the burden of a large external debt and its servicing. Leaving this judgment aside, however, there still remains the issue of Iran's cost of commercial borrowing.

U.S. sanctions could increase Iran's cost of capital for a number of reasons. The inability of U.S. commercial banks to lend to Iran would mean less competition to supply Iran with capital and thus a somewhat higher cost. The negative economic perception of Iran imparted by U.S. sanctions could affect third countries'

Table 4.9
Iran's External Debt, 1998–2002 ($ Millions)

	Total Debt Stock	Long-Term Debt	Short-Term Debt
1988	5,831	2,055	3,776
1989	6,519	1,862	4,657
1990	9,021	1,797	7,224
1991	11,330	2,065	9,226
1992	16,033	1,730	14,304
1993	23,362	5,759	17,604
1994	22,712	16,005	6,707
1995	21,879	15,430	6,449
1996	16,703	11,948	4,755
1997	11,823	8,469	3,354
1998	14,391	8,307	6,054
1999	9,900	6,400	3,500
2000	9,000	5,000	4,000
2001	8,000	4,000	4,000
2002	7,000	3,000	4,000

Source: 1988–98 figures from World Bank (2000b). All other figures are authors' estimates.

assessments of Iran's investment risk, again increasing the cost of borrowing. Additionally, the cloud of a secondary boycott (extraterritoriality) hanging over Iran could further raise the cost of lending to Iran.

Table 4.9 details Iran's commercial borrowing since 1988. While Iran's cost of capital is due largely to domestic economic conditions and outlook, U.S. sanctions have affected Iran's economic performance through a number of direct and indirect channels. It is difficult, if not impossible, to scientifically estimate the impact of U.S. sanctions on Iran's cost of capital, so we used three rough approaches instead.

First, we assessed Iran's cost of commercial borrowing using the borrowing costs of some comparable countries (Egypt and Indonesia) as a benchmark to estimate Iran's "extra" cost of capital attributable to sanctions. Second, the higher financing cost for Iran is also mirrored in Iran's high cost of LC confirmation. LC confirmation fees are a direct reflection of a country's short-term credit risk. In Iran's case, this fee is affected by domestic economic conditions, current account balance, oil prices and revenues, debt rescheduling, and arrears as well as by U.S. sanctions. The size of this fee in recent years has been 4 to 5.5 percent in 1991–92, 18 to 20 percent in 1993–94, 7 to 10 percent in 1995–96, 4 to 4.75 percent in 1997, 3 to 5 percent in 1998–99, and 1 to 1.4 percent in

Table 4.10
Iran's Higher Cost of Commercial Financing

	Higher Interest Expense (%)	Stock of Debt ($ millions)	Higher Cost of Financing ($ millions)
1995	0.5–0.75	21,879	109–164
1996	0.5–0.75	16,703	83–125
1997	0.5–0.75	11,823	59–89
1998	0.5–0.75	14,391	72–108
1999	0.5–0.75	10,900	54–82
2000	0.5–0.75	9,000	45–67
2001	0.5–0.75	8,000	40–60
2002	0.5–0.75	7,000	35–52

2000.[23] Third, we talked with a Middle Eastern banker who has loaned money to Iran to get a sense of his feel for the market.

Based on those three approaches we estimated, albeit unscientifically, that Iran's cost of capital may have been adversely affected by U.S. sanctions in the range of 0.5 to 0.75 percent. Using this estimate, we calculated the additional borrowing costs to Iran as a result of U.S. sanctions (see Table 4.10). Depending on the year and, thus, the size of Iran's external debt, this cost to Iran has been in the range of $135 million to $164 million.

Higher Debt Rescheduling Fees

During the period 1993–95, Iran's ability to finance its external debt deteriorated because of low oil prices, the depreciation of the dollar, and a surge in imports. In 1993–94, Iran managed to refinance its commercial debt. Iran wanted to reschedule its official debt generally under the auspices of the Paris Club as opposed to undertaking a number of bilateral negotiations. The United States opposed this effort, and Iran was forced to take the bilateral approach. The first agreement was with Germany, providing Iran with a two-year grace period, a four-year repayment period of principal, and interest at 5 to 7 percent per year.

If the United States had not opposed the Paris Club rescheduling, Iran would have received standard Paris Club terms. This would have entailed rescheduling at market interest rates (0.5 percent below Iran's rate), a repayment period of ten-plus years, and a five- or six-year grace period. Leaving aside the burden of a shorter grace period, Iran's interest payments (on its stock of official debt) were higher by 0.5 percent, translating to a cost of $13–55 million depending on the year (see Table 4.11).

Table 4.11
Iran's Higher Debt Rescheduling Fees

	Higher Rescheduling Rate (percent)	Stock of Bilateral Debt* ($ millions)	Higher Rescheduling Fee ($ millions)
1994	0.5	11,101	55
1995	0.5	10,974	55
1996	0.5	8,192	41
1997	0.5	8,258	41
1998	0.5	4,386	22
1999	0.5	3,058	15
2000	0.5	2,585	13

Sources: Figures for 1994–98 from World Bank (2000b); figures for 1999–2000 from International Monetary Fund (2000).

Reduced Foreign Direct Investment

Sanctions have reduced the overall attractiveness of investment in Iran, and this has been especially true as a result of U.S. threats of secondary boycotts. Still, with all of these negatives, Iran has attracted investors to its energy sector, with more than $5 billion committed for the three phases of the South Pars gas field.

In 1999, Elf and Agip agreed to invest $1 billion to develop an offshore field (Doroud). Elf, Agip, and Bow Valley Energy are investing $300 million to develop another offshore field (Balal), and in late 1999 Shell signed a contract to redevelop two other offshore fields (Soroush and Nowruz). Between Pars and these offshore fields, FDI committed to the energy sector during 1997–99 exceeded $7 billion. With the discovery of the Azadeghan oil field in 1999 and its estimated reserves of up to 25 billion barrels (and a capacity of 400,000–500,000 barrels per day), Iran will continue to attract foreign investors for its energy sector.[24] While U.S. sanctions have reduced the level of FDI in Iran's energy sector, their most important effect may have been to delay or postpone FDI (Iran's giant North Pars gas field is still not under development).

The story is different outside the energy sector, where Iran has not attracted a significant volume of FDI. The reasons for this failure are many: Iran's unattractive policies toward FDI, its sub-par economic performance and outlook, its less-than-attractive business climate, negative press coverage, and U.S. sanctions. Given the state of the Iranian economy, companies are not willing to jeopardize their relations with the United States unless it is worth their while, as may be the case with Iran's energy sector. For example, in

1999 total global FDI was $865 billion, with $9.2 billion in the Middle East and North Africa but only $85 million in Iran (compared to $4.8 billion in Saudi Arabia, $1.5 billion in Egypt, and $847 million in Morocco).[25] Iran has roughly 1 percent of the world's population, and if it attracted a commensurate share of the world's FDI, it would have received $8.6 billion. Similarly, Iran produces 0.5 percent of the world's GDP, and a commensurate share of the world's FDI would be $4.3 billion (World Bank 2000b).

What proportion of the shortfall in FDI is due to Iran's policies, to U.S. sanctions, and to other factors outside Iran's control? What has been the cost to Iran of lower FDI resulting from U.S. sanctions? Precise answers to these questions are beyond our scope. We can, however, offer educated guesses.

Investments in the energy sector should be separated from other investments. In the case of the energy sector, investments (with the exception of the trans-Iranian pipeline for Caspian oil) are moving ahead, albeit slowly. Our best guess is that these investments (totaling roughly $10–12 billion if North Pars is included) have been delayed by about five years. In the non-oil sectors, our best guess is that FDI in Iran would have been on the same order as in Egypt (excluding the energy sector), meaning Iran may have lost about $0.5–1.0 billion per year in non-oil FDI in recent years.

Under better political circumstances, including the absence of U.S. sanctions, much higher FDI might have been possible, especially with the development of the South and North Pars fields and peripheral petrochemical complexes. This would have benefited both Iran and the United States and could have resulted in significant exports to Iran.

What have the delayed (in the case of the energy sector) and reduced (in the case of non-energy sectors) FDI meant for Iran? In the case of the former, we estimate the loss at roughly 7 percent (as a discount factor) of the FDI that was delayed, or $700–840 million, but these losses are of limited duration and disappear when the projects come on line. In the case of non-energy sectors, we estimate that Iran lost about $0.5–1.0 billion in foreign exchange inflows per year.

Sanctions on FDI are a very sharp double-edged sword. They can impose a heavy loss on the target country by delaying FDI, but the burden on the sanctioning nation may be even more severe because its entities will not participate in major projects that will, instead, go to companies from other countries. This may, in turn, affect related joint-venture projects in the future. Moreover, the effects of this form of economic sanction may linger far beyond the lifting of sanctions.

Pipelines Across Iran and Oil Swaps

Three of the five Caspian littoral countries (Azerbaijan, Kazakhstan, and Turkmenistan) are landlocked; only Iran and Russia have access to the seas. There are a number of routes for transporting Caspian oil to market through pipelines. The most prominent routes are through Turkey (Baku-Ceyhan), Afghanistan-Pakistan, and Iran and expanded routes through Russia (Baku-Novorossiisk) and Georgia (Baku-Supsa). The United States has supported the Baku-Ceyhan route, while most oil companies privately favor the Iranian route because of the cost of construction, the number of countries to be transited, and the location of the terminal and its existing facilities. Assuming this to be the case, what has Iran lost (or what will Iran lose) because of U.S. opposition to an Iranian oil pipeline route?

Iran's potential benefits from Caspian oil pipelines fall into a number of categories: pipeline construction in Iran, pipeline operation and maintenance in Iran, annual payments for transit and loading fees, and a general enhancement of Iran's business reputation. There are two options for an Iranian oil pipeline route. The first option would be to build a new trans-Iranian pipeline dedicated to Caspian oil. The second option would be to build a new pipeline to hook up with Iran's existing network. As to the first approach, our best guess (based on the estimates of a person formerly in this business) is investment in the neighborhood of $2 billion for a 1 million barrel/day (b/d) pipeline, with roughly 30 percent of this in local Iranian content. With respect to the second approach, the Iranians have proposed a two-phase pipeline program. In the first phase, the Iranians propose 300,000 b/d and claim a construction cost of $450 million (50 percent local Iranian content), as they will be using part of an existing pipeline network. For the second phase they see an additional 1 million b/d at a cost of $1.2 billion, with 30 percent local content.

The cost of the Baku-Ceyhan route is placed at $3.2 billion (*Petroleum Economist* 2000). For our purposes, we assume a $2 billion cost for a 1 million b/d pipeline through Iran. This $2 billion of FDI would involve $600 million in Iranian contracts over roughly a two-year period, or $300 million in contracts per year. Our estimates for pipeline operation and maintenance are on the order of $50 million/year. As for transit fees, loading fees, and annual lump sum payments, our best guess (looking at Stevens' historical discussion and talking to various executives familiar with such transactions) is an amount close to $1 per barrel. This number is a matter of negotiation and also depends on the attractiveness of alternate routes. Finally, we assume volume would be

Table 4.12
Iran's Projected Foreign Exchange Earnings from a Trans-Iranian Oil Pipeline and Oil Swaps ($ Millions)

	Year 1 (1 Million b/d)	Year 2 (1.5 Million b/d)	Year 3	Year 4
Construction	300	300	0	0
Maintenance	0	0	50	50
Transit and Other Fees	0	0	547	547
Subtotal	300	300	597	597
Oil Swaps	90	90	90	135
Total	390	390	687	732

on the order of 1 to 1.5 million barrels/day. In Table 4.12 we summarize these results.

In addition to these benefits from pipelines, better U.S.–Iranian relations could allow Iran to swap oil from Caspian sources for its northern refineries for Iranian crude on the Persian Gulf. Based on current refinery deliveries, Iran could today conservatively use 500,000 b/d of Caspian crude for its northern refineries and expand this to 750,000 b/d in two years. In the past, such a swap could have benefited Iran to the tune of $0.50/barrel or roughly $90 million per year, rising to $135 million per year in 2002. The annual losses from oil swaps ($90–135 million) and transit fees ($365 million) are financial losses, whereas the annual loss from construction and maintenance ($50–350 million, depending on the year) is largely a loss in foreign exchange because Iran would have to devote real resources to these endeavors.

Reduced Tourism Receipts

Before the revolution, Iran was beginning to develop a reputation for its historic attractions. The revolution tarnished this reputation, and Iran's depiction in the international press discouraged tourism. The Islamic regime's strict enforcement of the female dress code and other restrictions has deterred all but the truly adventurous. The absence of a first-class tourist infrastructure has been another negative factor.

We believe that U.S. sanctions have played little direct role in dissuading tourists. The regime's rules and regulations and the negative depiction of Iran in the Western press have been the major deterrents. Sanctions may have played an indirect role in the absence of foreign investment in hotels and other tourist facilities in Iran. But again, Iran's own policies deter such activities.

By any standard, Iran should be a popular destination for foreign tourists. It is a nation with some of the greatest cultural sites and most breathtaking scenery in the world, plus beautiful beaches and great skiing. Prior to the revolution, Iran was becoming an exotic tourist attraction for Europeans and Americans and was increasing its traditional pull of Persian Gulf Arabs. U.S. sanctions have had some negative effect on tourism: Travel by U.S. citizens to Iran has declined from a significant figure prior to the revolution to almost nothing today.

Non-participation of U.S. Entities in Iran-Related Business

International business is much more than simple trade deals. It is built on deep-rooted business and personal relations and nurtured by constant contact and dialogue. It grows from dreams into projects designed, developed, and financed by would-be partners from across the globe. The realization of such projects, in turn, results in FDI, increased trade in goods and services, and the sharing of profits.

The ruptured relations between the United States and Iran have had business consequences that will be felt for years to come. In this sullied atmosphere, a few oil-related projects are going ahead (at South Pars, a number of offshore fields, and the newly discovered Azadeghan field), but others cannot be nurtured and developed because of U.S. non-participation. Americans have essentially lost all direct contact with their Iranian business counterparts. Under U.S. law there can be very little discussion, let alone cooperation, between U.S. and Iranian business interests.

The cost of these lost opportunities—to the United States as well as Iran—is difficult to quantify. Besides the lost FDI in the oil and gas sector and the attendant trade that invariably would have followed, the rupture of business has indefinitely postponed the potential for joint venture projects in a number of other sectors unrelated to energy. Our estimates of economic losses from U.S. sanctions are thus underestimated in all of the components we have considered.

Psychological Effects of U.S. Sanctions on Iranians and Non-Iranians

By cutting off the U.S. economy (by far the largest on earth) from Iran, sanctions have cast a shadow on the Iranian economy. It is common in Iran to hear Iranians say the economy will improve when sanctions are lifted. The psychological impact of sanctions means that capital flight is higher and domestic investment lower. This attitude, in turn, affects the views of non-Iranians toward the future of the Iranian economy. All of this, although not quantifiable, is an important factor in Iran's economic performance.

Impact on Iranian Economic Policies

Although Iran's economic policies are driven by domestic political and social considerations, U.S. sanctions have had an impact. The regime is concerned with the perceived impact of sanctions and is anxious to show they are of no real consequence and, in fact, of greater harm to the United States than to Iran. Thus, Iran's leaders are attracted to high-profile projects with European and Japanese companies that may not always be in Iran's best interest. Moreover, because the United States is not a participant in these projects (e.g., South Pars), Iran's bargaining power is somewhat reduced. The cost of this impact on Iran is difficult to quantify.

SUMMARY OF THE IMPACT OF SANCTIONS ON IRAN

Direct merchandise trade between the United States and Iran has declined significantly because of sanctions, but the broader trade impact (incorporating third-country effects) has been limited. As for Iran's exports, its oil revenues have been little affected by sanctions, while its non-oil exports, though modestly affected, have not been a total loss because some goods may have been diverted to other countries and some may have been consumed domestically. As for its imports, Iran can buy most goods previously imported from the United States from other countries and has continued to import many U.S. goods, especially through Dubai (albeit at a 20 percent markup). Only the higher cost of U.S. imports through third countries is a real out-of-pocket cost to Iran.

To the extent sanctions have had a deleterious effect on Iran, it has been indirect and imposed through other channels—higher financing costs, retarded or stalled oil and non-oil joint venture projects (which, in turn, have impeded oil capacity development and thus possibly reduced oil production and oil exports), and the like. Moreover, the non-quantifiable, longer-term, indirect effects of sanctions may turn out to be their most significant impact.

In Table 4.13, we summarize our estimate of the direct and indirect impacts of U.S. unilateral sanctions on Iran. Depending on the year, the annual cost to Iran of U.S. sanctions ranges from a low of

Table 4.13

Summary of Iran's Losses from U.S. Sanctions, 1995–2001[1] ($ Millions)

	1995	1996	1997	1998	1999	2000	2001
Higher Import Prices	2	5	20	18	25	27	27
Lower Export Receipts[2]	21–28	36–48	36–48	36–48	36–48	36–48	36–48
Official Export Financing	36–51	34–48	16–19	11–18	11–18	11–18	11–18
World Bank Lending	?	?	?	?	22	22	22
Commercial Financing	109–164	83–125	59–89	72–108	54–82	29–43	20–30
Rescheduling Fees	55	55	41	41	22	15	13
Lost and Delayed FDI (energy sector)	700–840	700–840	700–840	700–840	700–840	700–840	700–840
Lost and Delayed FDI (non-energy)	?	?	?	?	?	?	?
Tourism Receipts	?	?	?	?	?	?	?
Oil Pipelines	?	?	?	?	300	300	415
Oil Swaps	90	90	90	90	90	90	135
Intangibles	?	?	?	?	?	?	?
Total	1,013–1,230	1,003–1,211	952–1,147	968–1,168	1,260–1,447	1,230–1,403	1,379–1,548
Total Losses from Trade	23–30	41–53	56–68	54–66	51–73	63–75	63–75

[1]These figures represent estimated real costs to Iran. Iran's total non-oil exports are somewhat lower due to sanctions, but these losses are more precisely a loss of foreign exchange as opposed to a real burden. The lower estimated total export figures are in the range of $25–$110 million annually. Similarly, while we cannot estimate the cost of foregone non-energy FDI to Iran, we estimate the loss of foreign exchange at $0.5–1 billion per year.

[2]These figures would be increased by $25–110 million annually to arrive at foreign exchange losses.

$952 million to a high of $1.47 billion.[26] These estimates exclude the effects of a number of factors resulting from sanctions that we could not quantify, such as reduced non-energy FDI. Still, these figures are quite revealing with regard to the relative size of trade losses and other losses to Iran because of sanctions.

Our estimate for total annual trade losses is $33–182 million. As mentioned earlier, most of the trade losses are more precisely losses of foreign exchange—in the case of Iran, the real trade loss burden is $23–75 million, depending on the year—whereas non-trade losses are both a loss of foreign exchange and a loss of net resources.

The preoccupation with trade losses, though understandable because of the relative ease of quantification, may be misplaced in the case of countries such as Iran. Iran's major export is oil, a largely fungible commodity that easily can be diverted to other markets. For other countries that export a significant percentage of their manufactured goods to the United States (especially goods customized for the U.S. market), these losses could be much more significant. On the import side, Iran has managed to find other sources for most goods previously imported from the United States.

THE IMPACT OF SANCTIONS ON THE UNITED STATES

As is to be expected, the losses to the United States, though broadly similar, are different in nature and size than those to Iran.

Ruptured U.S.–Iran relations and the imposition of sanctions may have reduced direct U.S. merchandise exports to Iran by as much as $0.3–2.4 billion, depending on the year in question (see Table 4.4). This loss should not be seen as a total cost to the United States but instead viewed as an upper bound of foreign exchange losses. In part, these goods could have been exported to other countries or consumed domestically, or the inputs used to produce other goods for export or domestic consumption. Most importantly, when sanctions are lifted, this level of exports to Iran can be expected to be restored over time.

The loss to U.S. banks from not lending to Iran would be minimal in our view. Yes, U.S. banks would have marginally fewer lending opportunities, but they could increase their loans elsewhere and get slightly less return and/or reduced risk diversification. But the cumulative effect of ruptured financial relationships, if continued for some time, could impose a cost on the United States, especially after Iran's economic performance improves.

The implied losses for the U.S. energy industry from non-participation in Iran are somewhat different than those for Iran. The U.S.

energy industry can no longer participate in South Pars (all phases are already contracted), North Pars (in all likelihood), Doroud, Balal, Souroush, Nowruz, and Azadeghan (in all likelihood). This is a tremendous loss for the U.S. energy industry that could be further magnified over time because non-U.S. firms will have much more information about, and be more familiar with, Iranian oil and gas fields. Thus, even when sanctions are relaxed, U.S. firms may be less competitive in bidding on related and new projects in Iran.

To place a rough estimate on the losses for the U.S. energy industry, we assume that the United States could have won about 60 percent of these projects and that the extra return (over and above opportunities in the United States) would have been 10 percent on the total investment. This results in a loss of profits of about $700–840 million (excluding new projects), and losses will continue to accrue even after sanctions are lifted. As for FDI in non-energy sectors, we believe the situation is very different, as U.S. corporations could have found attractive investments elsewhere.

U.S. companies would be the major beneficiaries of any pipeline construction, trans-Iranian or otherwise. If U.S. sanctions ultimately mean that a Baku-Ceyhan or some other non-Iranian route is chosen, U.S. companies (engineering firms and oil companies) may lose little, if anything. If, however, U.S. sanctions mean that pipeline construction is postponed for a number of years, a loss will be felt. But even in the latter case the maximum loss (spread over a number of years) to U.S. firms would be the difference in the construction cost of the Baku-Ceyhan route and an Iranian route, since, theoretically, the U.S. government could pay this cost difference above the cost of a route through Iran and the pipeline would go ahead. This cost difference is estimated at $1.2 billion over three years, and we assume that as much as 50 percent of this could accrue to U.S. companies.

In the case of oil swaps, the outcome would depend on relative negotiating skills. We assume the oil companies would receive a benefit equal to that of Iran, with 50 percent of this benefit accruing to U.S. companies for a figure of $45 million per year (increasing to $67.5 million in 2002). In Table 4.14, we summarize the results of our assumptions. As in the case of Iran, the major loss for the United States may lie in the long-term impact of unquantifiable items, namely ruptured business relations on developing and financing projects and supplying the real resources required. These losses, while exceeding estimated direct trade losses, will continue for many years after the lifting of sanctions.

Table 4.14

Summary of Losses from U.S. Sanctions for the United States[1] ($ Millions)

	1995	1996	1997	1998	1999	2000	2001
Real losses due to lower trade	?	?	?	?	?	?	?
FDI (Non-energy)	5–10	5–10	5–10	5–10	5–10	5–10	5–10
FDI (energy sector)	700–840	700–840	700–840	700–840	700–840	700–840	700–840
Oil pipeline	110–140	110–140	110–140	110–140	110–140	110–140	110–140
Oil swaps	45	45	45	45	45	45	67.5
Financial services							
Intangibles							
Total	860–1035	860–1035	860–1035	860–1035	860–1035	860–1035	882–1057

[1]These figures represent estimated real costs to the United States. Losses associated with energy sector FDI can be expected to continue for a number of years even after sanctions are lifted. Losses to the United States from non-participation in Azadeghan field are not shown here as the impact of this field would occur after 2001. The losses with this field could potentially (if the field matches some expectations) be on the order of these total losses. U.S. total exports are lower due to sanctions, but these are more precisely a loss of foreign exchange as opposed to a real burden.

THE EFFECTIVENESS OF SANCTIONS AND THEIR BROADER IMPLICATIONS

U.S. economic sanctions on Iran were meant to influence various alleged Iranian policies, including Iran's opposition to the U.S.–led Middle East peace process, Iran's support for Hezbollah and Hamas, Iran's attempt to acquire nuclear and ballistic weapons, Iran's general support for international terrorism, and Iran's general hostility toward the United States.

After 20 years of sanctions, Iran still opposes the U.S.–led peace process, and its alleged support for Hezbollah and Hamas does not appear to have diminished. Iran denies it is trying to acquire nuclear weapons (a claim supported by international inspections), and even if it were it is unclear how general U.S. economic sanctions could thwart such efforts. Would not a ban on the trade of nuclear technology (with the threat of secondary boycotts against countries that engage in such trade with Iran) be more effective?

According to press reports, Iran apparently has tested some longer-range ballistic missiles. General U.S. economic sanctions on Iran have reduced Iran's foreign exchange earnings, but if Iran is determined to acquire such weapons it could do so by cutting other expenditures. As for Iran's general encouragement of international terrorism, there is little hard evidence to support this U.S. claim. Again, if Iran is in fact a force behind international terrorism, it is unclear how U.S. economic sanctions would change Iranian policies unless the economic hardship on Iran was sufficient to pressure the government. Focused policies against Iran would be more cost-effective than this "shotgun" approach.

Lastly, it appears that the behavior and policies to which the United States objects have changed very little since 1995. Secretary of State Madeline Albright confirmed much of this on 17 March 2000:

> As a step towards bringing down that wall of mistrust, I want today to discuss the question of economic sanctions. The United States imposed sanctions against Iran because of our concern about proliferation, and because the authorities exercising control in Tehran financed and supported terrorist groups, including those violently opposed to the Middle East peace process.
>
> To date, the political developments in Iran have not caused its military to cease its determined effort to acquire the technology, materials, and assistance needed to develop nuclear weapons. Nor have those developments caused Iran's Revolutionary Guard Corps or its Ministry of Intelligence and Security to get out of the terrorism business. Until these policies change, fully normal ties between our governments will not be

possible and our principal sanctions will remain. The purpose of our sanctions, however, is to spur changes in policy. (Albright 2000)

While it is unclear whether and how U.S. sanctions have changed Iranian policies, it is obvious that they have resulted in economic losses to both sides. Moreover, these losses will continue to accrue for many years after the sanctions have been lifted. For example, if a non-Iranian pipeline is built for Caspian oil, Iran will forever lose the associated transit fees. If non-U.S. companies develop Iran's newly discovered Azadeghan oil field, the United States will lose business in all future years, even after sanctions have been lifted. In addition, Iran is unlikely to resume normal relations with U.S. banks for many years after the sanctions are lifted (especially given the past freezing of Iranian deposits), with losses for both sides.

U.S. economic sanctions have done little to damage Iran's trade. The value of Iran's exports has not declined significantly, and the cost of Iran's imports has not increased appreciably. While Iran's foreign exchange earnings may have been reduced by as much as $183 million annually, the real cost to Iran has been less, on the order of $23–75 million annually. However, specific non-trade sanctions (e.g., a ban on FDI in Iran and opposition to an oil pipeline across Iran for Caspian oil and to oil swaps) have hurt Iran significantly. These same sanctions also have been preeminent in adversely affecting U.S. business interests. Careful analysis before the imposition of sanctions probably would have indicated such an impact. Focused or "smart" sanctions would have had about the same impact on Iran as the much broader sanctions imposed.

CONCLUSION

Over roughly the past twenty years, U.S. sanctions on Iran have imposed a significant economic burden on the United States as well as Iran. Direct merchandise trade between the United States and Iran has declined significantly, but the real cost of sanctions for each country is not reduced bilateral trade, since much of this trade is diverted to third countries. The real cost of sanctions for both countries is impeded FDI, missed joint-venture opportunities, and broken financial relationships. These costs will continue to accrue even after sanctions are lifted, while bilateral direct trade may be restored much more quickly.

International business is much more than merchandise trade. It is built on deep-rooted business relations and nurtured by continual contact and dialogue. It grows from dreams into projects designed, developed, and financed by would-be partners from across the globe. The realization of such projects in turn results in FDI, technology transfer, increased trade in goods and services, and the sharing of profits. Even when sanctions are removed, economic relations generally will not improve to their pre-sanctions level because the legacy of broken economic and financial relations can take many years to repair and reestablish.

Sanctions are one of the many ways that countries interfere with international trade and finance. When countries use tariffs or traditional non-tariff barriers (NTBs), their goal is limited to affecting some aspect of international economic or financial relationships with the target. In the case of sanctions (a nontraditional NTB), the goals are usually much more ambitious—to change economic relations and inflict economic hardship on the target, in turn causing a fundamental change in policies, government behavior, and more. Invariably, however, there is little or no connection between the sanction and the policy goal. Sanctions thus represent a shotgun approach to international economic, financial, and political relations.

While the imposition of tariffs or NTBs usually invites retaliation and is thus avoided, retaliation is hardly mentioned in the case of sanctions. The practical reason for this blind spot is that only one major country, the United States, uses this instrument with frequency, and the countries that are its targets invariably are not in a position to retaliate. Thus, while economists warn against the dangers of tariffs and NTBs, very little is said about the dangers of sanctions.

But sanctions impose a significant cost, both on target countries and on the United States. The costs of sanctions are underestimated for a number of reasons, including the fact that estimates (1) usually incorporate only the reduction in direct merchandise trade and ignore services, costs of capital, FDI, and other capital flows; (2) assume that sanctions have an effect only while they are in force (the residual effect after the lifting of sanctions is not taken into account); and (3) ignore the impact on long-term business relations, such as reducing the perceived reliability of U.S. firms, with the target and with third countries.

The success of sanctions, meanwhile, is exaggerated, because policies in the target country eventually change—not necessarily in response to the sanctions, but because of the passage of time. Yet because sanctions do not cost U.S. lives, require no budgetary allocation (their cost is thus somewhat hidden), and do not make daily headlines, their success can always be claimed to be around the corner, making them a popular instrument for politicians.

The experience with U.S. sanctions against Iran confirms much of the above. The United States was frustrated with Iran and U.S. politicians wanted to appear "tough" toward Tehran, resulting in a policy of continually escalating sanctions over a period of roughly twenty years. While these sanctions have affected direct bilateral merchandise trade (with losses largely in foreign exchange only), their non-trade impact appears to have been much more important because it represents a real cost to both sides. This cost will continue to accrue even after sanctions are lifted. Meanwhile, the objectionable policies followed by Iran have not changed, and there is little indication of any impact on Iranian policies except that U.S.–Iranian business relations are likely to be adversely affected for some time.

NOTES

1. Former U.S. Sen. Al D'Amato as a politician and Patrick Clawson (1998) as an expert exemplify this position.

2. U.S. Vice President Richard Cheney as a politician and Jeffrey J. Schott (1997) as an expert support this position. Zbigniew Brzezinski, Brent Scowcroft, and Richard Murphy (1997) also have concluded that unilateral U.S. sanctions against Iran have been ineffectual and attempts to coerce others into following America's lead a mistake.

3. See the Web site of USA Engage, an organization established and widely supported by U.S. business interests, at www.usa.engage.com.

4. Some private clinics are up to western standards, but most modern drugs generally are available only on the black market in the streets, with the attendant risk of not knowing whether one is getting the "real thing."

5. See Askari and Jaber (1999). The average annual GDP per capita growth rates of most oil-exporting countries have been quite dismal since 1975.

6. In 1977 this ratio was 36 percent, but it has declined steadily over time (IMF 1978; IMF 1999). For data on other countries, see Askari and Jaber (1999).

7. This ratio was 97 percent for Iran in 1977 (IMF 1977).

8. This strict policy seems to have been relaxed in late 2000. In order to attract FDI, Iranian policies have become more flexible.

9. Oil production is not, strictly speaking, under Iranian control. It is subject to output quota decisions made by Iran and the other members of the Organization of Petroleum Exporting Countries (OPEC).

10. This is only the direct damage figure. The total economic cost of the war, which would include the loss in output and the like, is much higher and is even harder to estimate (Askari 1994).

11. Nationalized businesses consist of 15 percent of the total number of enterprises and contribute around 70 percent of industrial GDP and more than 22 percent of total GDP (IMF 2000).

12. This increased pressure on domestic oil consumption has in turn been a factor in reducing oil exports.

13. This subsidy does not appear in the budget, as the government owns the oil and its refining, transportation, and distribution facilities.

14. For a comparison of Iran's subsidies to those of Saudi Arabia, see Askari (1990).

15. The TotalFina group includes Gazprom (Russia) and Petronas (Malaysia).

16. We say "as a result of *sanctions*" (emphasis added) because severed U.S.–Iranian relations may have affected Iran's exports to the United States irrespective of any sanctions.

17. A renowned oil expert told us in private discussions that he did not believe U.S. sanctions resulted in any significant loss to Iran in oil exports. To his mind, any loss more likely would have been due to prevailing market conditions when Iran switched to different buyers of its crude.

18. It should be noted that some of the markup in prices of re-exported goods goes to Iranians engaged in such activity and is not all strictly an extra expense to Iran as a whole.

19. A 20 percent markup was the average upper bound estimate of a "well-seasoned" Iranian businessman operating in Dubai.

20. The first assumption underestimates the cost to Iran, the third and fourth overestimate the cost, and the second is neutral.

21. Excluded from this figure is a celebrated gas flaring project that never came before the World Bank's executive board. It was economically sound and would have reduced global warning by about 1 percent, but the United States objected to it because the country proposing it was Iran!

22. This estimate was obtained from a large non-U.S. bank. Iran's financing cost declined significantly (to 7.5 to 7.75 percent) in 2000 because of higher oil prices and improved domestic economic conditions.

23. This data was supplied by a large non-U.S. commercial bank.

24. A private oil company source speculates that the size of Azadegan is even higher.

25. The investment figure for Iran may appear to be low given the recent FDI announcements in the energy sector. But the global figures are current flows, whereas the FDI in Iran's energy sector represents commitments that will flow over a number of years.

26. Preeg (1999c) estimates the impact on Iran of U.S. sanctions at $1.2–2.3 billion per year during 1995–97 and $1.5–2.6 billion per year during 1998–2000. These figures represent losses in five categories: prohibition on U.S. imports, prohibition on U.S. exports, prohibition on marketing to third countries, prohibition on U.S. investments and ILSA sanctions, and U.S. pressures to limit economic assistance. These figures are much larger than ours. Preeg's single largest item is the prohibition on U.S. imports ($0.5–1.0 billion).

Appendixes

Appendix 4.1
Iran's Non-Oil Exports by Country Destination, 1973/74–1998/99[1] ($ Millions)

	1973/74	1974/75	1975/76	1976/77	Preliminary 1977/78
U.S.S.R.	85	78	92	69	80
Germany, Federal Republic of	88	77	68	75	83
United States	46	38	39	31	63
Italy	19	14	25	29	29
Kuwait	12	18	22	15	29
Hungary	11	11	19	13	15
China, People's Republic of	6	6	19	7	10
Japan	36	26	16	16	6
France	20	22	14	13	14
Saudi Arabia	7	11	14	22	27
Egypt	—	8	13	—	—
United Kingdom	24	18	12	14	20
Bulgaria	11	2	11	—	—
Dubai	6	9	10	9	12
Czechoslovakia	10	8	9	8	5
Yugoslavia	11	3	8	—	—
India	5	6	8	—	—
Romania	12	11	8	12	6
Poland	8	5	7	12	10
Jordan	B	3	7	—	—
Switzerland	12	11	6	6	8
Bahrain	7	6	6	6	13
South Africa	12	3	5	1	32
Austria	4	2	5	16	5
Other	74	84	52	95	100
Total[2]	526	480	495	469	567

Appendix 4.1 (continued)
Iran's Non-Oil Exports by Country Destination, 1973/74–1998/99 ($ Millions)

	1980/81	1981/82	1982/83	1983/84	1984/85	1985/86	1986/87	1987/88
West Germany	291.9	108.2	53.3	73.4	64.2	749	885	447
United Arab Emirates	4.3	4.1	18.1	50.2	33.0	65.2	163.3	155.1
Italy	52.5	46.3	35.6	33.0	38.6	54.1	68.8	116.0
Switzerland	55.6	26.3	9.8	13.2	24.1	34.1	55.4	94.1
Soviet Union	80.2	39.8	55.5	40.0	43.2	30.3	22.0	90.9
Japan	4.2	1.2	7.0	8.4	5.2	3.9	12.9	31.9
France	20.1	8.0	9.9	7.9	3.5	4.3	16.9	29.2
Netherlands	6.0	2.6	4.3	3.8	3.5	4.0	20.2	26.2
United Kingdom	22.6	9.2	8.6	16.3	17.7	15.3	20.3	25.1
Austria	10.4	4.4	2.0	3.7	4.3	8.0	15.1	18.2
China	—	—	—	—	—	2.5	0.4	15.7
Belgium	8.4	3.3	4.1	2.3	2.8	2.4	9.4	11.6
Czechoslovakia	7.6	8.1	7.9	5.1	24.4	0.3	6.2	10.8
Turkey	0.1	1.0	0.3	2.0	5.8	11.0	6.2	10.3
East Germany	3.5	8.9	4.4	5.8	9.9	13.6	18.1	10.1
Canada	3.2	2.2	1.2	0.9	1.3	1.6	4.5	9.1
India	2.2	1.0	1.4	1.2	0.8	4.2	12.1	7.0
Hungary	3.5	1.2	1.4	10.7	16.5	16.2	6.3	5.8
Denmark	3.1	1.0	0.7	1.0	0.8	1.0	4.7	5.7
Others	65.8	62.7	58.2	77.7	61.5	79.0	169.6	127.4
Total	645.2	339.5	283.7	356.6	361.1	465.0	915.5	1,160.8

Appendix 4.1 (continued)
Iran's Non-Oil Exports by Country Destination, 1973/74–1998/99 ($ Millions)

	1990/91	1991/92	1992/93	1993/94	1994/95[3]
Germany	113.6	283.1	355.9	400	763
United Arab Emirates	153	390	336	352	152
Italy	159	211	22	260	152
Switzerland	100	191	161	176	86
Soviet Union	27	59	—	—	—
Japan	57	71	83	109	96
France	36	62	86	90	38
Netherlands	—	30	24	15	13
United Kingdom	50	103	74	82	27
Austria	18	30	38	46	23
China	4	18	147	329	104
Belgium	10	41	19	25	18
Czech Republic	2	2	1	2	1
Turkey	106	321	357	385	139
Canada	18	30	51	75	53
India	24	29	17	81	38
Hungary	2	1	1	2	1
Denmark	5	7	4	9	3
Others	139	293	616	825	446
Total	1,312	2,649	2,988	3,747	1,837

Appendix 4.1 (continued)
Iran's Non-Oil Exports by Country Destination, 1973/74–1998/99 ($ Millions)

	1994/95	1995/96	1996/97	1997/98	1998/99
Germany	1,128	722	570	392	410
United Arab Emirates	499	298	257	286	516
Italy	469	263	205	276	202
Switzerland	264	129	71	72	57
Russia	74	43	49	46	36
Japan	182	130	99	104	43
France	113	61	54	40	62
Netherlands	40	30	49	67	75
United Kingdom	82	656	32	41	23
Austria	62	35	33	12	15
China	157	73	74	62	92
Belgium	51	28	29	15	22
The Czech Republic	2	2	2	2	2
Turkey	279	164	134	90	158
Canada	131	48	37	55	59
India	136	150	120	95	145
Hungary	2	3	3	3	4
Denmark	10	9	10	9	9
Others	1,150	1,003	1,292	1,243	1,255
Total	4,831	3,257	3,120	2,910	3,185

[1]Exports according to Customs returns.
[2]Excludes exports of gas.
[3]Data for the first six months.
Source: Bank Markazi Jomhouri Islami Iran.

Appendix 4.2
Iran's Exports by Leading Destinations, 1975–98 (Values in $ Millions)

Rank		1975	1976	1977	1978	1979	1980	1981	1982
	Total	18,283	20,751	21,864	22,539	19,371	15,531	10,013	16,125
1	Country	Japan	Japan	Japan	USA	USA	Japan	Japan	Italy
	Value	4,526	4,049	3,881	4,345	3,904	3,745	1,732	2,523
	%	24.8	19.5	17.8	19.3	20.2	24.1	17.3	15.6
2		Netherlands	USA	USA	Japan	Japan	Germany	India	Japan
		1,458	2,646	3,762	3,869	3,864	1,710	1,655	2,331
		8.1	12.8	17.2	17.2	19.9	11.0	16.5	14.5
3		UK	Germany	Germany	Germany	Germany	India	Spain	Netherlands
		1,412	1,807	1,696	1,910	2,110	1,281	1,226	1,592
		7.7	8.7	7.8	8.5	10.9	8.2	12.2	9.9
4		USA	UK	Netherlands	Italy	France	Bahamas	Romania	India
		1,398	1,709	1,454	1,421	940	1,216	777	1,180
		7.6	8.2	6.7	6.3	4.9	7.8	7.8	7.3
5		Germany	Netherlands	Italy	Netherlands	Bahamas	Spain	Italy	Spain
		1,334	1,565	1,357	1,362	928	973	637	970
		7.3	7.5	6.2	6.0	4.8	6.3	6.4	6.0
6		France	France	UK	France	Netherlands	Turkey	Germany	Singapore
		1,150	1,309	1,245	1,093	862	701	612	816
		6.3	6.3	5.7	4.8	4.4	4.5	6.1	5.1
7		Italy	Italy	Spain	UK	Brazil	Brazil	Turkey	France
		1,036	1,155	1,078	928	804	696	439	804
		5.7	5.6	4.9	4.1	4.2	4.5	4.4	5.0
8		Virgin Islands	Spain	France	Spain	Spain	Romania	France	Romania
		807	842	998	829	657	691	434	741
		4.4	4.1	4.6	3.7	3.4	4.4	4.3	4.6

Appendix 4.2 (continued)
Iran's Exports by Leading Destinations, 1975–98 (Values in $ Millions)

Rank	1975	1976	1977	1978	1979	1980	1981	1982
9	Canada	Canada	Belgium	Belgium	UK	France	Belgium	Syria
	744	705	678	707	471	630	389	717
	4.1	3.4	3.1	3.1	2.4	4.1	3.9	4.4
10	Belgium	India	India	Bahamas	India	USA	Singapore	Turkey
	434	496	621	640	408	435	323	680
	2.4	2.4	2.8	2.8	2.1	2.8	3.2	4.2
11	India	Belgium	Canada	Canada	Italy	Italy	UK	Germany
	419	432	506	523	374	309	285	639
	2.3	2.1	2.3	2.3	1.9	2.0	2.8	4.0
12	Singapore	Brazil	Brazil	Brazil	Romania	Netherlands	Portugal	USA
	397	343	381	520	362	274	176	556
	2.1	1.7	1.7	2.3	1.9	1.8	1.8	3.4
13	Spain	Romania	Singapore	India	Belgium	Korea	Bahamas	UK
	315	303	367	509	353	247	144	356
	1.7	1.5	1.7	2.3	1.8	1.6	1.4	2.2
14	Sweden	Norway	Bahamas	Turkey	Korea	Belgium	Netherlands	Belgium
	262	292	351	444	307	246	140	267
	1.4	1.4	1.6	2.0	1.6	1.6	1.4	1.7
15	Denmark	Singapore	Romania	Singapore	Canada	UK	Finland	Hungary
	259	286	295	343	285	226	128	218
	1.4	1.4	1.3	1.5	1.5	1.5	1.3	1.4
USA share:							USA	
							60	

Appendix 4.2 (continued)
Iran's Exports by Leading Destinations, 1975–98 (Values in $ Millions)

Rank		1983	1984	1985	1986	1987	1988	1989	1990
	Total	19,207	15,641	13,668	8,019	10,999	8,100	11,282	15,476
1		Japan	Japan	Japan	Japan	USA	Japan	Japan	Japan
		3,852	2,602	2,296	1,281	1,592	1,058	1,622	3,151
		20.1	16.7	16.8	16.0	14.5	13.1	14.4	20.4
2		Italy	Italy	Italy	Singapore	Japan	Romania	Romania	Italy
		2,389	1,713	1,366	865	1,426	1,042	1,087	1,435
		12.4	11.0	10.0	10.8	13.0	12.9	9.6	9.3
3		Spain	Netherlands	Turkey	Italy	Italy	Netherlands	Belgium	France
		1,652	1,631	1,150	183	953	955	977	1,236
		8.6	10.4	8.4	9.8	8.7	11.8	8.7	8.0
4		Netherlands	Turkey	Singapore	USA	Netherlands	Turkey	France	Brazil
		1,357	1,423	1,025	556	878	600	940	927
		7.1	9.1	7.5	6.9	8.0	7.4	8.3	6.0
5		Turkey	Spain	India	Romania	Turkey	Germany	Netherlands	Netherlands
		1,111	1,101	810	522	861	579	936	919
		5.8	7.0	5.9	6.5	7.8	7.1	8.3	5.9
6		Syria	India	Spain	Germany	Romania	Belgium	Spain	Belgium
		1,080	953	807	470	724	529	752	882
		5.6	6.1	5.9	5.9	6.6	6.5	6.7	5.7
7		USA	Syria	Netherlands	Netherlands	Spain	Italy	Italy	Spain
		1,061	849	800	388	605	503	738	822
		5.5	5.4	5.9	4.8	5.5	6.2	6.5	5.3
8		India	France	Romania	Spain	France	Spain	Germany	Germany
		1,003	710	741	367	577	441	574	727
		5.2	4.5	5.4	4.6	5.2	5.4	5.1	4.7

Appendix 4.2 (continued)
Iran's Exports by Leading Destinations, 1975–98 (Values in $ Millions)

Rank	1983	1984	1985	1986	1987	1988	1989	1990
9	France	Romania	France	France	Germany	Singapore	UK	Romania
	881	703	730	328	455	362	373	549
	4.6	4.5	5.3	4.1	4.1	4.5	3.3	3.5
10	Germany	USA	USA	India	Singapore	UK	Singapore	Indonesia
	561	664	693	256	417	226	368	459
	2.9	4.2	5.1	3.2	3.8	2.8	3.3	3.0
11	Romania	Germany	Syria	Turkey	Belgium	Brazil	Brazil	Turkey
	531	589	642	201	343	193	338	446
	2.8	3.8	4.7	2.5	3.1	2.4	3.0	2.9
12	Singapore	UK	Germany	Yugoslavia	Brazil	Yugoslavia	Greece	UK
	526	433	584	182	337	189	259	442
	2.7	2.8	4.3	2.3	3.1	2.3	2.3	2.3
13	Brazil	Singapore	Belgium	Belgium	UK	Sweden	Phillipines	India
	383	311	252	162	283	169	255	438
	2.0	2.0	1.8	2.0	2.6	2.1	2.3	2.8
14	Yugoslavia	Portugal	Yugoslavia	Canada	Syria	Phillipines	Turkey	Singapore
	309	197	212	150	186	136	212	424
	1.6	1.3	1.6	1.9	1.7	1.7	1.9	2.7
15	Portugal	Belgium	Finland	UK	Yugoslavia	UAE	India	Greece
	293	170	147	132	143	115	177	343
	1.5	1.1	1.1	1.6	1.3	1.4	1.6	2.2
USA share:						USA	USA	USA
						8	8	2
						0.1	0.1	0.0

Appendix 4.2 (continued)
Iran's Exports by Leading Destinations, 1975–98 (Values in $ Millions)

Rank		1991	1992	1993	1994	1995	1996	1997	1998
	Total	16,428	19,868	18,080	19,434	18,360	22,391	18,381	12,861
1		Japan	Japan	Japan	Japan	Japan	UK	UK	UK
		2,538	2,524	2,476	2,941	2,775	3,908	3,037	3,037
		15.4	12.7	13.7	15.1	15.1	17.5	16.5	23.6
2		Italy	USA	UK	USA	Italy	Japan	Japan	Japan
		1,496	2,116	1,975	2,707	1,587	3,835	2,787	2,230
		9.1	10.7	10.9	13.9	8.6	17.1	15.2	17.3
3		France	UK	USA	UK	UK	Italy	Italy	Italy
		1,199	1,537	1,409	1,790	1,439	1,822	1,631	1,169
		7.3	7.7	7.8	9.2	7.8	8.1	8.9	9.1
4		Netherlands	Switzerland	Germany	Germany	Korea	Korea	Korea	Korea
		1,063	1,272	939	1,203	1,108	1,716	1,280	904
		6.5	6.4	5.2	6.2	6.0	7.7	7	7
5		Brazil	Korea	Switzerland	Korea	South Africa	Greece	Greece	UAE
		946	930	927	927	873	1,119	989	760
		5.9	4.7	5.1	4.8	4.8	5	5.4	5.9
6		Korea	Brazil	Korea	UAE	France	Spain	UAE	France
		930	862	780	780	848	748	695	661
		5.7	4.3	4.3	4.0	4.6	3.3	3.8	5.1
7		Belgium	Italy	Greece	Italy	Greece	India	Singapore	Greece
		882	815	615	758	839	722	695	553
		5.4	4.1	3.4	3.9	4.6	3.2	3.8	4.3
8		Germany	Germany	Singapore	Greece	UAE	France	France	India
		820	794	542	704	809	721	684	523
		5.0	4.0	3.0	3.6	4.4	3.2	3.7	4.1

Appendix 4.2 (continued)
Iran's Exports by Leading Destinations, 1975–98 (Values in $ Millions)

Rank		1991	1992	1993	1994	1995	1996	1997	1998
9		Spain	Greece	Belgium	Singapore	Germany	UAE	Spain	Phillipines
		651	622	489	702	783	695	634	510
		4.0	3.1	2.7	3.6	4.3	3.1	3.4	4
10		Greece	Bermuda	France	Switzerland	Spain	HK	China	China
		563	618	450	552	781	673	543	508
		3.4	3.1	2.5	2.8	4.3	3	3	3.9
11		India	France	Italy	India	USA	Singapore	India	Singapore
		532	609	397	493	762	586	531	454
		3.2	3.1	2.2	2.5	4.2	2.6	2.9	3.5
12		Singapore	Belgium	India	Belgium	India	Germany	Germany	Germany
		460	554	364	477	555	570	428	451
		2.8	2.8	2.0	2.5	3	2.5	2.3	3.5
13		Poland	Singapore	UAE	Spain	Belgium	Azerbaijan	Thailand	Spain
		422	460	352	403	536	224	252	435
		2.6	2.3	1.9	2.1	2.9	1	1.4	3.4
14		Romania	Poland	China	France	Singapore	Switzerland	Russia	Netherlands
		406	422	329	398	392	86	250	424
		2.5	2.1	1.8	2.0	2.1	0.4	1.4	3.3
15		Sweden	India	Portugal	Brazil	Portugal	China	HK	Azerbaijan
		378	375	258	374	305	74	249	232
		2.3	1.9	1.4	1.9	1.7	0.3	1.4	1.8
	USA share:	USA					USA	USA	
		237					3	5	
		1.4					0.0	0.0	

Source: International Monetary Fund, Direction of Trade Statistics Yearbook (various issues). Where the same year was reported in more than one book, figures from the most recent issue are shown here.

Appendix 4.3
Iran's Imports from Leading Sources, 1975–98 (Values in $ Millions)

Rank		1975	1976	1977	1978	1979	1980	1981	1982
	Total	10,346	12,887	14,642	19,533	8,840	12,824	12,898	11,161
1	Country	USA	USA	USA	USA	USA	Japan	Germany	Germany
	Value	2,051	2,133	2,347	4,153	1,181	1,697	1,766	1,536
	%	19.8	16.6	16.0	21.3	13.4	13.2	13.7	13.8
2		Germany	Germany	Germany	Germany	Germany	Germany	Japan	Japan
		1,804	2,304	2,807	3,719	1,413	1,657	1,629	1,033
		17.6	17.9	19.2	19.0	16.0	12.9	12.6	9.3
3		Japan	Japan	Japan	Japan	Japan	UK	UK	Turkey
		1,662	2,098	2,322	2,991	1,013	1,006	888	870
		16.1	16.3	15.9	15.3	11.5	7.8	6.9	7.8
4		UK	UK	UK	UK	USSR	France	Italy	Italy
		877	992	1,031	1,585	565	793	829	796
		8.5	7.7	7.0	8.1	6.4	6.2	6.4	7.1
5		France	Italy	Italy	Italy	UK	USSR	France	USSR
		415	686	810	1,173	542	712	735	712
		4.0	5.3	5.5	6.0	6.1	5.6	5.7	6.4
6		Italy	France	France	France	France	Italy	USSR	UK
		338	630	661	970	468	632	712	635
		3.3	4.9	4.5	5.0	5.3	4.9	5.5	5.7
7		India	Switzerland	Netherlands	Switzerland	Italy	UAE	Romania	Romania
		322	434	489	423	455	402	456	494
		3.1	3.4	3.3	2.2	5.1	3.1	3.5	4.4
8		Netherlands	Belgium	Switzerland	USSR	Netherlands	Netherlands	Netherlands	France
		278	421	445	419	261	386	430	367
		2.7	3.3	3.0	2.1	3.0	3.0	3.3	3.3

Appendix 4.3 (continued)
Iran's Imports from Leading Sources, 1975–98 (Values in $ Millions)

Rank	1975	1976	1977	1978	1979	1980	1981	1982
9	Belgium	Netherlands	Belgium	Belgium	UAE	Spain	Spain	Spain
	251	394	348	358	253	360	371	361
	2.4	3.1	2.4	1.8	2.9	2.8	2.9	3.2
10	Switzerland	India	USSR	Netherlands	Switzerland	Romania	USA	Netherlands
	213	394	273	346	245	321	330	298
	2.1	3.1	1.9	1.8	2.8	2.5	2.6	2.7
11	Australia	Australia	Australia	Spain	Korea	Australia	Belgium	Singapore
	162	173	229	285	204	311	281	283
	1.6	1.3	1.6	1.5	2.3	2.4	2.2	2.5
12	Romania	Sweden	Sweden	Sweden	Belgium	Switzerland	Switzerland	Hungary
	150	149	193	247	175	304	260	243
	1.4	1.2	1.3	1.3	2.0	2.4	2.0	2.2
13	Sweden	Korea	South Africa	Australia	Czech	Kuwait	Turkey	Brazil
	137	146	193	218	158	301	257	231
	1.3	1.1	1.3	1.1	1.8	2.3	2.0	2.1
14	Turkey	Romania	India	Romania	Australia	Belgium	New Zealand	Sweden
	86	142	193	198	146	297	253	219
	0.8	1.1	1.3	1.0	1.7	2.3	2.0	2.0
15	Kuwait	USSR	Romania	Korea	Romania	Brazil	Thailand	Australia
	84	126	192	181	142	263	233	219
	0.8	1.0	1.3	0.9	1.6	2.1	1.8	2.0
USA share:						USA		USA
						25		134
						0.2		1.2

Appendix 4.3 (continued)
Iran's Imports from Leading Sources, 1975–98 (Values in $ Millions)

Rank		1983	1984	1985	1986	1987	1988	1989	1990
	Total	18,989	14,829	11,622	93,55	9,369	8,171	12,746	15,789
1		Germany	Germany	Germany	Germany	Germany	Germany	Germany	Germany
		3,310	2,518	1,812	1,708	1,795	1,472	2,024	2,835
		17.4	17	15.6	18.3	19.2	18	15.9	18
2		Japan	Japan	Japan	Japan	Japan	Japan	Japan	Japan
		3,102	1,862	1,496	1,267	1,053	836	973	1,782
		16.3	12.6	12.9	13.5	11.2	10.2	77.6	11.3
3		Turkey	Italy	Turkey	UK	Italy	UK	UAE	Italy
		1,197	1,039	1,187	634	569	556	949	1,218
		6.3	7	10.2	6.8	6.1	6.8	7.4	7.7
4		UK	UK	UK	Italy	Brazil	Turkey	Italy	UAE
		1,047	1,030	745	609	552	425	803	1,044
		5.5	6.9	6.4	6.5	5.9	5.2	6.3	6.6
5		Italy	Turkey	Italy	Turkey	UK	Italy	Turkey	UK
		994	826	672	587	550	417	699	766
		5.2	5.6	5.8	6.3	5.9	5.1	5.5	4.9
6		USSR	USSR	USSR	UAE	Turkey	Belgium	UK	France
		676	608	548	537	474	393	567	663
		3.6	4.1	4.7	5.7	5.1	4.8	4.4	4.2
7		Pakistan	Sweden	Singapore	Belgium	UAE	Brazil	Belgium	Argentina
		539	522	436	341	390	343	493	564
		2.8	3.5	3.8	3.6	4.2	4.2	3.9	3.6
8		Sweden	Argentina	Argentina	Netherlands	Argentina	Netherlands	Korea	Turkey
		462	473	345	293	381	286	477	545
		2.4	3.2	3	3.1	4.1	3.5	3.7	3.5

Appendix 4.3 (continued)
Iran's Imports from Leading Sources, 1975–98 (Values in $ Millions)

Rank		1983	1984	1985	1986	1987	1988	1989	1990
9		Netherlands	Netherlands	Spain	Argentina	Australia	UAE	Argentina	Netherlands
		460	417	312	254	327	276	457	542
		2.4	2.8	2.7	2.7	3.5	3.4	3.6	3.4
10		Spain	Australia	Netherlands	Brazil	Belgium	France	Australia	Australia
		452	411	298	246	316	243	451	471
		2.4	2.8	2.6	2.6	3.4	3	3.5	3
11		Argentina	Singapore	Romania	Australia	Korea	USSR	Netherlands	Brazil
		436	374	261	243	242	217	410	469
		2.3	2.5	2.2	2.6	2.6	2.7	3.2	2
12		Singapore	Brazil	Australia	Korea	Netherlands	Australia	Canada	Belgium
		426	328	235	234	232	216	384	376
		2.2	2.2	2	2.5	2.5	2.6	3	2.4
13		France	Spain	Brazil	Switzerland	Switzerland	Switzerland	Brazil	Austria
		408	327	234	229	212	215	362	373
		2.1	2.2	2	2.4	2.3	2.6	2.8	2.4
14		Romania	Switzerland	Switzerland	Austria	USSR	Austria	Switzerland	Switzerland
		392	311	219	163	198	161	306	345
		2.1	2.1	1.9	1.7	2.1	2	2.4	2.3
15		Brazil	Pakistan	New Zealand	New Zealand	New Zealand	Argentina	France	Canada
		382	298	213	161	166	159	266	331
		2.0	2	1.8	1.7	1.8	1.9	2.1	2.1
	USA share:	USA	USA	USA					USA
		209	178	81					140
		1.1	1.2	0.7					0.9

Appendix 4.3 (continued)
Iran's Imports from Leading Sources, 1975–98 (Values in $ Millions)

Rank		1991	1992	1993	1994	1995	1996	1997	1998
	Total	21,339	29,870	20,037	11,795	12,313	15,117	14,165	13,107
1		Germany	Germany	Germany	Germany	Germany	Germany	Germany	Germany
		4,473	6,939	3,997	2,209	1,777	2,100	1,854	1,518
		21	23.2	19.9	18.7	14.4	13.9	13.1	11.6
2		Japan	Japan	Japan	Italy	Japan	Belgium	Japan	Italy
		2,724	3,639	2,341	1,008	886	928	882	1,002
		12.8	12.2	11.7	8.5	7.2	6.1	6.2	7.6
3		Italy	Italy	Italy	Japan	Belgium	Japan	Argentina	Japan
		1,924	2,869	1,939	894	663	844	833	962
		9	9.6	9.7	7.6	5.4	5.6	5.9	7.3
4		UAE	UK	UAE	Belgium	Argentina	Switzerland	Italy	Korea
		1,044	1,668	1,120	651	544	812	795	843
		4.9	5.6	5.6	5.5	4.4	5.4	5.6	6.4
5		UK	UAE	UK	UAE	Italy	Argentina	Russia	China
		1,000	1,588	1,007	647	535	798	704	723
		4.7	5.3	5.0	5.5	4.3	5.3	5.0	5.5
6		France	Belgium	USA	UK	Switzerland	Australia	UK	France
		985	1,052	824	544	509	741	681	697
		4.6	3.5	4.1	4.6	4.1	4.9	4.8	5.3
7		Sweden	France	France	France	UK	UK	France	UK
		781	814	663	479	505	685	675	615
		3.7	2.7	3.3	4.1	4.1	4.5	4.8	4.7
8		Korea	USA	Thailand	Azerbaijan	France	Italy	Canada	UAE
		613	812	541	392	498	675	616	551
		2.9	2.7	2.7	3.3	4.0	4.5	4.3	4.2

Appendix 4.3 (continued)
Iran's Imports from Leading Sources, 1975–98 (Values in $ Millions)

Rank	1991	1992	1993	1994	1995	1996	1997	1998
9	USA	Switzerland	Belgium		USA	Russia	UAE	Argentina
	580	760	539	347	476	644	562	548
	2.7	2.5	2.7	2.9	3.9	4.3	4.0	4.2
10	Netherlands	Korea	Switzerland	Korea	Canada	UAE	Korea	Brazil
	565	669	525	320	458	473	552	538
	2.6	2.2	2.6	2.7	3.7	3.1	3.9	4.1
11	Turkey	Netherland	Korea	Canada	UAE	Canada	Switzerland	Russia
	536	666	469	293	441	449	531	491
	2.5	2.2	2.3	2.5	3.6	3.0	3.7	3.7
12	Brazil	Canada	Australia	Argentina	Australia	Korea	Australia	Belgium
	471	600	402	287	412	445	522	431
	2.2	2.0	2.0	2.4	3.3	2.9	3.7	3.3
13	Belgium	Austria	Austria	Russia	Russia	France	Belgium	Spain
	439	558	394	268	372	437	457	352
	2.1	1.9	2.0	2.3	3.0	2.9	3.2	2.7
14	Austria	Sweden	Netherlands	Netherlands	Korea	Thailand	China	Netherlands
	414	513	174	263	342	405	395	285
	1.9	1.7	1.9	2.2	2.8	2.7	2.8	2.2
15	Argentina	Brazil	Argentina	Australia	Netherlands	Brazil	Brazil	Australia
	356	400	263	260	281	349	294	263
	1.7	1.3	1.8	2.2	2.3	2.3	2.1	2.0
USA share:						USA	USA	
						83	38	
						0.5	0.3	

Source: International Monetary Fund, Direction of Trade Statistics Yearbook (various issues). Where the same year was reported in more than one book, figures from the most recent issue are shown here.

Appendix 4.4
Value of Iran's Imports, 1980/81–1998/99 ($ Millions)

	1980/81	1981/82	1982/83	1983/84	1984/85	1985/86	1986/87	1987/88
Food and live animals	1,541	2,161	2,164	2,368	2,070	1,538	1,039	1,066
Dairy and eggs	357	482	351	530	364	255	151	206
Grains and derivatives	562	943	673	1018	156	723	455	611
Sugar, its derivatives and honey	157	32	395	86	70	112	99	101
Coffee, tea, cocoa, spices, etc.	39	61	37	54	147	84	84	50
Fruits and vegetables	7	12	8	17	15	3	5	2
Others	419	631	700	663	518	361	245	496
Beverages and tobacco	46	88	7	90	82	99	109	107
Raw non-edible products (excluding petroleum fuels)	661	667	461	802	522	314	282	257
Raw caoutchouc	35	49	54	75	58	35	43	52
Textile fibers unlisted elsewhere	182	301	199	410	199	94	80	59
Various raw fertilizers and minerals	54	50	45	68	48	31	20	26
Others	390	267	163	249	217	154	139	120
Mineral products, fuel, oil products and their derivatives	88	214	207	205	299	247	401	411
Vegetable and animal shortening	113	294	192	338	361	310	184	373
Vegetable shortening	51	207	171	304	344	292	163	339
Others	62	87	21	34	17	18	21	34
Chemical products	1,521	2,180	1,679	2,084	1,768	1,163	1,369	1,428
Chemicals and their compounds	161	291	267	351	252	268	274	288
Raw materials for paints, dyes & tanning	90	124	71	132	213	71	50	62
Medical and pharmaceutical products	468	525	398	356	206	156	258	259
Plastic, celluose, and artificial resins	425	450	304	514	393	218	275	212
Other unlisted chemicals	124	297	253	306	348	157	211	317
Others	253	493	386	425	356	293	301	291

Appendix 4.4 (continued)
Value of Iran's Imports, 1980/81–1998/99 ($ Millions)

	1980/81	1981/82	1982/83	1983/84	1984/85	1985/86	1986/87	1987/88
Goods classified according to their compositions	3,335	3,986	3,507	5,326	3,561	3,356	2,258	1,952
Paper, cardboard, and derivatives	276	333	216	285	207	193	138	224
Various textile yarns and related products	655	921	739	1476	998	595	450	218
Non-metal mineral goods	310	150	84	174	131	87	97	87
Iron and steel	1,033	1,415	1,557	1,902	1,105	1,768	1,031	820
Others	1,061	1,167	911	1,489	1,120	713	542	603
Transportation vehicles, machinery and tools	3,055	3,527	3,331	6,317	5,452	3,896	3,315	3,066
Non-electric machinery	1,403	1,854	1,732	3,042	2,828	1,873	1,798	1,717
Electric machinery, tools and appliances	987	894	693	1346	1089	834	792	787
Transportation vehicles	665	780	906	1929	1535	1189	725	562
Miscellaneous finished products	484	393	284	530	358	293	392	307
Scientific and professional tools	321	236	202	365	251	206	250	221
Artificial goods unlisted elsewhere	135	118	58	119	71	69	106	68
Others	28	39	24	46	36	18	36	18
Goods not classified according to their type	6	5	13	43	21	192	6	2
Total	10,850	13,515	11,845	18,103	14,494	11,408	9,355	9,369

Appendix 4.4 (continued)
Value of Iran's Imports, 1980/81–1998/99 ($ Millions)

	1990/91	1991/92	1992/93	1993/94	1994/95[1]
Food and live animals	2,138	2,124	2,276	2,446	643
Dairy and eggs	150	230	166	178	28
Grains and their derivatives	1,240	965	1,047	1,376	379
Sugar, its derivatives and honey	351	373	308	167	79
Coffee, tea, cocoa, spices, etc.	133	126	248	147	17
Fruits and vegetables	27	87	92	119	2
Others	237	243	415	459	138
Beverages and tobacco	47	109	95	80	21
Raw non-edible products (excluding petroleum fuels)	753	860	768	551	295
Raw caoutchouc	102	82	76	58	36
Textile fibers unlisted elsewhere	180	300	213	200	115
Others	471	478	469	293	144
Mineral products, fuel, oil products and their derivatives	422	385	406	83	42
Vegetable and animal shortening	323	278	300	431	98
Vegetable shortening	279	235	274	414	92
Others	44	43	26	17	6
Chemical products	2,876	2,892	2,689	2,023	624
Chemicals and their compounds	633	632	524	405	125
Raw materials for paints, dyes and tanning	166	183	198	123	37
Plastic, celluose, and artificial resins	790	572	690	516	122
Other unlisted chemicals	559	821	636	509	160
Others	728	684	641	470	180
Goods classified according to their compositions	5,153	7,075	5,507	3,344	790
Paper, cardboard and derivatives	404	516	395	249	93
Various textile yarns and related products	460	730	637	343	120
Non-metal mineral goods	247	306	383	250	55
Iron and steel	2,927	4,004	2,481	1,667	370
Others	1,115	1,519	1,611	835	152
Transportation vehicles, machinery and tools	6,264	14,924	16,498	10,036	2,534
Non-electric machinery	3,886	8,576	10,193	6,957	1,842
Electric machinery, tools and appliances	1,344	2,516	2,913	1,780	421
Transportation vehicles	1,034	3,832	3,392	1,299	271

Appendix 4.4 (continued)
Value of Iran's Imports, 1980/81–1998/99 ($ Millions)

	1990/91	1991/92	1992/93	1993/94	1994/95[1]
Miscellaneous finished products	683	925	1,317	760	201
Scientific and professional tools	498	685	883	564	153
Artificial goods unlisted elsewhere	155	211	387	168	44
Others	30	29	47	28	4
Goods not classified according to their type	63	105	24	283	46
Total	18,722	29,870	20,037	5,294	

	1994/95	1995/96	1996/97	1997/98	1998/99
Food and live animals	1,369	2,404	2,581	2,508	1,583
Dairy and eggs	60	96	60	35	77
Grains and their derivatives	693	1444	1881	1705	878
Sugar, its derivatives and honey	251	376	335	405	23
Coffee, tea, cocoa, spices, etc	52	40	28	38	37
Fruits and vegetables	34	7	4	4	3
Others	279	442	273	321	565
Beverages and tobacco	36	2	11	8	9
Raw non-edible products (excluding petroleum fuels)	649	660	770	647	596
Raw caoutchouc	73	119	113	72	52
Textile fibers unlisted elsewhere	207	204	226	200	201
Others	369	337	431	375	343
Mineral products, fuel, oil products and their derivatives	423	228	377	265	186
Vegetable and animal shortening	392	490	602	434	654
Vegetable shortening	376	455	580	420	633
Others	16	35	22	14	21
Chemical products	1,376	1,733	1,931	1,890	1,774
Chemicals and their compounds	306	430	571	494	458
Raw materials for paints, dyes and tanning	86	101	116	169	135
Plastic, celluose, and artificial resins	237	259	385	403	413
Other unlisted chemicals	313	293	242	267	316
Others	434	650	617	557	452

Appendix 4.4 (continued)
Value of Iran's Imports, 1980/81–1998/99 ($ Millions)

	1994/95	1995/96	1996/97	1997/98	1998/99
Goods classified according to their compositions	1,654	2,533	3,704	2,720	2,520
Paper, cardboard, and derivatives	256	527	569	392	266
Various textile yarns and related products	224	206	304	324	310
Non-metal mineral goods	129	136	137	163	166
Iron and steel	686	820	2049	1290	1287
Others	359	844	645	551	491
Transportation vehicles, machinery and tools	5,525	3,656	4,205	5,045	6,348
Nonelectric machinery	4,054	2,285	2,325	2,672	3,501
Electric machinery, tools and appliances	834	892	1,184	1,444	1,521
Transportation vehicles	637	479	696	929	1,326
Miscellaneous finished products	403	306	353	384	538
Scientific and professional tools	316	222	217	271	3880
Artificial goods unlisted elsewhere	79	75	130	108	155
Others	8	9	6	5	3
Other	67	301	583	295	115
Total[2]	11,795	12,313	15,117	14,196	14,323

[1]Data for first six months.

[2]Customs clearance data (c.I.f. base) including registration fee, but not including defense-related imports and refined-oil products, which are included in f.o.b. import data in the balance of payments table. Registration fee is included in trade statistics because customs are levied on a registration-fee-inclusive base.

Source: Bank Markazi Jomhouri Islami Iran.

CHAPTER 5

Costs and Benefits of Sanctions: A Contingency Perspective

INTRODUCTION

Our review and analysis of economic sanctions imposed unilaterally by the United States against China, Cuba, and Iran have provided important insights into our primary research concern regarding the efficacy of sanctions. As we concluded in our precursor volume, *Economic Sanctions: Examining Their Philosophy and Efficacy,* a valid assessment of a particular sanction requires a deliberate examination of the rationale for the sanction. Given the differences among possible sanction rationales—purposeful, palliative, punitive and partisan—an efficacy assessment must be nuanced and matched to the initial rationale.

It must be said in all cases that sanctions are barriers to trade and investment flows, and as such they reduce the level of global welfare. Thus, there is a *global cost* to sanctions that persists independent of the net impact on any given nation—sender, target, or third country.

Case Diversity

Our case analyses revealed significant diversity in terms of sanction rationale; sanction scale and scope; the extent to which multilateralism has "crept" into an otherwise unilateral sanction; the degree of economic dependency between target and sender as well as each nation's relationship with the rest of the world; the organization, location, and influence of various stakeholder groups; and the political and/or moral justification for sanctions given their rationale and intended outcome. Thanks to this diversity, we can further our collective understanding of the impact of sanctions beyond the basic trade effects that are captured by extant gravity and related models, which are common vehicles for gauging sanction efficacy.

As a starting point for framing our discussion of conclusions, we illustrate in Table 5.1 the breadth of rationales provided for U.S. economic sanctions against China, Cuba, and Iran. Table 5.1 is not intended to be exhaustive, but rather indicative of the variety of rationales invoked for each country we examined.

Our conclusions regarding the efficacy of sanctions stem from our findings from these three diverse cases. We have organized our conclusions to respond to the original impetus behind our case approach: to more accurately assess the total costs and benefits of U.S. unilateral economic sanctions to sender, target, and third countries. For each conclusion we draw about costs and benefits, we outline important contingency factors guided by our diverse cases.

Contingency Perspective

The complexity of national (and global) economic and political environments makes it impossible to draw definitive quantitative conclusions that provide precise formulas to policymakers for crafting sanctions that perfectly reflect their motivating rationales. Our analysis does provide, however, a clear delineation of relevant contingency factors in assessing costs and benefits. Given the diversity of the three cases we studied, we can provide subtle but instructive guidance to policymakers on the critical considerations relevant to unilateral economic sanctions.

COSTS OF SANCTIONS TO TARGET COUNTRIES

Reduced Trade

In all three of our cases, economic sanctions are (and were) intended to affect exports to, and imports from, the target country. Thus, in each case there have been measurable reductions in imports and exports compared to levels of trade that would have been achieved without sanctions (as estimated by a gravity model). Since sanctions on China are limited to specific economic sectors,

Table 5.1
Rationales for U.S. Sanctions Against Three Target Countries

Target	Scope of Sanction	Rationale(s)	Purpose
China	Total trade	Purposeful; palliative	Inhibit spread of communism
	Dual-use goods	Partisan	Hinder development of Chinese military capability; prevent arms proliferation
	Partial trade/investment	Punitive; purposeful	Punish for Tiananmen incident
	Partial trade/investment	Palliative; purposeful	Promote democracy and freedom of religion; curb certain social policies
	Partial trade/investment	Partisan; purposeful	Promote market access and intellectual property rights
Cuba	Most trade/investment	Purposeful; palliative	Inhibit spread of communism in Americas
	Most trade/investment	Partisan	Satisfy Cuban diaspora in United States
	Most trade/investment	Purposeful	Promote democracy and human rights
	Stepped-up sanctions enforcement	Punitive	Retribution for aggressive acts (e.g., downing of plane)
Iran	Comprehensive	Punitive	Punish taking of hostages at embassy and alleged support for terrorism
	Comprehensive	Purposeful	Deter creation/spread of weapons of mass destruction; promote support of Middle East peace process
	Comprehensive	Purposeful; palliative	Promote human rights (e.g., women's rights)
	Comprehensive	Partisan	Promote energy security and access to energy resources

the relative trade impact has been smaller than in the cases of Cuba and Iran, where near-comprehensive sanctions are in place.

In all cases, the target countries effected some degree of trade diversion to third countries, thus dulling the direct trade impact of sanctions. In addition, Iran's use of the United Arab Emirates and China's use of Hong Kong as pass-through countries effectively allowed at least partial reclamation of sanctioned exports to and imports from the United States. In predicting the ability of a target to mitigate a sanction's impact on trade, several important contingencies must be considered.

If a target nation produces goods that cannot be universally manufactured—such as non-renewable natural resources like petroleum (in the case of Iran) or a class of products resulting from specific factors in which a nation possesses a unique advantage (e.g., certain pharmaceutical and biotechnology products made in Cuba)—or for which many nations around the world have ready demand, diversion of exports from the target to third countries will likely result (perhaps with some negative price impact, depending on the price elasticity of demand for these products in other markets). Where targeted countries produce goods that are ubiquitous (such as textiles, produced by China) and/or in ample supply globally (such as sugar, produced by Cuba), trade diversion to markets in third countries may be less likely if entrenched alternative supply arrangements with other countries exist.

Ubiquitous goods may, however, be fungible goods, as is the case with oil, where trade restrictions have promoted flexible trade diversion by rearranging the refining and shipment of oil around the globe. Iranian crude previously destined for the United States was directed to other markets, while oil from other sources was shipped to the United States.

If targets and senders are geographically proximate, like Cuba and the United States, diverting goods to third countries becomes particularly expensive owing to heightened transportation costs. If targets are unable to either consume the goods domestically and/or redeploy productive assets to the production of other goods in demand, real losses to the target (as opposed to potential foreign exchange losses through domestic consumption) are incurred. Cuban tourism exports exemplify such deadweight losses. Local consumption of tourism services is limited by low discretionary incomes, and assets committed to tourism (e.g., hotels and golf courses) are not readily adaptable to the provision of other exportable services or goods.

By restricting a target's ability to import goods and services from the sender, a sanction can limit the availability of those products, especially if they are scarce and/or unique. For example, U.S. expertise in many high-tech sectors, including computer software and heavy equipment in infrastructure, is often unmatched by competitors in other nations. Even where such products are available elsewhere, they may be of lower quality and/or cost more and/or be incompatible with the existing infrastructure in the target country—any of which would produce a negative consequence for the target.

Where target countries are economically diverse, sanctioned imports could be replaced through local production, though this may involve significant costs to utilize production factors in the target. Cuba, for example, has had an explicit economic policy in place since the Soviet withdrawal to diversify its economy in hopes of reducing dependency on outside nations. But Cuba's small domestic market and limited natural resources have impinged on its ability to diversify sufficiently to substitute local production for trade. Iran would face similar difficulties in diversifying its internal production sufficiently, while China, which has the most diverse of the three economies, has geared itself to promoting exports.

This or any other strategy for replacing sanctioned imports limits potential gains from trade for the target through specialization and the comparative advantage of nations. As with exports, however, sanctioned imports might find a ready replacement source in patron countries. When target nations are members of another trading bloc, such as China and Cuba with the former Soviet bloc at different points in time, any harm that a sender can cause in reducing or eliminating exports from the target previously sent to the nation imposing the sanction will be largely thwarted.

Although the direct trade impacts of sanctions are clear, restricted exports and imports also impose costs on the target by reducing upstream and downstream industrial activity, thus multiplying the impact of trade reductions throughout the economy. Where exports from a target are in sectors that are relatively uncoupled from the remainder of the economy (as in the case of Iranian caviar), these multiplier effects will be minimal. The same is true for some targeted imports, as in the case of wine imports into Cuba.

Less Access to Investment and Credit Funds

U.S. direct investment in Cuba and Iran is prohibited; in China it is restricted to prevent the transfer of technology. Such sanctions clearly reduce the pool of potentially available funds for promoting industrial development and expansion in the target nations.

Firms invest abroad in productive assets to take advantage of business opportunities. They also use strategic investments in nations to position themselves competitively on the global stage. All things being equal, firms will invest in countries that offer good profit opportunities locally and in markets representing good opportunities for blocking or weakening competitors in other markets.

If a target country is relatively small or poor or offers limited growth prospects, few attractive investment opportunities may exist. The net impact of sanctions on investment in such a country will be small, as is the case with Cuba. If, however, a target offers competitive positioning opportunities, sanctions may provide an incentive to firms in third countries to invest in the target to earn profits protected from sender competition—profits that could be used to cross-subsidize competitive activities elsewhere in the world. Many European firms' investments in the petroleum sector in Iran would comport with such an investment incentive.

Where a target represents a unique opportunity to exploit scarce resources (as in the case of energy reserves in Iran), third countries likely will step in to fill any investment void created by sanctions. Under these conditions, a sanction actually will *promote* investment by third countries in the target. But where investment opportunities in the target are strategically or "naturally" linked with the sender country (e.g., the sender is the largest market for the output in question), a sanction may serve to dampen investment by third countries in the target. Cuba's tourism sector, for example, might present inferior investment opportunities for third countries since U.S. tourists are denied access to its services. The negative consequences of reduced foreign investment are exacerbated in target nations that lack domestic savings sufficient to fund investment internally, as is the case for all three studied nations.

U.S. financial institutions are prohibited from lending to entities in Cuba and Iran. Where target nations lack domestic savings and/or strong financial institutions that can provide sufficient credit funds for productive projects, they must look abroad to fund their industrial development. Since U.S. firms are not competing for these lending opportunities (and U.S. institutions do not even provide credit ratings for these countries), third-country lenders can charge higher lending rates to target borrowers.

The degree to which third-country lenders will be attracted to lending opportunities in a target will depend upon a repayment risk assessment of the borrower. Risk will vary based on the target economy's economic vulnerability (a function of production diversification, primary product dependence, domestic demand strength, and political stability) as well as the borrower's repayment history. Foreign lending to Cuba, for example, has come to a virtual halt owing largely to that government's reneging on prior borrowing obligations.

The role of multilateral institutions in guaranteeing credits to entities in a target country is important in providing incentives to third-country lenders. Sender influence in the decision-making process of such institutions has been shown to extend the reach of an otherwise unilateral sanction ("multilateralism creep") by reducing lending from such institutions and even negatively affecting export cover from third-country lenders to the target country.

Lockout from Technology

Technology access is critical for most nations' economic development. U.S. sanctions against China, Cuba, and Iran limit the free flow of technology to these nations. In sectors where the United States enjoys technological leadership, sanctions mitigate a target nation's ability to benefit from incorporating this technology into its domestic production processes. Denying Iran access to U.S. drilling and oil field construction technology, for example, limits its productive efficiency.

Furthermore, any research and development (R&D) activities undertaken by the target may not enjoy the leverage of innovating on top of existing technological platforms, putting the target at a disadvantage it may never overcome owing to the fast innovation-cycle times and extreme competitive pressures in the global R&D arena. Chinese investments in innovation in many high-tech sectors, including satellite technology, will suffer such delays. Lockout from technology access, however, may provide opportunities for innovations in target country R&D. Since China is prohibited from accessing certain U.S. satellite technology, it may have an incentive to "innovate around" the U.S. standard, with positive outcomes for its economy.

Assessing the impact of technology lockout depends critically on the absorptive capacity of the target nation. Where limited advanced R&D activity is taking place, as in Iran and in Cuba in most sectors beyond the life sciences, the costs from technology lockout will be small in the short run owing to the nation's inability to fully absorb and thus leverage the sanctioned technology.

Promotion of Internal Dissent

The imposition of a sanction on another country, particularly when motivated by palliative or punitive considerations, provides groups and individuals within the target nation some credibility and support for opposing the government regime. The degree to which a sanction can provoke and/or provide leverage to internal dissenters will vary depending on the degree to which the sanction affects different groups in the target society, the existence of political divisions in the target, the level of organization and coalescence among individuals in society, and the role and strength of business and the private sector in general in the target country.

In the case of Cuba, the Varela Project, which has organized a petition drive in hopes of forcing political liberalization on the island, has garnered some credibility in the nation from U.S. sanctions policy calling for democratic reforms in Cuba. The Falun Gong, declared a cult by the Chinese government, has similarly gained public support for its cause through U.S. sanctions intended to encourage protection of religious freedom. Thus, U.S. sanctions against target nations can have important repercussions in terms of undermining internal support for a regime.

Restricted Flows of Tourists and Ideas

Where travel to/from a target is restricted, as in the case of Iran and Cuba (although restrictions on travel to Cuba have been relaxed in recent years), the citizens of the target suffer from denial of family visitation rights. The costs to target citizens will be particularly acute if a large diaspora resides in the sender country. If the sender nation serves as a natural hub for travel to the rest of the world (as in the case of the United States vis-a-vis Cuban travel abroad), transaction costs for travel increase for the target's citizens.

Beyond tourism considerations, limits on travel (including restrictions on student education abroad) may impede the free flow of ideas and knowledge between countries and could hinder the target nation's citizens from engaging fully in matters of global importance. Where a target nation's citizens have access to global communications technology, such limits will be mitigated.

Diminished Ability to Act on the Global Stage

Unilateral sanctions reduce opportunities for the target to engage with other private- and public-sector actors around the world. At the simplest level, close allies of the sender typically are wary of offending the sender by exploiting close relations with the target (Iran has suffered in this respect). Where trade and investment restrictions are in place, the target nation will not enjoy full consideration by firms as they strategize how to configure their various assets and activities.

Firms need flexibility and unfettered access to upstream and downstream markets and seek out complementary private-sector activities to enhance the value of their products and services. Nations sanctioned by the largest, most diverse economy in the world may not be able to offer potential trading or investment partners such flexibility, especially if positioning in strategic networks and/or linkages with lead countries is critical.

Target countries may also suffer consequences on the geopolitical stage. Where sender nations are effective in using their political leverage to reinforce the impact of economic sanctions—in the case of China, for example, the United States has wielded important power over that nation's WTO accession—a target may find itself in a weakened position internationally. Where a target has other sources of leverage on the global stage (e.g., a large domestic market in the case of China, or a role in global energy security in the case of Iran), the impact of sanctions may be mitigated.

In sum, the range of costs to nations targeted by sanctions is considerable: lost trade (direct and indirect), diminished access to capital (investment and borrowing), restricted access to technology, increased internal dissent, limits on travel, and a weaker position in the global arena. As we have indicated, the importance and relevance of each of these costs to a target are contingent upon a variety of factors. Since many sanctions are imposed explicitly to harm the target (i.e., inflict costs), a thorough analysis of these factors is required to predict whether a particular sanction will be effective. In addition, although sanctions typically are thought of in terms of costs to the target, the target nation may also *benefit* from sanctions. We will now address the potential benefits to a target from sanctions and consider the contingent conditions that make these benefits possible.

BENEFITS OF SANCTIONS TO TARGET COUNTRIES

Target countries view many sanctions as double-edged swords. As discussed previously, even where a sanction causes harm in the short run, targets can effectively mitigate the intended harm from a sanction through strategies like import substitution or trade diversion.

Reduced Blame for Domestic Ills

Our case analyses demonstrated that many economic (and, as a result, social) problems in target nations resulted principally from failed domestic policies or other events beyond the scope of the sanctions imposed by the United States. A beleaguered regime facing economic crisis, however, can publicly point to a sanction as the source of its domestic ills. Leaders of sanctioned countries are often heard spouting rhetoric along the lines of "if only the United States would lift its embargo, we would all be prosperous."

The effectiveness of such a strategy depends critically on two factors. The first concerns the sector of society most harmed by the sanction. Where harm *owing to the sanction* is not readily apparent to most of society, yet where economic or societal hardship is pervasive, it is difficult for a regime to link general hardship to a particular harm from the sanction. The typical Chinese citizen, for example, can identify little harm from U.S. sanctions. Similarly, where a nation has suffered economic or societal problems across history (both before and after imposition of a sanction and regardless of its scope or level), a link between the sanction and suffering is hard to draw.

The case of Cuba may be instructive here. Despite U.S. sanctions being in force against the island for more than four decades, the Cuban economy enjoyed great prosperity under Soviet support. With the relaxation in U.S. sanctions on food and medicine exports to Cuba in recent years, the average Cuban can detect little impact on his/her caloric intake or incident or length of illness.

In any case, some public knowledge of the sanction must be present so that regimes can manipulate this information to "force" a link between a sanction and hardship in the society. In the case of Cuba, detractors of sanctions policy in the United States often argue against providing Fidel Castro with such an easy excuse for his failed economic policies.

Increased Sympathy from Third Parties

When a sender is a large and powerful country like the United States, and when the target is relatively weak and small (Cuba in particular, Iran less so), the global community may take exception to the wielding of economic power via a sanction. In egregious cases, other nations may even provide extra assistance to the target nation. Evidence of this sort of sympathy is demonstrated by Canada, one of the United States' most important allies, which actively supports training for public administrators in Cuba.

Where such power imbalances seem not to exist, the "bully" label is not so readily applied. For example, China's economic growth rate, large population, and important global security role insulates the United States from such claims, and third parties are less willing to "make China whole." As a related matter, if the brunt of a sanction's impact appears to affect "innocents" in a given target (e.g., Cuban children suffering the effects of restricted access to imported vitamin supplements) as opposed to inflicting harm across the board, third parties are more likely to redress the sanction through countervailing policies. In such instances, individuals and groups in the sender country may feel justified in subverting the sanction (e.g., by smuggling vitamins to Cuban relatives through third countries).

Third countries are most likely to try to thwart the impact of a sanction if it contains explicit or implied extraterritoriality provisions. For example, when the United States restricts overseas subsidiaries of U.S. firms and firms headquartered in third countries from trading with China, Iran, or Cuba (albeit in violation of international law), third countries are affected and seek redress. Mexico and Canada, for example, enacted "antidote" laws to the Helms-Burton legislation sanctioning Cuba, while foreign firms have threatened WTO action to counteract U.S. threats to sanction their American operations if they invest more than $20 million in Iran's energy sector. Clearly, where such third-country pressure exists, the sting of a sender's sanction is blunted.

Improved Strategic and/or Competitive Posturing

In our discussion of investment, we noted that third parties may be induced to invest in sanctioned countries because their competitors in sender nations are blocked from enjoying investment opportunities in the target. Similarly, developing a relationship with a target firm provides third-country participants a market protected from a whole set of competitors. Such relationships offer performance gains to the third-country firms as compared to a purely competitive environment.

In industries where global rivalries exist and important network economies are relevant (as in the case of a U.S.–based airline maintenance firm providing seamless service coverage for a Latin American airline), the incentive for third parties to engage commercially with a target are strengthened, as firms from sender nations are blocked from effectively competing in those settings.

Avoided and/or Reduced Dependence on a Given Nation

Imposing an economic sanction on a target may be sufficient to force that country to forego depending on a trading relationship with one country (namely, the sender). The case of Cuba is particularly instructive here. Prior to 1960, the United States was Cuba's largest trading partner, largely owing to geographic proximity.

Once the United States imposed an embargo, Cuba shifted gears and reoriented its trade to the Soviet Union, effectively trading one dependency for another. The fall of the Soviet Union (and with it the subsidization of the Cuban economy) forced Cuba to broaden its scope of commercial partners. This diversification in trading partners has proven somewhat useful in insulating Cuba from the vagaries of relying on a given trading partner.

A sanction may also spur a nation to further develop its industrial capacity. China, for example, has made important advances in high technology in response to U.S. restrictions on technology-based exports and the absence of viable third-country alternatives. In effect, U.S. sanctions served to boost productive possibilities for the nation, possibilities that may never have been explored in the absence of sanctions. Domestic industrial development and diversification of trading partners are thus indirect benefits of sanctions and reduce the net harm of a sanction to a target.

Sympathy from Diaspora and Global Society

Hardships on citizens in the target can evoke feelings of sympathy among citizens elsewhere. Where the target country has a significant diaspora community abroad, this sympathy can be mobilized in support of citizens (often family members) in the target nation. In the case of Cuba, this support takes the form of hundreds of millions of dollars in annual remittances sent by the diaspora to family members on the island. These dollars are the largest source of foreign exchange for the country as a whole and an important force in the Cuban economy. A sender country may specifically limit or prohibit such remittance flows, reducing this potential benefit to target countries.

Sanctions also may affect other organized members of civil society. Religious groups, business service organizations, and professional associations (e.g., of doctors) may be moved to provide humanitarian assistance to groups within a targeted nation. Such aid flows may be permitted from the sender country; third-country civil society groups are also active in providing this sort of assistance. In the absence of sanctions, target nations might not enjoy the same benevolence from civil society groups.

Target nations thus have clear opportunities to benefit from sanctions. An analysis of the net impact of sanctions on the target, then, must consider both the costs and benefits under the various contingent conditions we have described. Policymakers, in assessing ex ante the likelihood of a sanction's efficacy, must evaluate these costs and benefits for the target, particularly where a sanction is purposeful in rationale. Without a net cost to the target, it is unlikely the target will alter its behavior. Where punishment is intended (punitive rationale), the net impact of the sanction on the target must be negative to claim sanction victory.

Policymakers in the sending country must assess the net impact on *their* country as well. In fact, some popular press accounts of sanctions have addressed the aggregate economic costs of sanctions to the sender country alone. In the following section we highlight the direct trade impacts (as well as other important costs) of sanctions on senders.

COSTS OF SANCTIONS TO SENDER COUNTRIES

Sender countries incur both direct and indirect trade impacts of sanctions. By limiting or prohibiting economic linkages between the sender and target countries, a sanction can affect an extensive range of economic activities.

Reduced Trade

The dynamics of, and contingencies associated with, trade costs to senders parallel our previous discussion of costs to targets, since the impact on, say, imports by a sender is linked to the impact on exports from a target. There may be some important trade impact differences, though, owing to third-country effects and trade diversion. Important contingencies affecting trade diversion and/or domestic replacement for trade, including substitute availability, elasticity, geographic proximity, availability of excess production capacity, and existing trading relationships all pertain to assessments of net impacts of sanctions on senders.

The distinction between real (deadweight) and foreign exchange losses is critical in this analysis. Lost exports (i.e., exports not diverted to third countries) may be consumed domestically or the factors used to produce them diverted to produce other goods.

In regard to the United States as a sender country, however, it is important to note that given the large size, wealth, and diversity of the U.S. market as well as the breadth of trade and investment relationships that the United States enjoys globally, any trade impact of sanctions will be felt more acutely by the target (i.e., goods will not be diverted as readily or absorbed into local production or consumption). Potential multiplier effects from lost exports or imports may be more significant for the United States, however, since up- and downstream linkages are more relevant to advanced economies.

Restricted Investment Opportunities

Where a target nation represents an important profit-making opportunity for investors, a sanction might cause direct financial harm to the sender. If similar investment opportunities are not available domestically or in third countries, as when the investment's attractiveness is tied to a geographic location—beaches in Cuba, production platforms in China (with its proximity to Asian markets), or pipeline construction in Iran—potential profits are lost.

Where a target market does not present viable or attractive opportunities—owing to weak institutions, poor economic conditions, fierce competition, or incompatibility with a sending country's competitive advantages—the costs to senders from investment sanctions will be low. Poor economic prospects in the domestic markets of Cuba and Iran and bureaucratic obstacles in China point to limits to investor attraction regardless of sanctions.

Where opportunities exist in target nations for one-time investments, a sanction may impose immediate and lingering costs to the sender. In many industries, there are important first-mover advantages: Only one or two pipelines will be built to transport Caspian crude to market, and only one telecommunications network will be installed in Cuba. Even in industries where such effects are not present, first-mover firms from third countries can enter targets that are sanctioned, establish working relations with up- and downstream actors, and effectively continue to block firms from sender countries even after sanctions are lifted.

That Iranian and Cuban consumer markets are filled with branded products from outside the United States speaks to another source of lingering sanctions effects. If consumers become loyal to non-U.S. branded products, they will resist purchasing U.S. products should sanctions be lifted. China, for example, has effectively diversified its import sources in response to economic sanctions. The U.S. share of China's total imports consequently has been declining, from more than 20 percent in the early 1980s to less than 10 percent in 2000.

Restricted Knowledge Flows

Each target nation is unique and thus provides potential for individuals and organizations from sender countries to learn and improve. Where investments, commerce, and travel are restricted, knowledge flows between nations are limited. Medical research in Cuba is known to be very advanced, yet collaboration with the scientific community in the United States is impeded by travel restrictions and other sanctions.

Where a target is distinct (culturally, economically, etc.) from a sender, learning opportunities might be strongest. Alternatively, such distinctions may make effective learning between the countries more difficult, as language, cultural, and political differences can all serve as barriers to knowledge flows.

Diminished Moral Authority and/or Global Reputation

The mere act of imposing sanctions often implies that the sender nation is effecting a moral judgment against the target. Where a sender enjoys a reputation for global leadership, imposing sanctions unilaterally may threaten its position in the eyes of the world.

In situations where sanctions have an extraterritorial reach—for instance, application to overseas subsidiaries of firms headquartered in the sender country—and where sanctions are clear violations of international law or other binding multilateral agreements (such as the WTO), they pose clear threats to a sender's reputation. Such has been the case with the extraterritorial reach of U.S. sanctions against Iran.

Where sanctions are directed against target behaviors or policies the sender deems morally unsound (palliative and/or purposeful sanctions), the degree to which this view is shared around the globe will enhance or diminish the sender's position of global leadership. For instance, one-child family planning arguably forms a basis for some U.S. sanctions against China. If this social policy is not universally accepted across countries, broad acceptance of the sanctions is more likely.

Sanction rationale and scope also affect a sender's ability to maintain a reputation for global leadership. Protection or promotion of parochial domestic constituencies is unlikely to be viewed as sufficient rationale to sanction a target. "Smart" sanctions that target specific sectors of society deemed worthy of punishment or relevant for prompting policy change in the target will likely induce less ire among third countries than comprehensive sanctions. As we have argued, comprehensive economic sanctions are rather blunt instruments for addressing what often are circumscribed policy concerns. The objectionable policies may not even be economic in nature, calling into question the use of economic tools for noneconomic ends.

A sender nation's consistency in its sanctions policy will influence its ability to maintain a position of global leadership. When a sender sanctions a target for failing to adhere to democratic processes in selecting its government, third parties might reasonably expect that similar sanctions are due other nations failing to adhere to said processes. We saw in our three case analyses significant variations in the reasons for, and resulting scope of, sanctions, thus threatening the reputation of the United States for fair dealing. Human rights violations in China, Cuba, and Iran have been invoked as a reason for U.S. sanctions, but these same behaviors in Saudi Arabia, Egypt, and Pakistan have not provoked similar sanctions.

An important cost to sender nations is the resentment that sanctions may cause among citizens in the target nation. As we have noted, target regimes can use U.S. sanctions as a scapegoat for domestic policy failures. In all three case studies we found some evidence of a soiled U.S. reputation in the eyes of target citizens.[1] It is difficult to gauge the potential consequences of this resentment. In the case of Iran, for instance, stated U.S. sanctions policy is geared toward eliminating Iran's alleged support for terrorism. In a society where sanctions provoke resentment, this goal may be at odds with the reality of the sanction's impact.

The costs of a tarnished reputation for moral authority or global leadership are seen directly in acts by third countries (e.g., Mexican and Canadian passage of antidote laws countering U.S. sanctions against Cuba) as well as by targets (regime intransigence). In the case of purposeful sanctions, where few or no policy changes occur in a target, the sender's reputation for global leadership, which connotes an ability to get things done, is challenged.

Altered Domestic Politics

As a final cost to senders, we note that domestic policy within the sender country may be disproportionately affected by sanctions policy toward a particular target. The political might of the Cuban exile lobby in shaping national political outcomes in the United States (as evidenced by the 2000 U.S. presidential election) points to the potentially far-reaching effects of sanctions on the rest of the sender's society.

Although sanctions exact costs on sender countries, they also provide some important benefits beyond those implied by a given sanction's rationale. In the following section we highlight some of these benefits.

BENEFITS OF SANCTIONS TO SENDER COUNTRIES

Given the stepped-up use of unilateral economic sanctions noted in our previous volume, it is clear that policymakers believe sanctions provide important benefits to the sender country. We delineate here the most salient benefits and note important contingencies gleaned from our case analyses.

Lower Costs Than War

Economic sanctions are considered by policymakers to be important weapons in the foreign policy arsenal. No nation enters into war lightly, given the inevitable casualties and losses associated with most military initiatives. Thus, sanctions are viewed as tools that *cause* harm to the target but do not *inflict* harm on the sender. Of course, this view assumes a priority for physical (as opposed to economic or emotional) harm in terms of causing pain.

Considering the cases we have examined, it is hard to argue that U.S. sanctions policy per se has caused significant pain to citizens in the target nations beyond that caused by domestic policies. It is also difficult to conclude that harm inflicted upon citizens in the United States by sanctions has been limited. Imagine, for example, the plight of an individual employed in a firm that is driven to bankruptcy when sanctions render it unable to provide its largest client with services in Cuba, China, or Iran. Such an example might make one question the normative judgment on harm and costliness.

Enhanced Global Leadership

Global leaders are expected to take stands on important issues, including those relating to the protection of otherwise weak or disempowered groups. Where global leadership rests on foundations of a particular form of society, such as democracy, promoting the spread and stability of such foundations may be seen as a legitimate rationale for imposing sanctions on non-conforming societies. In the cases of China and Cuba (and, to a lesser extent, Iran), U.S. sanctions policy explicitly identifies promotion of democratic systems as a basis for sanctions.

Whether taking such a stand will produce a benefit for the sender depends principally on two factors. If a significant segment of the target society does not share a desire for the outcome motivating the sanction (such as the adoption of a democratic system), the sanction likely will be viewed as patronizing or meddling in the sovereign affairs of another state. But if a visible group in the target (e.g., the Varela Project in Cuba) advocates the goals of the sanction, the sender can justify the sanction as supporting an oppressed group.

The prevailing attitude among citizens in the sending nation also affects the degree to which a given sanction is deemed consistent with global leadership. If a sender cannot point to broad domestic consensus in support of a sanction, its actions will be questioned and its leadership legitimacy may be threatened.

Changed Target and/or Third-Country Behavior

There is some evidence in all three case analyses that target regimes have made (or allowed) changes consistent with the outcomes intended by U.S. sanctions policy. The spread of communism from Cuba throughout the Western Hemisphere has not occurred; a more progressive regime is in power in Iran; and some improvement in human rights has been noted in China. Whether U.S. sanctions influenced these outcomes is impossible to determine, but the changes provide evidence of a potential benefit of purposeful sanctions. Our studies show that there is greater likelihood of change when the costs to the target are great (such as potential denial of WTO membership for China), when members of the target community support a behavior change (e.g., the Varela Project, which favors democratic reforms in Cuba), or when a regime is not insulated from public pressure.

Sanctions also can induce third countries to refrain from engaging in undesirable behaviors and policies. Sanctions imposed against Iran, for example, may dissuade other states from supporting terrorism or otherwise promoting instability in their region. The degree to which sanctions actually induce behavior changes in other countries depends upon the extent to which such nations view their situations as parallel to that of the target country. Saudi Arabia, for instance, may appreciate U.S. allegations of state sponsorship of terrorism yet feel that that given its importance to the United States as an "ally" in the Middle East, the likelihood of sanctions imposition is slight.

Protected Economic and/or Strategic Sectors

Partisan sanctions are imposed to benefit certain parochial interests in the sender country, such as the U.S. military (as in the case of certain sanctions against China) or the U.S. tobacco industry (in the case of certain sanctions against Cuba). Whether partisan sanctions benefit a sender depends on the degree to which relevant parochial interests are able to leverage the protections provided by sanctions to create sustainable advantages.

For instance, restrictions on exports to China of high-technology products with potential military applications (such as supercomputers) may induce Beijing to seek alternative sources of these products or develop them internally. Under this scenario, any protections a sanction might provide will be temporary at best. Allowing China access to U.S. supercomputer technology, on the other hand, ensures that any Chinese military applications will be based on technology platforms in which the United States has expertise.

In the case of tobacco, sanctions against Cuba provide U.S. producers of the crop with little in the way of sustainable advantage since third countries (e.g., the Dominican Republic) are well-suited to fill any voids in world markets left by Cuban producers. As with developing nations trying to protect infant industries, countries that seek protection via sanctions rarely enjoy long-term benefits in a global economy.

Avoided Bad Deals

Given the pressures created by global competition and the demonstrated tendency of firms to rush together into business opportunities without exercising sufficient due diligence regarding a particular investment or transaction (the "bandwagon effect"), sanctions might protect domestic firms in sender nations from engaging in hazardous business climates. Cuba's decision to renege on debt repayments, costly bureaucratic delays in China, and concerns about upstream supply access in Iran all have resulted in consequences for private-sector entities operating in these sanctioned environments. Thus, where economic, political, legal, and social conditions in target countries might not be conducive to effective business dealings but bandwagon effects are in play, sanctions may protect sender firms from harm in target nations.

In addition to the benefits and costs of sanctions to senders and targets, our case analyses have demonstrated significant impacts on third countries as well. In the following section we address these third-country effects.

COSTS OF SANCTIONS TO THIRD COUNTRIES

Direct Economic Losses

Many third countries have investments in target countries. When these investments are made prior to the imposition of a sanction and are predicated on inputs from or access to the market of the sender country, their profitability will be affected, at least in the short term. For instance, investments in Cuban sugar production prior to the imposition of U.S. sanctions undoubtedly were predicated on demand estimates based on preferential access to the U.S. market under its sugar quota system.

Sanctions also limit the strategic flexibility of firms from third countries. If a firm wishes, for example, to concentrate its production of textile products destined for the North American market, the option of a Chinese production platform may be denied if exports from that nation to the United States are sanctioned owing to concerns over the use of prison labor in textile manufacturing.

Losses from Extraterritorial Sanctions

Extraterritorial sanctions exact the clearest cost to third countries. When third-country firms and U.S. subsidiaries abroad are prohibited from conducting business in a sanctioned country (as in Iran and Cuba), their parent nations lose tax revenues and other "spillover" benefits. If third countries are influenced or dominated by a sender country in a multilateral forum such as the World Bank (as in the case of U.S. opposition to a project to reduce gas flaring in Iran) or the WTO (as in the case of U.S. concern about China's accession), they may face retribution from the sender should they not "toe the line" on sanctions against target countries, even though such extraterritoriality generally is considered inconsistent with international law.

Attacks on third-country sovereignty via extraterritorial sanctions and increased economic costs resulting from sanctioned activities have been demonstrated in our case analyses to cause harm to third countries. However, many third countries *benefit,* both directly and indirectly, from sanctions. We outline these benefits in the following section.

BENEFITS OF SANCTIONS TO THIRD COUNTRIES

Our three case studies focused on target countries being sanctioned unilaterally by a single sender,[2] the United States. Rarely were other countries willing to join the United States in imposing sanctions against these targets, in stark contrast to high-profile multilateral sanctions against South Africa and its apartheid policies and against Iraq for that country's alleged holdings of weapons of mass destruction. Although most observers argue that other nations do not join the United States in imposing sanctions because they do not feel sanctions are an appropriate tool in these situations, some experts offer an alternative explanation: that U.S. sanctions confer (unwittingly or otherwise) advantages upon third countries.

Reduced Competition in Trade and Investment

When trade and investment are sanctioned, third-country firms gain protection from U.S. trade competition and U.S. bidding on investment projects. If a third country is similar to the United States and/or the target in terms of size, wealth, production factors, location, or other characteristic, advantages from sanction protection will readily result.

The profits that third-country firms can generate from participating in trade and investment with a target country can be utilized to cross-subsidize their other global activities. Firms from the sender country may then face stiffer competition from these third-country firms elsewhere. Thus, the benefits to third countries depend upon the degree to which their firms are engaged in global business activities.

The United States, for example, has long prohibited American companies from selling nuclear power-generating equipment to China. Consequently, China has imported nuclear power facilities from France, Canada, and Russia. Firms from these nations can use profits generated in China to subsidize their efforts in markets where they compete with U.S. firms.

Preferred Access

According to the resource-based view of firms, commercial enterprises that are best able to compete are those with access to key strategic resources. Sanctions deny sender-country firms access to strategic resources in target nations while allowing third-country firms to take full advantage of them. Such resources are especially valuable when they are rare and not readily replaced by substitutes or copied. Two resources that are particularly valuable are technology and knowledge.

Third-country firms can access technology developed in target nations to improve their products, processes, and management. Where these firms have sufficient capabilities and experience, they have "absorptive capacity" to effectively utilize the technology provided by the target. Canadian and Brazilian pharmaceutical firms, for example, are able to license immune-deficiency treatment technology from Cuba; their U.S. counterparts, however, must develop these advances internally or license them from other countries where alternatives exist.

Other knowledge-based assets also are likely to be valuable to third-country firms competing globally. By trading with or investing in the target country, third-country firms gain valuable experience and expertise in consumer behavior, dealing with intermediaries, utilizing unique production factors, learning about novel application areas, and so on. Since this process takes time and the experience and expertise acquired are not readily bought or otherwise accessed quickly, sender firms lose opportunities to learn by participating in economic activities concerning the target. The knowledge that third-country firms gain from these experiences may be used profitably to compete against sender-country firms elsewhere.

Improved Scale and Scope Advantages

Third-country firms that trade with and invest in a target country can combine these activities with their other global pursuits to achieve scale benefits (e.g., access to larger markets and volume purchasing opportunities) and scope benefits (by optimally configuring activities to best leverage factor complements, minimize coordination costs, and reduce risk). Firms from sender countries are prohibited from fully considering all options for scale and scope advantages because sanctioned nations are off-limits. Thus, third-country firms can leverage scale and scope benefits to lower costs beyond levels attainable by sender-country competitors in global industries.

CONCLUSION AND FUTURE DIRECTIONS

We have argued here that, based upon our detailed case analyses, a full and complete assessment of the efficacy of sanctions requires consideration of costs and benefits to sender, target, and third countries. We highlighted the contingent factors at play in determining these costs and benefits and noted that the underlying rationale for a sanction provides the focal scope for the assessment. We concluded each of our cases with a summary of the impact and efficacy of U.S. unilateral economic sanctions with regard to that particular target.

We are pleased with the additional insights into sanctions that our case examinations have provided. By moving beyond the extant aggregate examinations of direct trade impacts on sender countries contained in typical gravity models, we provided a much fuller perspective of the range of costs and benefits from sanctions. Our conclusions in this volume will provide policymakers with a concise inventory of relevant factors to consider when crafting and gauging sanctions policies in the future.

Our casework here, however, is insufficient to address other considerations relevant to the study of sanctions. We hope to explore some of these remaining issues in a subsequent volume based on further analysis of key stakeholders' perceptions of sanctions. We conclude by briefly delineating some of the important unanswered questions about sanctions.

1. To what degree are different political systems more or less vulnerable to economic sanctions? Which specific economic sanctions have the most influence over certain political systems and regimes? Are comprehensive sanctions better or worse than focused sanctions in terms of achieving political ends?
2. What forms of sanctions tend to produce lingering effects (both costs and benefits)? Are long-term, lingering costs and benefits more or less important to key stakeholders than immediate, direct costs and benefits? Why?
3. How do sanctions affect the strategy of firms headquartered in target, sender, or third countries? What is the role of multinational enterprises and their headquarters locations in determining the impact of sanctions?
4. How is a nation's competitiveness affected by sanctions? What forms of sanctions have long-term implications for competitiveness in target, sender, and third countries?
5. What specific role do linkages (economic, political, legal, or cultural) among countries and among citizens within countries play in promoting or thwarting the intended impact of sanctions? How do extraterritoriality provisions of sanctions and "multilateralism creep" interact with other linkages?
6. What role do supranational institutions such as the WTO play in circumscribing sanctions as a legitimate foreign policy tool?

We look forward to continuing this work on sanctions by investigating the perspectives of diverse stakeholders—citizens, civil society, governments, and firms in sender, target, and third countries. By observing and assessing similarities and differences among these stakeholders' perspectives, we can further refine our conclusions regarding the impact and efficacy of imposing unilateral sanctions in a global economy.

NOTES

1. It is important to note that anti-U.S. sentiments may predate sanctions. Where sanctions exacerbate such sentiments, however, we believe our arguments to be justified.

2. The three nations we analyzed are not subject to "pure" unilateral sanctions. Most western countries (including Japan) joined the United States in sanctioning China after the Tiananmen incident, and members of the Organization of American States sanctioned Cuba for several years while the United States was doing likewise.

References

Albright, Madeline K. 2000. "American and Iranian Relations: A New Chapter in Our Shared History." Remarks at a meeting of the American-Iranian Council, 17 March, in Washington, D.C.

Alvarez, Jose, and Lazaro Pena Castellanos. 2001. *Cuba's Sugar Industry.* Gainesville: University Press of Florida.

Amuzegar, Jahangir. 1997. "Adjusting to Sanctions." *Foreign Affairs* 76 (May/June): 31–41.

Askari, Hossein. 1990. *Saudi Arabia: Oil and the Search for Economic Development.* Greenwich, Conn.: JAI Press.

———. 1994. "It's Time to Make Peace with Iran." *Harvard Business Review* 72 (January/February): 50–63.

Askari, Hossein, John Forrer, Hildy Teegen, and Jiawen Yang. Praeger, 2003. *Economic Sanctions: Examining Their Philosophy and Efficacy.* New York: Quorom Books.

Askari, Hossein, and Mohamed Jaber. 1999. "Oil Exporting Countries of the Persian Gulf: What Happened to All That Money?" *Journal of Energy Finance and Development* 4 (2): 185–218.

BP Amoco. 1999. *Statistical Review of World Energy, 1999.* London: BP p.l.c.

———. 2000. *Statistical Review of World Energy, 2000.* London: BP p.l.c.

Bergsten, C. Fred. 1998. "Sanctions Against Rogue States: Do They Work?" Debate sponsored by Council on Foreign Relations, 20 April, in New York.

Berry, Nicholas. 2002. "U.S. National Missile Defense: Views from Asia." In *National Missile Defense: What Does It All Mean?* Washington, D.C.: Center for Defense Information.

Bertsch, Gary K., and Richard T. Cupitt. 1993. "Nonproliferation in the 1990s: Enhancing International Cooperation on Export Controls." *The Washington Quarterly* 16 (4): 53–70.

Betancourt, Ernesto. 2000. "Cuba's Balance of Payments Gap, the Remittances Scam, Drug Trafficking and Money Laundering." *Cuba in Transition* (10): 149–161. Silver Spring, Md.: Association for the Study of the Cuban Economy.

Boehm, Peter. 2002. "Cuba and the Western Hemisphere." Presentation to the Interamerican Dialogue, 6 June, in Washington, D.C.

Bonetti, Shane. 1998. "Distinguishing Characteristics of Degrees of Success and Failure in Economic Sanctions Episodes." *Applied Economics* 30 (June): 805–813.

Bottelier, Pieter. 2001. "Was World Bank Support for the Qinghai Anti-Poverty Project in China Ill-Considered?" *Harvard Asia Quarterly* 5 (1): 47–55.

Brzezinski, Zbigniew, Brent Scowcroft, and Richard Murphy. 1997. "Differentiated Containment." *Foreign Affairs* 76 (May/June): 20–30.

Burstein, Daniel, and Arne De Keijzer. 1998. *Big Dragon.* New York: Simon & Schuster.

Business Coalition for U.S.-China Trade (BCUSCT). 1997. *Restructuring U.S.-China Trade Relations: Advancing American Interests.* Washington, D.C.: Business Coalition for U.S.-China Trade.

Cable News Network (CNN). 2000. "Cuba Tells U.S. Business Leaders Embargo is Costing Them." 9 June.

Canada Trade and Economic Section (CTES). 2001. *Cuba: A Guide for Canadian Business.* 3d edition. Havana, Cuba: Embassy of Canada.

Carranza Valdez, Julio. 2001. *La economia cubana: Un balance breve de una decada critica.* London, England: Institute of Latin American Studies, University of London.

Carter, Jimmy. 2002. "Openings to Cuba: We Must Find A Common Ground." *Washington Post,* 24 May, editorial.

Census Bureau. 2002. "U.S. Trade with China in 2001." Washington, D.C.: U.S. Census Bureau.

Central Intelligence Agency (CIA). 1999. *Cuba: Handbook of Trade Statistics, 1999.* Washington, D.C.: Directorate of Intelligence, Central Intelligence Agency.

China Atomic Energy Authority (CAEA). 2002. "Peaceful Uses of Nuclear Energy: Nuclear Energy Development in China." Beijing: China Atomic Energy Authority.

China National Bureau of Statistics. 2002. "Statistical Communique of the People's Republic of China on the 2001 National Economic and Social Development." Beijing: China National Bureau of Statistics.

China Trade Relations Working Group. 2000. "Summary of U.S.-China Bilateral WTO Agreement." Washington, D.C.: The White House, Office of General Counsel.

Clawson, Patrick. 1996. Remarks at a conference on the effects of economic sanctions sponsored by the Petroleum Industry Research Foundation and the Middle East Institute, 29 April, in Washington, D.C.

———. 1998. "U.S. Sanctions on Iran: What Has Been Achieved and At What Cost?" Testimony before the Committee on International

Relations, U.S. House of Representatives. 105th Cong., 2d sess. Washington, D.C.: Washington Institute for Near East Policy.

Code of Federal Regulations. 2002. Title 22, Chapter 1, Part 126, Sec. 126.1: *Prohibited Exports and Sales to Certain Countries.* Washington, D.C.: U.S. Government Printing Office.

Cohen, Jerome A., Robert F. Dernberger, and John R. Garson. 1971. *China Trade Prospects and U.S. Policy.* New York: Praeger.

Collins, Joseph J., and Gabrielle D. Bowdoin. 1999. *Beyond Unilateral Economic Sanctions—Better Alternatives for U.S. Foreign Policy.* Washington, D.C.: Center for Strategic and International Studies.

Congressional Budget Office (CBO). 1999. *The Domestic Costs of Sanctions on Foreign Commerce.* Washington, D.C.: Congressional Budget Office.

Coughenour, Amy. 2002. "Cuba." *Hemisphere Highlights* 1 (2). Washington, D.C.: Center for Strategic & International Studies.

Council for Economic Planning and Development (CEPD). 1995. *Taiwan Statistical Data Book 1995.* Taipei: Republic of China, Council for Economic Planning and Development.

Council on Foreign Relations. 1999. *U.S.-Cuban Relations in the 21st Century: An Independent Task Force Report.* New York: Council on Foreign Relations.

Crespo, Nicolas, and Charles Suddaby. 2000. "A Comparison of Cuba's Tourism Industry with the Dominican Republic and Cancun, 1988–1999." *Cuba in Transition* (10): 352–359. Silver Spring, Md.: Association for the Study of the Cuban Economy.

Cuba Policy Foundation. 2002. "Where do Americans Stand on Cuba Policy?" Washington, D.C.: Cuba Policy Foundation.

Davis, Lester A. 1996. *U.S. Jobs Supported by Goods and Services Exports, 1983–94, Including Special Focus on Exports by High Technology Industries.* Washington, D.C.: U.S. Department of Commerce, Office of International Macroeconomic Analysis.

Department of Agriculture. 2000. *What's New.* 16 November. Washington, D.C.: U.S. Department of Agriculture.

Department of Commerce (DOC). 1995. *Comparison of the 1992–1993 Merchandise Trade Statistics of the United States and the People's Republic of China.* Washington, D.C.: U.S. Department of Commerce, Bureau of the Census, Economics and Statistics Administration.

———. 2002a. "International Investment Data." Washington, D.C.: U.S. Department of Commerce, Bureau of Economic Analysis.

———. 2002b. "U.S. Foreign Trade Highlights." Washington, D.C.: U.S. Department of Commerce, International Trade Administration.

Department of Energy. 2000. *International Energy Outlook 2000.* Washington, D.C.: U.S. Department of Energy, Energy Information Administration.

Department of State. 2002. "Sanctions Imposed on Chinese Entities Pursuant to the Iran Nonproliferation Act." Washington, D.C.: U.S. Department of State.

Diaz-Briquets, Sergio. 1994. "Emigrant Remittances in the Cuban

Economy: Their Significance During and After the Castro Regime." *Cuba in Transition* (4). Silver Spring, Md.: Association for the Study of the Cuban Economy.

Dominguez, Jorge. 2002. "The Cuban Political System." Presentation to the Interamerican Dialogue, 6 June, Washington, D.C.

Donohue, Thomas J. 2000. "A Counterproductive Approach to China." *The Washington Post,* 10 July.

Dorn, James A. 1996. "Trade and Human Rights: The Case of China." *Cato Journal* 16 (1): 77–98.

Drezner, Daniel. 2000. "Bargaining, Enforcement, and Multilateral Sanctions: When is Cooperation Counterproductive?" *International Organization* 54 (Winter): 73–102.

DuBois, Frank. 2002. "Location, Location, Location: How Integration Through Trade Agreements and Transportation Corridors Affect FDI in the Americas." Paper presented at the 44th Annual Meeting of the Academy of International Business, 1 July, in San Juan, Puerto Rico.

Economic Commission for Latin America and the Caribbean (ECLAC). 2000. *Economic Survey of Latin America and the Caribbean: 1999–2000.* Santiago, Chile: United Nations Economic Commission for Latin America and the Caribbean.

Economist Intelligence Unit (EIU). 2002. *Country Report: Cuba.* London: The Economist Intelligence Unit.

Erickson, Daniel P. 2002. "The New Cuba Divide." *The National Interest* 67 (Spring).

Espino, Maria Dolores. 2001. "Cuban Tourism: A critique of the CEPAL 2000 Report." *Cuba in Transition* (11): 343–349. Silver Spring, Md.: Association for the Study of the Cuban Economy.

European-American Business Council (EABC). 1997. *Is the Price Too High? The Cost of U.S. Sanctions Policies.* Washington, D.C.: European-American Business Council.

Executive Order 13222. 2001. "Continuation of Export Control Regulations." In *Federal Register* 66 (163): 44025–44026. Washington, D.C.: The White House.

Export Administration Act of 1979 (EAA). U.S. Public Law 96–72. 96th Cong., 1st sess., 29 Sept. 1979.

Export Administration Regulations (EAR). 2002. *Part 738: Commerce Control List Overview and the Country Chart.* Washington, D.C.: Department of Commerce, Bureau of Industry and Security.

Export-Import Bank of the United States (Ex-Im Bank). 2002a. "Country Cover Policy and Risk-Taking Practices." In *Competitiveness Report for 2001.* Washington, D.C.: Export-Import Bank of the United States.

Export-Import Bank of the United States (Ex-Im Bank). 2002b. "Ex-Im Bank Programs—Overview." Washington, D.C.: Export-Import Bank of the United States.

Falcoff, Mark. 2000. "Cuba after Castro." *Chief Executive* 155 (April): 28–30.

Fauriol, Georges. 2000. "U.S. Policy Outlook on the Caribbean." Testimony before the Subcommittee on the Western Hemisphere,

Committee on International Relations, U.S. House of Representatives. 106th Cong., 2d sess. 17 May. Washington, D.C.: Center for Strategic & International Studies.

Fisk, Daniel W. 1999. "Cuba Alert: New Policy Initiatives Reaffirm Fundamentals of U.S. Policy toward the Castro Regime." Washington, D.C.: Center for Strategic & International Studies.

Foreign Agricultural Service (FAS). 2000. "FASonline: U.S. Trade With Cuba." Washington, D.C.: Foreign Agricultural Service, U.S. Department of Agriculture.

Frank, Marc. 2001. "France Freezes $175 Million in Cuba Trade Cover." Reuters, 4 September.

Garve, Lucas. 2001. "El picaro, el gerente y la corrupcion." *CUBANET,* 26 June.

Gejdenson, Sam. 2000. "Gejdenson Introduces Satellite Exports Bill." Washington, D.C.: U.S. House of Representatives, Committee on International Relations, Democratic staff.

General Accounting Office (GAO). 1993. *Export Controls: Issues in Removing Militarily Sensitive Items from the Munitions List.* Washington, D.C.: U.S. General Accounting Office.

———. 1998. *Export Controls: Information on the Decision to Revise High Performance Computer Controls.* Washington, D.C.: U.S. General Accounting Office.

———. 2002. *Export Controls: Rapid Advances in China's Semiconductor Industry Underscore Need for Fundamental U.S. Policy Review.* Washington, D.C.: U.S. General Accounting Office.

Gerth, Jeff, and James Risen. 1999. "Spying Charges Against Beijing Are Spelled Out by House Panel." *The New York Times,* 26 May.

Gonzalez Gutierrez, Alfredo. 2001. "Aspectos estrategicos en el perfeccionamiento del modelo de planificacion." La Habana, Cuba: *El Economista de Cuba.*

Gutierrez-Castillo, Orlando. 2000. "Cuba, turismo y desarrollo economico." In *La Economia Cubana: Coyuntura, Reflexiones y Oportunidades.* La Habana: Centro de Estudios de la Economia Cubana/ Fundacion Friedrick Ebert.

Gutierrez Urdaneta, Luis, and Orlando Penate Rivero. 2000. "La Reforma de los Sistemas de Pensiones en America Latina: La Alternativa Cubana." La Habana: *Editorial Ciencias Sociales.*

Haass, Richard N. 1998. "Economic Sanctions: Too Much of a Bad Thing." *Policy Brief 34.* Washington, D.C.: The Brookings Institution.

———. 1999. "The Use and Effect of Unilateral Trade Sanctions." Testimony before the Subcommittee on Trade, Committee on Ways and Means, U.S. House of Representatives. 106th Cong., 1st sess. Washington, D.C.: Brookings Institution.

Haass, Richard N., and Meghan O'Sullivan. 2000. "Terms of Engagement: Alternatives to Punitive Policies." *Survival* 42 (Summer): 1–23.

Hamilton, John R. 1999. "Cuba: Economic Transition and U.S. Policy." Washington, D.C.: U.S. Department of State, Bureau of Western Hemisphere Affairs.

Harding, James. 1997. "China Urges End to High-tech Ban." *Financial Times,* 18 August.

Hays, Dennis. 2002. "Cuba and the United States." Presentation to the Interamerican Dialogue, 6 June, in Washington, D.C.

Hecker, JayEtta. 1996. "International Trade: Challenges and Opportunities for U.S. Businesses in China." Testimony before the Committee on Banking and Financial Services, U.S. House of Representatives. 104th Cong., 2d sess. Washington, D.C.: General Accounting Office.

Helms, Jesse. 1999. "What Sanctions Epidemic? U.S. Business' Curious Crusade." *Foreign Affairs* 78 (1): 2–8.

Hernandez-Cata, Ernesto. 2001. "The Fall and Recovery of the Cuban Economy in the 1990s: Mirage or Reality?" Working Paper 01/48. Washington, D.C.: International Monetary Fund.

Hong Kong Special Administrative Region (HKSAR). 2002. "Hong Kong in Figures: Gross Domestic Product at Current Prices by Economic Activity." Hong Kong: Government of the Hong Kong Special Administrative Region of the People's Republic of China.

Howlett, Bob. 1998. *Hong Kong 1998.* Hong Kong: Information Services Department.

Hufbauer, Gary Clyde, Kimberly Ann Elliot, Tess Cyrus, and Elizabeth Winston. 1997. *U.S. Economic Sanctions: Their Impact on Trade, Jobs and Wages.* Washington, D.C.: Institute for International Economics.

Hufbauer, Gary Clyde, Jeffrey J. Schott, and Kimberly Ann Elliot. 1990. *Economic Sanctions Reconsidered.* 2d ed. Washington, D.C.: Institute for International Economics.

Institute for International Economics (IIE). 2001. "Economic Sanctions Reconsidered: History and Current Policy." Washington, D.C.: Institute for International Economics.

International Monetary Fund (IMF). 1978. *Iran: Recent Economic Developments, 1978.* Washington, D.C.: International Monetary Fund.

———. 1995. *Islamic Republic of Iran: Recent Economic Developments, 1995.* Washington, D.C.: International Monetary Fund.

———. 1998. *Islamic Republic of Iran: Recent Economic Developments, 1998.* Washington, D.C.: International Monetary Fund.

———. 1999. *United Arab Emirates: Recent Economic Developments, 1999.* Washington, D.C.: International Monetary Fund.

———. 2000. *Islamic Republic of Iran.* Washington, D.C.: International Monetary Fund.

———. 2001a. *Direction of Trade Statistics Yearbook: 2001.* Washington, D.C.: International Monetary Fund.

———. 2001b. *Islamic Republic of Iran: Staff Report 2001.* Washington, D.C.: International Monetary Fund.

———. 2002a. "Direction of Trade Statistics, March 2002." Washington, D.C.: International Monetary Fund.

———. 2002b. "The World Economic Outlook, April 2002." Washington, D.C.: International Monetary Fund.

International Rivers Network (IRN). 2001. "IRN's China Campaigns." Berkeley, Calif.: International Rivers Network.

International Trade Commission (ITC). 1998. *Overview and Analysis of Current U.S. Unilateral Economic Sanctions.* Washington, D.C.: U.S. International Trade Commission.

———. 2001. *The Economic Impact of U.S. Sanctions with Respect to Cuba.* Washington, D.C.: U.S. International Trade Commission.

Jatar-Hausmann, Ana Julia. 1999. *The Cuban Way: Capitalism, Communism and Confrontation.* West Hartford, Conn.: Kumarian Press.

Johnson, Harold J. 2000. "Export Controls: National Security Risks and Revisions to Controls on Computers." Testimony before the Committee on Armed Services, U.S. Senate, 106th Cong., 2d sess. Washington, D.C.: U.S. General Accounting Office.

Journal of Commerce. 1990. "Cuban Trade with U.S. Subsidiaries." 12 April.

Kan, Shirley A. 1998. "U.S. Policy Regarding Satellite Exports to China." Testimony before a joint hearing of the Committees on International Relations and National Security, U.S. House of Representatives, 105th Cong., 2d sess. Washington, D.C.: Library of Congress, Congressional Research Service.

Kittredge, Frank D. 1999. *CBO Study Flawed, Inconsistent, and Underestimates Real Costs to U.S. of Unilateral Sanctions.* Washington, D.C.: USA*Engage.

Klintworth, Gary. 1995. *New Taiwan, New China: Taiwan's Changing Role in the Asia-Pacific Region.* New York: Longman St. Martin's Press.

Koo, Jeffrey. 1996. "MFN for China is Also Good for Taiwan." *The Wall Street Journal,* 7 May.

Kristof, Nicholas D. 2002. "Devastated Women." *The New York Times,* 26 April.

Lardy, Nicholas R. 1994. *China in the World Economy.* Washington, D.C.: Institute for International Economics.

———. 1996. "China and the WTO." *Policy Brief 10.* Washington, D.C.: The Brookings Institution.

———. 1997. "Is China MFN an Effective Foreign Policy Tool?" Testimony before the Subcommittee on East Asian and Pacific Affairs, Committee on Foreign Relations, U.S. Senate, 105th Cong., 1st sess. Washington, D.C.: The Brookings Institution.

———. 2001. "U.S.-China Economic Relations: Implications for U.S. Policy." Testimony before the Subcommittee on East Asia and the Pacific, Committee on International Relations, U.S. House of Representatives. 107th Cong., 1st sess. Washington, D.C.: The Brookings Institution.

Lieberthal, Kenneth. 2001. "U.S. Policy Toward China." *Policy Brief 72.* Washington, D.C.: The Brookings Institution.

Lubman, Stanley B. 1978. "Trade and Sino-American Relations." In *Dragon and Eagle: United States-China Relations, Past and Future,* ed. Michel Oksenbert and Robert B. Oxnam, 187–210. New York: Basic Books.

Mansfield, Edward D. 1995. "International Institutions and Economic Sanctions." *World Politics* 47 (July): 575–605.

Marquetti Nodarse, Hiram. 2000. "Cuba reanimacion del sector industrial." *Revista Bimestre Cubana* 13 (July–December): 5–30.
Mastel, Greg. 1997. *The Rise of the Chinese Economy: The Middle Kingdom Emerges.* Armonk, N.Y.: M.E. Sharpe.
Maybarduk, Gary H. 1999. "The State of the Cuban Economy, 1998–1999." *Cuba in Transition* (9). Silver Spring, Md.: Association for the Study of the Cuban Economy.
Mesa-Lago, Carmelo. 2001. "The Cuban Economy in 1999–2001: Evaluation of Performance and Debate on the Future." *Cuba in Transition* (11): 1–17. Silver Spring, Md.: Association for the Study of the Cuban Economy.
Monreal, Pedro. 2001. "Export Substitution Industrialization in Cuba." Paper presented at "Facing the Challenges of the Global Economy," a workshop sponsored by the University of London's Institute of Latin American Studies, 25–26 January, in London.
Morris, Emily. 2000. "Interpreting Cuba's External Accounts. *Cuba in Transition* (10): 145–148. Silver Spring, Md.: Association for the Study of the Cuban Economy.
Morrison, Wayne M. 2002. *China-U.S. Trade Issues.* Washington, D.C.: Library of Congress, Congressional Research Service.
Nathan, Andrew J., and Robert S. Ross. 1997. *The Great Wall and the Empty Fortress.* New York: W. W. Norton.
National Association of Manufacturers (NAM). 1999. "Response to Senator Jesse Helms on Unilateral Economic Sanctions." Washington, D.C.: National Association of Manufacturers.
National Bipartisan Commission on Cuba. 1998. "U.S.-Cuba History." Available on the World Wide Web at http://www.uscubacommission.org/history.html.
New York Times. 2002. "America as Nuclear Rogue." Editorial, 12 March.
Nicoll, Alexander. 1994. "Singapore's PM Warns U.S. over China." *Financial Times,* 21 April.
Odessey, Bruce. 1995. "No Agreement Yet on Bringing Russia into Post-COCOM Regime." United States Information Agency, 23 June.
Office of Foreign Assets Control (OFAC). 1998. *Terrorist Assets Report.* Washington, D.C.: Office of Foreign Assets Control, U.S. Department of the Treasury.
O'Sullivan, Meghan L. 2000. "The Dilemmas of U.S. Policy Toward 'Rogue' States" (in French). *Politique Etrangère* (Spring).
Overholt, William H. 1993. *The Rise of China: How Economic Reform is Creating a New Superpower.* New York: W. W. Norton.
Overseas Private Investment Corporation (OPIC). 2002. "What is OPIC?" Washington, D.C.: Overseas Private Investment Corporation.
People's Daily. 1997. "1997 Consumption Survey of Urban Residents in China." 22 December.
Perez, Omar. 1997. "El comercio exterior y la inversion extranjera en la economia cubana." In *La Economia Cubana en 1996.* La Habana, Cubana: University of Havana.
Perez-Lopez, Jorge F. 2000. "Cuba's Balance of Payments Statistics." *Cuba*

In Transition (10): 136–143. Silver Spring, Md.: Association for the Study of the Cuban Economy.

Perez Villanueva, Omar Everleny. 2001. "Ciudad de La Habana: Desempeno economico y situacion social." *La Economia Cubana en el 2000.* CEPAL/ECLAC Comision Economica para America Latina/ Economic Commission for Latin America and the Caribbean.

Petroleum Economist. 2000. "Oil Find Re-opens Debate About Export Routes." 67 (6): 78–79.

Portela, Armando H. 2002. "Fewer Tourists, Falling Sugar Prices Push Cuba into Recession." *Cuba News,* 14 June.

Preeg, Ernest H. 1998. "U.S. Economic and Trade Policy Toward Cuba." Testimony before the Subcommittee on Trade, Committee on Ways and Means, U.S. House of Representatives. 105th Cong., 2d sess. Washington, D.C.: Center for Strategic & International Studies.

———. 1999a. "China: Where It All Comes Together." In *Feeling Good or Doing Good with Sanctions.* Washington, D.C.: Center for Strategic & International Studies.

———. 1999b. "Cuba: A Western Hemisphere Anachronism." In *Feeling Good or Doing Good with Sanctions.* Washington, D.C.: Center for Strategic & International Studies.

———. 1999c. "Iran: National Security at Bay." In *Feeling Good or Doing Good with Sanctions.* Washington, D.C.: Center for Strategic & International Studies.

Quest Economics. 2000. *Iran: Review 2000.* Kent, England: Janet Matthews Information Services.

Ramkissoon, Harold. 2001. "Science and Technology in Cuba Today." St. Augustine, Trinidad: Caribbean Network of Scientists.

Ratliff, William, and Roger Fontaine. 2000. "A Strategic Flip-Flop in the Caribbean: Lift the Embargo on Cuba." Stanford, Calif: Hoover Institution on War, Revolution and Peace, Stanford University.

Rennack, Dianne E. 1997. *China: U.S. Economic Sanctions.* Washington, D.C.: Library of Congress, Congressional Research Service.

Rich Kaplowitz, Donna. 1998. *Anatomy of a Failed Embargo: U.S. Sanctions Against Cuba.* Boulder, Colo.: Lynne Rienner Publishers.

Richardson, J. David. 1993. *Sizing Up U.S. Export Disincentives.* Washington, D.C.: Institute for International Economics.

Riddell, Peter. 1989a. "U.S. Urges Clemency for Peking Protesters." *Financial Times,* 21 June.

———. 1989b. "World Bank Defers China Plans." *Financial Times,* 27 June.

Ross, Robert S. 1998a. "The Strategic and Bilatoral Context of Policy-Making in China and the United States: Why Domestic Factors Matter." In Robert S. Ross eds. In *After the Cold War: Domestic Factors and U.S.-China Relations.* New York: M.E. Sharpe.

———. 1998b. "China." *In Economic Sanctions and American Diplomacy,* edited by Richard N. Haass. New York: The Council on Foreign Relations.

Sandza, Raymond, and Mina Remy. 2002. "Cuba." *Hemisphere Highlights* 1 (7). Washington, D.C.: Center for Strategic and International Studies.

Sanguinetty, Jorge. 2002. "The Cuban Economy." Presentation to the Interamerican Dialogue, 6 June, Washington, D.C.

Schott, Jeffrey J. 1997. "The Iran and Libya Sanctions Act of 1996: Results to Date." Testimony before the Committee on International Relations, U.S. House of Representatives. 105th Cong., 1st sess. Washington, D.C.: Institute for International Economics.

Seiglie, Carlos. 2001. "Cuba's Road to Serfdom." *Cato Journal* 20 (Winter): 425–430.

Spadoni, Paolo. 2001. "The Impact of the Helms-Burton Legislation on Foreign Investment in Cuba." *Cuba In Transition* (11): 18–36. Silver Spring, Md.: Association for the Study of the Cuban Economy.

Stern Group. 2000. "The Impact on the U.S. Economy of Lifting the Food and Medical Embargo on Cuba." Washington, D.C.: The Stern Group.

Stevens, Paul. 2000. "Pipelines or Pipe Dreams: Lessons from the History of Arab Transit Pipelines." *Middle East Journal* 54 (Spring): 224–241.

Stuttard, John B. 2000. *The New Silk Road—Secrets of Business Success in China Today.* New York: Wiley.

Suchlicki, Jaime. 2000. "The U.S. Embargo of Cuba: Implications of Lifting the U.S. Embargo and Travel Ban." Miami, Fla.: Institute for Cuban and Cuban-American Studies.

Suettinger, Robert L. 2000. "The Taiwan Dilemma: Time for a Change in the U.S. Approach?" Presentation to *U.S.-China Relations Since the Cold War,* a conference sponsored by the Woodrow Wilson International Center for Scholars. Washington, D.C.: The Brookings Institution.

Sugawara, Sandra. 1996. "With Billions at Stake, Boeing Goes to Bat for China." *The Washington Post,* 7 July.

Togores Gonzalez, Viviana. 1999. "Cuba: Efectos sociales de la crisis y el ajuste economico de los 90s." In *Balance de la Economia Cubana a Finales de los 90s.* La Habana: Centro de Estudios de la Economia Cubana.

Toricelli, Robert G. 1998. "Sanctions Against Rogue States: Do They Work?" Debate sponsored by Council on Foreign Relations, 20 April, in New York.

Trade and Development Agency (TDA). 2001. "TDA Reopens U.S. Export Promotion Program in China." *TDA Update* 8 (1). Washington, D.C.: U.S. Trade and Development Agency.

———. 2002. "About TDA." Washington, D.C.: U.S. Trade and Development Agency.

Triana Cordovi, Juan. 2001. *La economia Cubana en el ano 2000.*

Truell, Peter. 1989. "The Outlook: Trading Places In Global Commerce." *The Wall Street Journal,* 14 August.

United Nations Conference on Trade and Development (UNCTAD). 2000. *World Investment Report 2000.* Geneva, Switzerland: United Nations Conference on Trade and Development.

United Nations Development Programme (UNDP). 2000. *Human Development Report 2000.* New York: Oxford University Press.

U.S.-Cuba Trade and Economic Council (USCTEC). 2000. "2000

Commercial Highlights." New York: U.S.-Cuba Trade and Economic Council.

———. 2001a. "Foreign Investment and Cuba." New York: U.S.-Cuba Trade and Economic Council.

———. 2001b. "Trademark and Patent Registration Procedures." New York: U.S.-Cuba Trade and Economic Council.

———. 2001c. "Certified Claims." New York: U.S.-Cuba Trade and Economic Council.

———. 2002. "BusinessWeek Magazine Ranks 100 Global Brands; 64% Available in Cuba." *2002 Commercial Highlights.* New York: U.S. Cuba Trade and Economic Council.

U.S. House of Representatives. 1999. *Report of the Select Committee on U.S. National Security and Military/Commercial Concerns with the People's Republic of China.* 105th Cong., 2d sess. H. Rept. 105–851.

Vivanco, Jose Miguel. 2002. "Time to End the U.S. Embargo on Cuba." Washington, D.C.: Human Rights Watch.

Wall Street Journal. 2002a. "Cuba Faces Hard Times Amid Slump in Sugar Prices, Cut-Off of Cheap Oil." 6 June.

———. 2002b. "Castro Rejects Reform Demands by Opposition." 17 June.

Weintraub, Sidney. 2000. "Cuba's Trade Policy After Castro." *Cuba in Transition* (10): 337–341. Silver Spring, Md.: Association for the Study of the Cuban Economy.

World Bank. 2000a. *Caspian Oil and Gas: Mitigating Political Risks for Private Participation.* Washington, D.C.: The World Bank.

———. 2000b. *Global Development Finance 2000.* Washington, D.C.: The World Bank.

———. 2001. *World Development Indicators 2001.* Washington, D.C.: The World Bank.

———. 2002. *World Development Indicators 2002.* Washington, D.C.: The World Bank.

World Trade Organization. 2001. "World Trade in 2000—Overview." Geneva, Switzerland: World Trade Organization.

Xu, Fu. 1999. *An Introduction to China's Foreign Trade.* Tianjin, China: Nankai University Press (in Chinese).

Yang, Jiawen. 1998. "Some Current Issues in U.S.-China Trade Relations." *Issues & Studies* 34 (7): 62–84.

Index

About the Authors

HOSSEIN G. ASKARI is Aryamehr Professor of International Business at The George Washington University. He is the author or coauthor of 15 earlier books and monographs, including *Economic Sanctions: Examining Their Philosophy and Efficacy* (Praeger, 2003), coauthored with Forrer, Teegen, and Yang.

JOHN FORRER is Director of the Institute for Global Management and Research at The George Washington University. He has consulted extensively on international energy and environmental issues.

HILDY TEEGEN is Associate Professor of International Business at The George Washington University. She has written extensively on international negotiations and business partnerships and Latin American economic affairs.

JIAWEN YANG is Assistant Professor of International Business at The George Washington University. He is the author of numerous articles and book chapters on exchange rate pass-through, international capital flows, and the financial crises in Latin America and Asia.